Yeats's blessings on von Hügel

By the same author

A Mirror for Anglo-Saxons
Re-Appraisals: Some Commonsense Readings in American
    Literature
Science and the Shabby Curate of Poetry
The Problem of Boston

Essays on literature and religion

Yeats's blessings on von Hügel

Martin Green

LONGMANS, GREEN AND CO LTD
48 Grosvenor Street, London W1
Associated companies, branches and representatives
throughout the world

© *Martin Green 1967*
First published 1967

Printed in Great Britain by
The Camelot Press Ltd
London and Southampton

for Carol Hurd

Contents

Acknowledgements

We are grateful to the following for permission to reproduce copyright material: William Collins, Sons & Co. Ltd for material from *Dr Zhivago* by Boris Pasternak; Darwen Finlayson Ltd for material from *Rilke's 'Duino Elegies': An Interpretation* by Romano Guardini, translated by K. G. Knight; J. M. Dent & Sons Ltd for material from *Selected Letters of Baron von Hügel*; Penguin Books Ltd for material from *Kruschev's Russia* by Edward Crankshaw; the author and Victor Gollancz Ltd for material from *Morte d'Urban* by J. F. Powers; Putnam & Co. and Alfred A. Knopf Inc. for material from *The Don Flows Home to the Sea* by Mikhail Sholokhov; Routledge & Kegan Paul Ltd and Wesleyan University Press for material from *Life Against Death* by Norman O. Brown; George Weidenfeld & Nicolson Ltd and G. P. Putnam's Sons for material from *Lolita* by Vladimir Nabokov, and Mr M. B. Yeats and Macmillan & Co. Ltd for lines from 'Vacillation' by W. B. Yeats from *The Winding Stair and Other Poems* by W. B. Yeats.

'Nabokov and Lolita' first appeared in *The Kenyon Review*, July 1966, under the title 'The Morality of Lolita'.

Must we part, Von Hügel, though much alike, for we
Accept the miracles of the saints and honour sanctity?
The body of Saint Teresa lies undecayed in tomb,
Bathed in miraculous oil, sweet odours from it come,
Healing from its lettered slab. Those self-same hands perchance
Eternalised the body of a modern saint that once
Had scooped out Pharaoh's mummy. I—though heart might find relief
Did I become a Christian man and choose for my belief
What seems most welcome in the tomb—play a predestined part.
Homer is my example and his unchristened heart.
The lion and the honeycomb, what has Scripture said?
So get you gone, Von Hügel, though with blessings on your head.

W. B. Yeats, 'Vacillation', Part VIII, 1932

When I first told literary friends how interesting I found von Hügel as a writer, I heard one of them ask, 'Who *was* von Hügel?' and another reply, 'He's a character in a poem by Yeats.' It seemed to me both that this was pretty much what Yeats himself implied, and that literary people today are all liable to a kind of corporate arrogance about other-than-literary things, a conspiratorial complacency; an arrogance which added a secret spice to that remark, and which has more serious manifestations worth quarrelling with. The second of those propositions it will take all of this book to substantiate; but about the first I can perhaps make my point in a few sentences.

Yeats takes no account of who von Hügel was. He imposes on him a rôle, of representing 'miraculous' religion, which is in fact positively inappropriate. Von Hügel was far from being a miracle-monger; within the spectrum of Catholic though the stood for a fairly extreme position of 'explaining' the supernatural, of making it accord with the natural—to put it crudely, a religious-rationalist position. And if this were not true, if von Hügel had been in any significant sense a preacher of miracles, he would have been all the more the wrong man to be saluted as 'much alike'. Yeats clearly meant something quite different, when he 'honoured sanctity', from what any Catholic could mean. If

St Teresa were eternalized by those self-same hands ('perchance') which scooped out Pharaoh's mummy, then her corporal preservation was no Christian miracle. On both counts, therefore, von Hügel's name is inappropriate to the function Yeats assigns it. Von Hügel stands for something important—Yeats obviously has heard of him and thinks he is confronting him—but he has not bothered to find out what. Indeed, one can't help suspecting that Yeats mistook St Teresa for St Catherine of Genoa, on whom von Hügel was an authority—though his book about her lays the least possible stress on miraculous oils and sweet odours.

With all this at the back of his mind, how can any reader of von Hügel react to Yeats's last two lines except as to a piece of arrogant condescension? Yeats does not know who von Hügel is. His blessings, consequently, are worth very little. And those who *do* know who von Hügel is, and find his comments on such subjects as are treated in the poem rather more interesting than Yeats's own, must find the condescension not only arrogant but arrant.

The poem, of course, remains a fine poem. My quarrel with Yeats's tone is (in one sense) not serious. It is (largely) my way of playing the game the poet wants me to play, the game which is a part of reading the poem. Yeats invited us to quarrel with him. He wanted to seem a foolish passionate man. My objection is only that he also wanted his foolish passionate utterances to have the dignity of prophetic truths; and the utterer thus to have a prophetic dignity superior to the criticisms of common sense, or morality, or exact learning, or any of the other voices that combine in culture. And my objection is much more that in literary circles he is effectively granted that superiority. This is shown not only in the kind of impromptu epigram I cited, but in considered interpretation and scholarship.

Thus in *The Identity of Yeats* Richard Ellman remarks, of this same poem, that Yeats does not repudiate the saint, or sanctity, but he absorbs them; he accepts the saint's point of view, but he regards it as only partial. Of course the critic is here expounding the poet's thought rather than offering any judgment of his own. But in other cases it seems clear that the expounding amounts to endorsement, and there is no line drawn between those cases and these. In any event, the act of exposition, in a chain of such acts hung like a garland of praise round the poet's neck, gives his thought a dignity quite different from —more marmoreal than—what it had in the poem. It puts back the pressure of critical common sense. Especially for the young student, but to some extent for any reader of Yeats, it inhibits critical response. It makes illegitimate my own reaction, 'No one has the right to assume that the poet's point of view is larger than the saint's.'

Of course, in the act of interpretation one must sympathize with the poet. But the act of evaluation, equally a part of criticism, derives from not sympathizing with him, too, from recognizing the limits of the sympathy he deserves. But in *The Identity of Yeats*, and generally in literary scholarship today, there is no well-defined or easily appealed to sense of those limits. And if we go all the way in sympathy with the heroes of modern literature, we find ourselves in very strange country.

For instance, in the same book Ellman takes up a question he says some readers ask about Yeats's philosophy and theology; could Yeats really have believed in what he said he did? 'But to ask this question is to show that one is several generations in time behind Yeats, who asked with more point whether the word *belief* belonged to our age at all; nothing is farther from his mind than simple credence....' Thus we have the possibility of belief (sorry, simple credence) filched from us as suavely as if no one today could seriously claim to believe in anything. Even to raise the question of belief is to show oneself several generations behind the times.

What replaces simple credence, for Yeats and Ellman, is what is expressed in this paragraph from a letter to the poet by his father, John Butler Yeats. 'There are two kinds of belief; the poetical and the religious. That of the poet comes when the man within has found some method or manner of thinking or arrangement of fact (such as is only possibly [*sic*] in dreams) by which to express and embody an absolute freedom, such that his whole inner and outer self can expand in a full satisfaction. In religious belief there is absent the consciousness of liberty. Religion is the denial of liberty. An enforced peace is set up among the warring feelings. By the help of something quite external, as for instance the fear of hell, some feelings are chained up and thrust into dungeons that some other feelings may hold sway, and all the ethical systems yet invented are a similar denial of liberty, that is why the true poet is neither moral nor religious.' This is clearly a dangerous principle if believed in passionately, dangerous not only to ethics, but to knowledge and even personal relations, since everything is subordinated to self-expression. But I suspect that everyone today whose major training is in the arts believes in that as an important principle, of action as well as of feeling, with the major exception of those who are also religious.

The explicit criteria by which all systems of belief are tested in that paragraph are 'absolute freedom' and 'full satisfaction' for the individual. The implicit criterion is the development of the personality to full strength. John Butler Yeats says in another letter, 'It seems to me that the intellect of man *as man*, and therefore of an artist, the most human of all, should obey no voice except that of emotion, but I would have a man know all emotions. . . . Art has to do with the sustaining and invigorating of the Personality. To be strong is to be happy. Art by expressing our feelings makes us strong and therefore happy . . .' Personality takes precedence over both morality and truth. Again, this is what Yeats the poet believed, and I think it is what most literary and artistic people believe; this is what lies behind, to take a very minor instance, his and their rough handling of half-known figures like von Hügel. But it is not what I believe, and my disagreement involves me in a whole series of dissents from the theory and practice of the modern literary world.

Let me be clear. It is not a disrespect for von Hügel in person, or in the abstract as a representative of religion, that I suspect, or not primarily. It is primarily a too great respect for Yeats, in person and in the abstract as a representative of poetry, with poetry's way of treating other kinds of human truth. What upsets me is the kind of disregard for fact, for reality, for truth, which Ellman expresses here: '. . . the capacity to imagine is redemptive; man, in a frenzy at being limited, overthrows much of that limitation. He defiantly asserts his imagined self against futility, and to imagine heroism is to become a hero.' But of course it is nothing of the kind, I protest; and however acceptable as paradoxes, statements of this kind are quite intolerable as habits of thought, as major principles of an interpretation of life and literature. 'Born incomplete, he conceives of completeness and to that extent attains it. We outfling ourselves upon the universe, people the desert with our fertile images. The hero does this unconsciously, the artist consciously, but all men do it in their degree. . . . In the poems which deal with artists or with heroes or with other men, he wishes also to show how brute fact may be transmogrified, how we can sacrifice ourselves, in the only form of religious practice he sanctions, to our imagined selves which offer far higher standards than anything offered by social convention. If we must suffer, it is better to create the world in which we suffer, and this is what heroes do spontaneously, artists do consciously, and all men do in their degree.'

We notice here the same wild talk about creating worlds, and transcending human limits, and imagining standards for ourselves far higher than any we could get from outside. But what is even more striking is the idea that the hero does something unconsciously, the artist consciously, and all men do it in their degree. This gives the artist the advantageous position of being, for one thing, the archetypal intellectual, the conscious mind; and for another, a more mature *person* than either the average man or the hero. And the artist here clearly covers all lovers of the arts, all users of their imaginations. The term can hardly be restricted to practising poets, if the trick is merely to conceive of completeness and to that extent attain it. We can all outfling ourselves upon the universe in that sense, if we are reckless enough. If anybody can't, he must either be a very dull and timid mind, or else he must refuse on principle to be reckless. If the latter, he must be either a humanist, with a strong loyalty to a variety of truths, or a man of religion, with a strong sense of the limits to his personal autonomy. Both these modes of being have very much the same quarrel with the unbridled literary sensibility (when that is erected into an autarchic guide to life) and the two go very much together for me. It is being a Catholic humanist (with both terms equally important) which makes me so resistant to Yeats's ideas.

My profession of Roman Catholicism is naturally as large and multiform a fact in my intellectual and imaginative life as my profession of teaching literature. I have to reconcile the claims of both professions, and von Hügel was such an important figure in my conversion to Catholicism just because he showed how much secular freedom could be reconciled with a limited and limiting creed. But he was a liberal humanist, not a creative artist, it was humanism he reconciled with Catholicism, not literature, and consequently it was a humanist's freedom he won for me, not Yeats's poetic kind. Humanism is a way of ordering professions rather than a profession in itself, a way of relating my literariness to other things, but what von Hügel did for me was no second-best alternative. It was humanism, not literature, I needed to see married to Catholicism. I already knew, after all, in 1951, quite a few imposing figures who combined the literary with the Catholic imagination, from Graham Greene and Evelyn Waugh to T. S. Eliot and C. S. Lewis. That combination was *anti*-humanist; and I think, looking back, that those imposing figures constituted one of the thorniest thickets in my path, through which von Hügel alone could have guided me. They struck me—though I don't know that I was putting it this way then—as exhibiting a quite unholy alliance of literature with religion, in vengeful betrayal of humanist freedom, of natural happiness, of all 'life'-values. Most manifestations of that alliance, including that prestigious 'sense of sin' we used to hear so much about in those days, appeal only to the worst parts of a temperament like mine. Only when they are in the hands of a great writer, and then only after an effort of self-discipline on my part, can I respond to them fully. What I wanted was what von Hügel gave me. He did not make that dangerously Romantic alliance—can it ever escape the taint of the Romantic death-wish?—between literature and religion. He showed instead how both belong with everything else in the massive inter-balancing whole of humanism. It is this opposite sort of truth I could respond to with the self I wanted to be.

In the course of the first three essays here I think most of the major facts of von Hügel's life and work get mentioned, but perhaps it is worth saying now that he was most importantly a philosopher of religion; that he was born in 1852 and died in 1925; that his father was an Austrian diplomat, soldier, traveller, his mother a Scotswoman; that he lived in England from the age of fifteen on and married an Englishwoman; that he was a leader of the Modernist Movement in the Roman Catholic Church, which in many ways foreshowed the contemporary movement of *aggiornamento*.

The liberal humanist as Roman Catholic

Though largely neglected since his death in 1925, Baron von Hügel was surely one of the great heroes of liberal humanism, one of the synthesizers of modern Western culture. His work was, in a dozen ways, an attempt to put together as many as possible of the separated elements of that culture; to put England together with the rest of Europe, Catholicism with other religions, religion itself with philosophy, the past with the present, science with the arts, morality with sensibility, and so on. And this was synthesis rather than systematization; the large motive behind the subordinations and explanations of all this material was the desire to accept everything, to make everything of value in life available to the person who places himself at the centre; the desire to be cut off from nothing. We may take as emblematic his remark about Professor Heiler's book on prayer, 'Indeed the Professor loves the "aut . . . aut"; whilst I believe real life mostly demands the "et . . . et".'

He pursued this aim, he obeyed this over-mastering drive, in different kinds of ways. Most obviously, in those books where he set forth his schemes of philosophical and theological thought; equally impressively, in those 'political' attempts to influence policy in the Roman church (the most famous is his rôle in the Modernist Movement) and to influence public opinion in England and to introduce leading thinkers to each other's work. But both these modes of activity are interesting to us now mostly for the personality we see at work in them. What was actually achieved thereby, his effectiveness as a philosopher and as a politician, was not so solid or so brilliant that time has not undermined or dimmed it. His philosophy, his 'political' achievement, need scholars to bring them to life for us; and that life will be (a layman gathers) largely their historical interest. But the personality we see engaged in them, the voice we hear booming through his prose, that is still remarkably alive. It is most fully expressed in his letters, and amongst them, in those he wrote as a kind of spiritual director. However, this personality is recurrently there in his most formal writing, and nowadays the best way to approach his work in general seems to be to read it for its expression of that personality; to read it as autobiographical essay. The Baron's systems are not (we gather) of the sort to much outlast their time and place. The mind we see at work within them is.

To call that personality heroic may well seem a paradox. Maude Petre described the Baron in a well-known epigram as a saint but not a martyr; in contrast with Father Tyrrell, the other leading figure in English Modernism, who was a martyr but not a saint. That 'not a saint', though largely sober in tone, coming from Miss Petre, has still some of its common overtones of lusty self-assertion. Father Tyrrell was 'no saint'; this is just what made him available for hero-worship. His books were put on the Index, he was driven out of the Jesuit Order, he was deprived of his priestly functions, he was, finally, excommunicated. And these things happened to him because he defied authority; because he was a stormy and reckless and rebellious personality; and for that reason—though for better ones too—he was Miss Petre's hero. These things did not happen to the Baron; because he was not stormy and reckless and rebellious; and so he was nobody's hero. He was prudent and passive and concessive. Even to his niece, who felt for him an emotional devotion comparable to Miss Petre's for Tyrrell, the Baron's personality and actions did not have the sharp, energetic profile of heroism.

Miss Petre even accused the Baron of moral failure in his part in Father Tyrrell's tragedy. The Baron felt almost exactly as Tyrrell did about the theories at stake; the theories of how Rome ought to act in the Modernist crisis, as well as the theories of Biblical criticism, etc. which caused that crisis. Indeed, the Baron had taught Tyrrell to feel as he did. But in the realm of practice, he counselled resistance only up to the verge of disobedience, and always in the most respectful and private style. But this was not moral failure, since it derived so necessarily from the Baron's consistently explicit policy, and indeed implicit *self*. The Church's being so wrong in this matter *could* not abrogate one's duty, one's need, one's desire, to belong fully to her. The situation was changed, one's feeling about it was changed, by the Church's obduracy; however wrong that obduracy was (and the Baron was perfectly clear about that) and fully granting Tyrrell the right to *his* rebellion (and here the Baron's liberality showed itself noblest) he himself was *bound*—by every law of his being—to obey. Because his being, in a profound sense, was that of a great humanist, a great synthesist. He was that, not by avocation, nor even by conviction, but by the structure of his personality; he was called to be that or nothing. His behaviour was not failure, but fulfilment, of that vocation. He was in many ways the Erasmus of the Modernist movement; and Tyrrell's tragic destruction cannot easily seem to us today any more *honourable* than the Baron's saddened survival; though there are of course legitimate personal preferences amongst styles of honour. But our point here is that the Baron's virtues and prudences and passivities all followed the outline of liberal humanism. It is because his personality so vividly represents that *Weltanschauung*, and develops those qualities to sometimes magnificent proportions, that we call him a hero of liberal humanism.

There is of course another sense in which the phrase could be applied to the Baron—as a leader and representative. As a leader in Biblical Studies, in a kind of ecumenicism, in a kind of *aggiornamento* indeed, he was a fore-runner of the contemporary liberalizing movement in the Church. In his own day he was a major focus for the hopes and aspirations of thousands of liberal intellectual Roman Catholics, in England, in France, in Italy, in Germany. Perhaps Wilfrid Ward's words are—by their unintentionality—the best accolade of von Hügel's knighthood in this respect. The Baron, he says, was not controversial enough to be a Catholic; indeed (quite unironically) he was not *narrow* enough. In his own way—by a quite risky ignoring of official disapproval —the Baron did battle for those causes. Certainly he suffered for them. He was nearly excommunicated; Cardinal Bourne consoled von Hügel's family with the words, 'I have never got him into trouble, and I never will'; words which surely reveal both how much trouble he was in, and how magisterial the expression of that disapproval would be. The Baron's wife remained loyal to him, without understanding his position at all; his mother and brother strongly disapproved of his activities; his son-in-law, who served in the Papal Guard, lost his commission apparently because of the connection. He suffered, then, and he represented; he was a hero of liberal humanism in that sense. But, because his 'practical' achievement is nowadays so much less relevant than his personal distinction, the authoritative movement of his mind in meditation, it is the other application of the phrase which is now the more interesting.

Perhaps the most large-scale way in which the Baron 'put things together' was in his reconciliation of Catholicism and Victorianism. He was very much a son of Victorian England, from his enthusiasm for Browning ('that grand Christian poet') to his dislike for Belloc ('a curiously *foreign* mind, and foreign of the poorer type'). Darwin was one of his heroes; 'grandly attractive' and 'not at all clever'. Lytton Strachey was exactly what he meant by clever; and something of what he meant by foreign. Macaulay was lovable but ordinary. Pater was affected and unhealthy.

The Baron, it will be clear, was not an original literary critic. In such matters, his opinions were typical; though in dealing with the literature of the past, where his mind moved more freely, he could make some interesting remarks—comparing Shakespeare with Milton, for example. And there was more than *mere* typicality in his responses to nineteenth-century literature. He drew on some of the best strengths of the Victorian mind. His vocabulary, his conception, his whole portrait of his saint in *The Mystical Element in Religion* is clearly 'derived from' George Eliot. St Catherine of Genoa, as conceived by the Baron, was another Dorothea Brooke. She was a 'grand' and 'noble' woman, a human being on a large scale, trapped into a wrong marriage, torn between its duties and her religious aspirations. She began by demanding appreciation and love, but ended by giving them; 'the noblest nature will begin by getting, not giving'. He speaks of the 'affectionate, ardent, aspiring, impatient, and absolute qualities and habits of her mind and heart and will'. She was all heart, all soul, all spirit; and the Baron is quite explicit about the correlative—no body, no appetite, no sex. There, in that frankness—and the Baron goes into the matter quite fully—we see how intelligently he responded to and used the great Victorian images. He presents plenty of evidence, from the historical records of St Catherine, to prove that the image fitted the facts. At the same time, the image clearly attracted him as an image, something derived from contemporary culture and quite unconnected with the facts. (This 'coincidence' presumably means only that he first began to investigate St Catherine just because she did answer to that image of a great soul and a great woman, so glamorous in his own mind.)

The Baron was no novelist; at his best he can only repeat some of George Eliot's effects, and his 'character' cannot compare with hers, except in one respect. Dorothea's likeness to St Teresa, and her whole potential for sainthood or its secular equivalent, is something no modern reader of *Middlemarch* can feel easy with. The Baron knew a lot more about Catholic sanctity, and the religious vocation, and their relation to the emotional and intellectual qualities George Eliot and he admired so much in their heroines. And this is typical of all the ways he extended the Victorian imagination out into areas which it hadn't, at its most typical, entered. He put together that broad and understanding and forgiving wisdom of George Eliot's—itself so much a matter of synthesis and compromise—with even those dogmatic rigidities, those ecclesiastical severities, those Vatican perspectives on truth and value, which seemed most foreign to it. At the same time, when we remember the date of *The Mystical Element in Religion*, 1908, and compare it with the date of Pater's *Studies in the Renaissance*, 1873, we realize how markedly the Baron's imagination was Victorian. He was out of touch with the liveliest sensibilities of his own time. *Sons and Lovers* came out in 1913, which is to all intents and purposes the same date as *The Mystical Element*. There was thus something ineffectual in the Baron's synthesizing, seen in relation to contemporary culture; but seen in relation to his own personality, as his attempt to put together different kinds of truth, it has great dignity. In this paragraph, for instance, expounding with authority the complexity, the obscurity, the many-levelled richness of experience, he makes us share in his enterprise in *The Mystical Element*.

'Experience indeed and its resultant feeling are always, in the first instance, coloured and conditioned by every kind of individual many-sided circumstances of time and place, of race and age and sex, of education and temperament, of antecedent and environment. And it is this very particular combination, just this one, so conditioned and combined, coming upon me just at this moment and on this spot, just at this stage of my reach or growth, at this turning of my way, that carries with it this particular power to touch or startle, to stimulate or convince. It is just precisely through the but imperfectly analysable, indeed but dimly perceived, individual connotation of general terms; it is by the fringe of feeling, woven out of the past doings and impressions, workings and circumstances, physical, mental, moral, of my race and family and of my own individual life; it is by the apparently slight, apparently far away, accompaniment of a perfectly individual music to the spoken or sung text of the common speech of man, that I am, it would seem, really moved and won.'

One must say that, on the whole, *The Mystical Element* does not succeed in its enterprise. But in such prose as that, in its combinations of categorical logic with concrete and poetic images, of stately music with dry and energetic thought, the Baron triumphs. He lives there, in the act of turning to his task, even though what he then built was not very useful for very long.

Historically, what he built is of course interesting, and was valuable. Of the other Victorian Catholics, the one best qualified by intellect to perform such a function of cultural synthesis was Newman, and he was disqualified by temperament. He was not Victorian enough. He was 'earnest' but hardly 'genial'; he did not participate in the Victorian syndrome of 'manly' qualities, and so his claims even to the 'human' qualities were narrow and feeble. He presented a narrow edge of sensibility and intellect to the world. The Baron himself took a Victorian and British attitude towards him. He described Newman as 'like a very refined sensitive old lady' and declared he could never be made a saint, because saints must be shown to have been deeply joyful. Though he understood and valued Newman intellectually and theologically —he was himself the same kind of Catholic in theology and church policy—he told his niece when he began to send her religious books that he had thought of starting her on a volume of Newman's sermons, but then had decided against it. 'But then these sermons are rigorist—how they have depressed me! Just the opposite from Fénelon, who always braces me.' And of other British Catholics, Wilfrid Ward may be said to have performed a similar function (of reconciling Catholicism and Victorianism) in his biographies of Wiseman, Newman, and Ideal Ward. But between the Baron's mind and Ward's there was no comparison, in range and strength, in vitality and distinction.

If he was more British, more Victorian, than Newman, he was certainly more European, less provincial, than Ward or almost anyone else. One of his biographers tells us that seven-tenths of his reading, all his life long, was in German. Kant was one of the major figures he laboured to answer, to understand, to learn from without yielding to; Troeltsch and Eucken were friends whose work he owed a great deal to, and which he introduced to British readers. In France he was a friend of both Blondel and Loisy, and their teaching, in philosophy and Biblical scholarship respectively, he absorbed. But it was even more essentially his kind of spirituality which he derived from France; the tradition of spiritual direction which includes St François de Sales and Fénelon, and develops through Père Grou and Père de Caussade to the Curé d'Ars, came to him from the Abbé Huvelin, and influenced him very profoundly. The Baron of the last decade of his life, the great man who reveals himself in his letters to his niece, could not have happened without that spiritual tradition. His share in Italian life seems to have been more external, and more limited to the period and the publications of the Modernist movement there. As long as that movement lasted, the Baron was an important figure in Italian religious life, but he does not seem to have been as much indebted to Italian thinkers or men of religion as he was to those of England, France and Germany. He used all four languages fluently, and was said to be the most learned man of his time in England. But from our point of view, the more relevant fact is his ability to *use* the best contemporary learning; to discriminate the better from the worse and to combine different kinds of things. Thus when a correspondent asked him for good books on the psychology of women, he replied that he knew of none. What he himself had learned had been from— besides personal observation—great plays and novels (he cites *Anna Karenina* and George Eliot), the great women letter-writers (Madame de Sévigné and Dorothy Osborne), and the psychological studies of Dr Janet. Despite the old-fashionedness of his literary taste—and indeed of other areas of his sensibility closely connected—the Baron was impressively in touch with contemporary thought. Freud's is the one system of thought of which he seems markedly and impoverishingly ignorant.

What we have described so far is perhaps the reconciliation of Victorianism with Catholicism. The reverse process may be exemplified by this quotation from a letter to Wilfrid Ward. He has said that he 'expects to agree with much of' an essay which Ward has been writing.

'I put my anticipation in this way, because I have to admit that I am generally a little fearful of finding that you have treated the questions *under the aspect of their orthodoxy, and the limits of the latter*. Now whilst quite prepared to think or declare such and such a view or such and such a man, inadequate, impoverishing, or even downrightly untrue, I find I would be acting quite against my whole interior movement and spontaneous conscience, if I allowed myself to shift it on to the ground of orthodoxy, and drawing the line as to who and what is within, who or what is without its pale. I should wish to work all these questions into a very devoted spiritual life, and, as to the results, leave the question of true orthodoxy to God and the Church authorities.'

Truth known by conscience as opposed to truth known by orthodoxy is an issue he is always ready to raise, and ready to settle in favour of the first; and he insists that this is the Catholic solution. The best Catholic solution, that is, for he was quite aware of how often the other is in effect preferred, and how much more often the issue is not raised. His correspondence with Tyrrell is particularly energetic in its expression of these points. Tyrrell wrote to him, 'Rome does terrorize even good men into scepticism about the plainest dictates of their conscience. . . . *Unqualified* obedience is too often viewed as merely a fault on the right side, and not as the profoundest idolatry and immorality.' There we hear the sharp voice of the Victorian Protestant conscience, and the Baron wholly respected that voice. He strove to reconcile its virtues with those of Catholic orthodoxy. At the beginning of *The Mystical Element* he says:

'Hence the following book would condemn itself to pompous unreality were it to mimic official caution and emphasis, whilst ever unable to achieve official authority. It prefers to aim at a layman's special virtues and function; complete candour, courage, sensitiveness to the present and future, in their obscurer strivings towards the good and true, as these have been in their substance already tested in the past, and in so far as such strivings can be forecasted by sympathy and hope.'

Nor was this reconciliation merely a matter of the distinction between the layman's rôle in religion and 'authority's'. Religion itself had a place to keep, and limits to observe. 'However much man may be supremely and finally a religious animal, he is not *only* that; but he is a physical and sexual, a fighting and an artistic, a domestic and social, a political and philosophical animal as well.' This was a principle the Baron was ready to follow out to all kinds of consequences. Thus he warns his niece against Church societies and Church newspapers and so on. 'To love Holy Communion, yet tactfully, unironically, to escape from all Eucharistic guilds, etc.'; never to open a Church newspaper or magazine—this is for him necessary. To be a devoted child of the Church it is not necessary to be *churchy*. And he puts it in larger terms thus:

'If there is one danger for religion—if there is any one plausible, all-but-irresistible trend which, throughout its long rich history, has sapped its force, and prepared the most destructive counter-excesses, it is just that—that allowing the fascinations of Grace to deaden or to ignore the beauties and duties of Nature. What *is* Nature? I mean all that, in its degree, is beautiful, true and good, in this many-levelled world of the one stupendously rich God? Why, Nature (in this sense) is the expression of the God of Nature; just as Grace is the expression of the God of Grace. And not only are *both* from God, and to be loved and honoured as His: but they have been created, they are administered and moved, by God, as *closely interrelated parts of one great whole*—of the full and vivid knowledge and service of Him and happiness of ourselves.'

The Church's task, in fact, is not only to spiritualize civilization, but to civilize spirituality. It is this kind of idea which is most typically von Hügel, and which—worked out with some range and boldness, but without losing touch with more conventional teachings about the Bride of Christ—constitutes one of his great claims on our attention.

The Baron found moral and indeed spiritual values outside the Church; some of which he looked for in vain inside the Church. As Michael de la Bedoyère puts it, during the Modernist controversy he found in science, in criticism, and in historical scholarship an *integrity* and *seriousness* he did not find in Rome. But his most characteristic achievement was the confidence and continuity of tone with which he moved on from acknowledging the Church's rights, her claims, her triumphs, to condemning her failures and her shames. Surely no one else in modern times has more fully acknowledged her special status and—at the same time—so fully maintained the integrity of his judgments of her. He manifested some real sense of shame at her failures. Thus he speaks of critical and historical studies of the Bible.

'And yet such work is but little good, if disavowed, or even if only

tolerated, for we are so behind-hand with it, that for a long time
to come, honest work on our part in this department will necessarily have to be a spreading amongst ours of the sound results of
outside scholarships; the only originality of such work would
just exactly consist in its finding a home in the Church.'

He accepted the age in which he lived. Though he had a favourite
historical period, the thirteenth century, he shows no impulse
to condemn or even reproach the present for being unlike the
past. He was even ready to believe in a kind of progress in religion,
as he explains in his essay of that title.

'Now a fairly steady improvement is possible, desirable, and largely
actual, in the critical sifting and appraisement, as to the dates of
the historical documents, and as to the actual reality and details
of these Accessions; in the philosophical articulation of their
doctrinal and evidential content; in the finer understanding and
wider application of their ethical demands; and in the greater
adequacy (both as to firmness and comprehensiveness) of the
institutional organs and incorporations special to these same
Accessions. . . . Still, we can speak of progress in the Science of
Religion more appropriately than we can of progress in the
Knowledge of Religion.'

Here we see the Baron carrying out the Abbé Huvelin's maxims,
'*Connaître son temps avec amour: Faut-il dire beaucoup de mal de son
siècle? Non . . . marchez avec votre siècle, donnez à votre foi la parure de
vos connaissances intellectuelles. . . . Il ne faut pas non plus se scandaliser
de ce qui est nouveau.*' This was a time when intellectual Catholics
were already conscious of the post-Tridentine quarantine they had
imposed on themselves, and were hoping to emerge from what
is now, in the contemporary liberalizing movement, called the
ghetto. Wilfrid Ward had already coined the phrases 'State of
siege' and 'siege mentality' to describe the Catholic thought of the
previous three centuries. He even spoke of a Roman period,
characterized by legality and militarism and organization, 'now'
to be replaced by a Greek period, of spontaneity and loveliness
and freedom. This was all the more significant, as a theory of
Church history, for being a contrast popular among non-Catholics
to express their hopes for twentieth-century England as opposed
to nineteenth-century. Reconciliation, therefore, and synthesis,
were hopes to be found in many young Catholics' minds, for

perhaps fifteen years before 1907. But the Evangelical *Pascendi*, of that year, putting a final end to Modernism, put an end to Catholic liberalism, too. With Tyrrell driven out of the Church, and Ward driven into conservatism, the Baron was left alone.

The Baron was thereafter the only 'Grecian' of contemporary Catholic leaders, and one of the few manifestations of 'loveliness and freedom' in Catholic thought was his teaching on the religious value of other religions, Christian and Pagan. The one Jesuit theologian he was never tired of citing was the Spanish Cardinal de Lugo (1583–1660) who taught that all the sects teach some truth about God, and that through apprehending that truth all their members *may* achieve salvation. The Baron's application of this lays a characteristic stress on the way it liberalizes a Catholic's *intellectual* life.

'The Unincarnate God has thus a wider range, though a less deep message, than the Incarnate God; and these two Gods are but one and the same God, Who, mysteriously, mostly slowly and almost imperceptibly, prepares or supplements, expresses and otherwise aids Himself, in each way by the other way . . . [and thus some Pagan thinking served and supplemented Christian thinking] . . . Only thus can we be freed from anxiety, and can we sincerely rejoice and be confirmed in our faith in God the Omnipresent, when we discover how largely the Old Testament Book of Wisdom borrows from Plato, how appreciable is St Paul's indebtedness to the Greek Mysteries, how much in the form of the Fourth Gospel comes from Philo, how greatly Tertullian learnt from Roman Law, how important was St Augustine's indebtedness to Plotinus, how almost wholesale was the Dionysian writer's incorporation of Proclus, and how systematic and gratefully avowed was St Thomas of Aquino's utilization of Aristotle.'

At the same time, the movement of his mind was not simply towards tolerance, or not towards a simple tolerance. Thus we find him writing to Tyrrell even as early as 1908:

'And then I feel sure too that, somehow, ever *two* things and not simply *one* have to be attended to: that not only bigotry but also indifference is to be fought and daily overcome. And I must, very simply, confess that if such and such people stand out, in my soul, as illustrations of the former, such and such others stand out in it as examples of the latter. And I notice that all these latter treat good faith, search for the light, self-renouncement, etc., as things *"of course"*, things universal, and lightly, rather irritatedly, to be assumed as operative all round. Now I know well that there is no enclosure within which there flourishes that full (*i.e.* ever operative, ever renewed) good faith, and outside which it does not exist. I merely mean that I have, for myself and in trying to help others, to guard against the *"of course"* business. I find it as impoverishing here, as in Science and Criticism is the assumption of the ease of accuracy: the latter is destructive of the alone fully fruitful disposition for scientific work.'

The Church, then, with all its severities and disciplines, all its rigidities and injustices, must be accepted as humanly useful and necessary, as humanly justified.

'Even vigorous persecution or keen exclusiveness of feeling have —*pace* Lord Acton—saved for mankind, at certain crises of its difficult development, convictions of priceless worth—as in the Deuteronomic Reform and the Johannine Writings. In proportion as men become more manysidedly awake, they acquire at least the capacity for greater sensitiveness concerning the laws and forces intrinsic to the various ranges and levels of life; and, where such sensitiveness is really at work, it can advantageously replace, by means of the spontaneous acceptance of such objective realities, the constraints of past ages—constraints which now, in any case, have become directly mischievous for such minds. None the less will men, after this change as before, require the corporate experience and manifestation of religion as, in varying degrees and ways, a permanent necessity for the vigorous life of religion.'

This too is a part of his teaching on 'Progress in Religion'.

The Baron's mind included, as we have seen, even the principle of exclusiveness. Its characteristic movement was outward, in more and more freedom, towards more and more various goods, but only then to return upon itself more and more insistently, to weave together everything into a coherence, a pattern of mutual accessibility; a movement caught in these typical sentences. 'Daring to the verge of presumption, prudent to the verge of despair. . . . Variety to the verge of dissipation, recollection to the verge of emptiness. . . . A tension to the verge of strain, and a *détente* to the verge of relaxation. . . . Otherworldliness

without fanaticism, and Thisworldliness without philistinism. . . .
A happiness that is not superficial, and a depth that is not morbid. . . .
A fervour without fanaticism, and a generous sympathy without
indifference.'

The one thing he hated was the enforcement of absolute
contrasts and absolute choices; not in the sphere of moral action,
where he was traditionally ascetic, and of which he spoke quite
rarely, but in the sphere of moral-spiritual imagination and
theological *Weltanschauung*. God is the God of Nature as well as of
Grace, he tells his niece; the Maker of the meal as well as of the
yeast. The distinction between the Supernatural and Nature is of
course of prime importance, but it is a distinction which leads to a
fruitful tension and interaction between the two. Understanding
that tension is a prime task for the philosopher of religion. In
fact, though the conflict between Good and Evil looks like the
more promising mental problem for the religious thinker, as it is
the more pressing practical problem, the Baron disagrees.

'Yet I have come to the conclusion, with many another recent or
still-living thinker belonging to the most various religious groups,
races, avocations and temperaments, that a certain monotony,
dullness, oppression, besets much of the spiritual practice and
principles of many religious persons; that these qualities are fatal
to the charm, freshness and freedom essential to religion at its
best; and that, not the contrast between sin and virtue, but the
difference between Nature and Supernature can furnish a solid
starting point for the recovery, the resuscitation of religion, as by
far the richest, the most romantic, the most entrancing and
emancipating fact and life extant or possible anywhere for man.'

Certainly one must not be chosen over the other.

'Those who most exalt the power and need of grace do so usually
by most depreciating nature. God thus gets glorified in direct
proportion as man gets vilified. The more holy I find God, the
more wicked I feel myself to be. This is touching and real, and
almost irresistible to vehement natures, but it is dangerous and
excessive. The inconstancy, variety and insufficiency of nature—
this is the central fact with us—with its profound need of grace,
and its incapacity to gain grace of itself.'

From this developed his own turning away, in later years, from
the emphasis on sin itself.

'It may even be questioned whether a man's apprehensions of the human which are in the most close contact and in the most constant contrast with the same man's apprehensions of the Super-human, are indeed Evil, Suffering, Sin. I believe those closest and most constant concomitants of the superhuman intimations to be, in actual fact, the feelings of Weakness, Instability, Dependence. And these feelings and apprehensions are clearly involved, as concomitant contrasts, in the experiences and concepts of Revelation, Miracle, Creation and Personality, which we deliberately include in our study.'

He refused to identify the supernatural with the miraculous, finding the former manifest in much of man's spiritual life, even that part not professedly religious—in some acts of moral heroism, for instance. For this reason, he was not much interested in miracles. He was uneasy with ecstatic states, inner voices, etc. As for diabolic manifestations, he was sharply disapproving. This is clear in his treatment of such manifestations in the life of St Catherine. Her deathbed vision of a devouring beast in the bedroom he dismisses as having

'all the opaque, uninteresting character of mere, given, unrelated, and unsuggestive fact, which all such purely nervous projections always have; and stands thus in complete and instructive contrast to her finely suggestive and transparent, spiritually significant *Viste,* which contributed so largely to the volitional stimulation and moral and religious witness and truth of her life.'

But what he really values St Catherine for are such things as her doctrine of Purgatory, so gradual in its workings, so purely supernatural in his sense.

'The self-marring of some, probably, in her view, of most souls, gets slowly and blissfully albeit painfully unmade by the voluntary acceptance, on the part of these souls, of the suffering rightly attaching, in a quite determinist manner, to all direct, deliberate, and detached pleasure-seeking of the false self. And this is Purgatory, which is essentially the same whether thus willed and suffered in this world or in the next.'

And as one would expect, he laid considerable stress on the idea of Limbo, which offered yet another modification of the black and white either-or.

The moral struggles and moral achievements which filled the Victorian novel at its best were thus shot through with the supernatural, as von Hügel understood the term, and religious experience was continuous with moral experience. Not that von Hügel was in any danger of confusing the two categories; the 'isness' of religion as opposed to the 'oughtness' of ethics is one of the major themes of *Letters to His Niece,* and the givenness, the transcendence, of God ('religion is adoration') seemed to some the obsession of his later thinking. But his feelings about the two, the moral imperatives he derived from them, were in close relation with each other. Creatureliness, his favourite virtue, partakes of the nature of both. He defines it somewhere as the absence of self-infatuation, and it derives properly from one's sense of being entirely the work of one's Creator. But during the crisis of his daughter's faith he wrote to Tyrrell that he could bear her leaving the Church, and even her ceasing to be a Christian, if she could retain her creatureliness; which then appears as a largely moral virtue, a dutifulness towards 'life', of a George Eliot kind.

Christianity was for von Hügel essentially a matter of personality.

'For its originality consists not so much in its single doctrines, or even in its teaching as a whole, and in the particular place each doctrine occupies in this teaching, as in its revelation, through the person and example of its Founder, of the altogether unsuspected depth and inexhaustibleness of human Personality, and of this Personality's source and analogue in God, of the simplicity and yet difficulty and never-endingness of the access of man to God, and of the ever preceding condescension of God to man.'

The kind of interest taken in personality here, the reverence, the connection with the idea of freedom, is very close to the interest of George Eliot and Tolstoy.

'Here again the true solution will be found in an ever fuller conception of Personality, and of its primary place in the religious life. For even the bare possibility of the truth of all religion, especially of any one of the characteristic doctrines of Christianity, involves a group of personalist convictions. Here a human person begins more as a possibility than a reality. Here the moral and spiritual character has to be built up slowly, painfully, laboriously, throughout all the various stages and circumstances of life, with their endless combinations of pleasure and pain, trouble and temptation, inner and outer help and hindrance, success and failure. Here the simply Individual is transformed into the truly Personal only by the successive sacrifice of the lower, of the merely animal and impoverishingly selfish self, with the help of God's constant prevenient, concomitant, and subsequent grace. And here this constantly renewed dropping and opposing of the various lower selves, in proportion as they appear and become lower, to the soul's deepest insight, in the growing light of its conscience and the increasing elevation of the moral personality, involves that constant death to self, that perpetual conversion, that unification and peace in and through a continuous inner self-estrangement and conflict, which is the very breath and joy of the inner life.'

This conception of the moral life is very much that of the great nineteenth-century novelists, and—once granted the changes in interest and emphasis brought by time—probably all novelists interested in moral life, in all ages, must have this conception somewhere in their minds. But for von Hügel, this is part of the specifically religious life, and these connections are 'involved in' the characteristic doctrines of Christianity. It is then religion and literature he is here interconnecting, through their common interests in morality.

This idea of personality obviously includes a strong sense of the rôle played by feeling and will even in truths of the understanding, and this was important to von Hügel. Philosophically, it seems to have been Blondel and Newman who taught him this point of view, but temperamentally he must have been prepared for it already, and have needed it. Maurice Nédoncelle puts it this way: 'The first confused findings of nature do not develop into truths of the understanding save through the mediation of the moral will. It is only through the capacity to live and to act in conformity with an ideal, that our capacity for recognizing reality is awakened and becomes able to take charge. Conduct is thus the metaphysical field where nature and thought, the immanence of the subjective act and the transcendence of objective truth, meet.' The great enigma he propounds at the very beginning of *The Mystical Element*, an 'enigma of life', is that the Universal and Abiding does not move the will; and that what does move it is individual and evanescent. The practical solution to which is of course a biography of the kind he is writing.

'Only a life sufficiently large and alive to take up and retain, within its own experimental range, at least some of the poignant question and conflict as well as of the peace-bringing solution and calm: hence a life dramatic with a humble and homely heroism which, in rightful contact with and in rightful renunciation of the Particular and Fleeting, ever seeks and finds the Omnipresent and Eternal; and which again deepens and incarnates (for its own experience and apprehension and for the stimulation of other souls) this Transcendence in its own thus gradually purified Particular: only such a life can be largely persuasive at least for us Westerns and in our times.'

This approach makes him see all forms of thought and study as modes of moral action, with their own characters *as* forms. Hence he describes modern (that is, post-Newtonian) science thus, at the beginning of *The Mystical Element*.

'This study was perceived, even by the shallower thinkers, to be fair and rational and fruitful in itself; and it was found, by some few deep spirits, to be a strangely potent means of purifying, enlarging, "deprovincializing" man himself. The severe discipline of a rigorous study of man's lowly, physical conditions and environment, things hitherto so despised by him, was now at last to purify him of his own childish immediacy of claim. The pettily selfish, shouting Individual was to pass through the broad, still, purgatorial waters of a temporary submergence under the conceptions, as vivid as though they were direct experiences, of ruthless Law, of Mechanism, of the Thing; so as to pass out, purified and enlarged, a Person, expressive of the Universal and Objective, of Order and of Law.'

And seeing science this way, he was free from that resentment of it so almost inescapable for non-scientists, especially for such lovers of 'personality' as the Baron.

He had a clear sense of the moral dangers in the predominance of science. He blamed our blindness to the possibility of the higher sins, pride, vanity, self-sufficiency, on that predominance, on the triumph of mathematical, mechanical, natural sciences. They make us believe only what is absolutely clear, and prevent us from blaming those who claim to have no responsibility for what is

not clear. But he goes on, asking how then moral responsibility
can enter into scientific work.

'The answer is, that certain dispositions of the will very certainly
enter into all deep and delicate apprehensions, be they of the life-
history of a clematis-plant, or of the doings of a spider. A certain
rare disoccupation with the petty self is here a *sine qua non* condition
of any success; it is this noble freedom from all self which makes
the character, *e.g.* of a Charles Darwin so very great. And the
answer is further that, if a certain parental temper, a loving
humility which joyfully bends down and contracts itself into the
life of creatures lower than man, be necessary for the understanding of the orchid or the earth-worm, so a certain filial
temper, a loving humility which joyfully reaches up, and stretches
itself out wide towards the life above it, is necessary for our
apprehension of God.'

But perhaps most striking of all is his vivid sense of the moral
dignity of all abstract intellectual work.

'Such science will help to discipline, humble, purify the natural
eagerness and wilfulness, the cruder forms of anthropomorphism,
of the human mind and heart. This turning to the visible will thus
largely take the place of that former turning away from it; for only
since the Visible has been taken to represent laws, and, provision-
ally at least, rigorously mechanical laws characteristic of itself,
can it be thus looked upon as a means of spiritual purification.

Such science again will help to stimulate those other, deeper
activities of human nature . . . perhaps never has man turned to
the living God more happily and humbly, than when coming
straight away from such rigorous, disinterested phenomenal
analysis, as long as such analysis is felt to be both other than, and
preliminary and secondary to, the deepest depths of the soul's life
and all ultimate Reality.'

He had therefore a sense of the progress of the mind in this way;
a sense of history as growing and changing and bringing gifts as
well as curses; as not the dreary cycle it seems to so many literary
humanists. He wrote to Tyrrell, 'It would be easy, I think, to
show how, even still in St Catherine's day, science represented by
such fantastic anthropomorphic conceptions as those of Paracel-
sus, and scholarship, by such pretentious omniscience as that of

Pico della Mirandola, could not as yet be the ready found purification I think they both can now be easily turned to.'

So what we have is a vigorous synthetic mind, mastering a remarkable number of elements in contemporary thought, and making them into patterns which, if not solid enough to outlast their generation, are quite solid enough to support his claims on our attention as a pattern-maker. A mind, moreover, eminently able, by its skill with language, to capture for us the dignity and the excitement of the thinking function, and so to satisfy our attention. In that sense, as Man Thinking, it is still possible to find Baron von Hügel a significant thinker.

A liberal humanist was of course the last thing Yeats wanted to be. A liberal humanist is a man who sets up for moderateness, due proportion, doing everything justice—for wisdom; and Yeats explicitly renounced all claim to wisdom. 'God guard me,' he says in 'A Prayer for Old Age',

From all that makes a wise old man
That can be praised of all;
O what am I that I should not seem
For the song's sake a fool?

He was ready to be foolish because to be sensible, to be moderate, to be wise, no longer seemed an act of life. He was reacting—for the song's sake—against the wisdom, the humanism, of the nineteenth century, with which von Hügel had identified himself. For instance, commenting on George Eliot and her insistence on the moral law, Yeats said, 'Surely the tongue of the poet is for other teaching?', and the style as much as the substance of the remark indicates his refusal to obey the sadly earnest suasions of that humanism. And in this he was like his great symbolist contemporaries, like Rilke in Germany and Blok in Russia, Rilke with his amateur spiritualism and mysticism, Blok with his explicit attacks on humanism.

These were poets, concerned primarily with poetry, but they spoke for all men, demanding a kind of experience which nineteenth-century humanism had made impossible, and which men needed not only in order to write poems but in order to live. Poet is simply another name for man using his imagination rather than his reason or his faith.

The artist, John Butler Yeats said, is man *as man,* the most human of all types. 'For the song's sake' was closely related to 'for the imagination's sake' and 'for life's sake'. For Blok, music was *the* symbol, in the largest sense of symbol, of all the sacred, irrational, and anti-conventional forces that add up to life.

In *The Downfall of Humanism* (1919) Blok wrote, 'The mistake of the inheritors of humanistic culture, the fatal contradiction into which they fell, originated in their exhaustion. The spirit of integrity, the "spirit of music", abandoned them, and so they blindly put their trust in historical time. . . . There are two kinds of time, one historical according to the calendar, and the other "musical", without date or number. In the consciousness of civilized man the first kind alone is immutably present: but it is only when we realize how near we are to Nature, only when we abandon ourselves to the wave of music issuing from the chorus of the Universe, that we live in the second.' Blok, Rilke, and Yeats turned their backs on 'the consciousness of civilized man', and made themselves over into 'uncivilized men' with a recklessness the world has rarely seen. This process of self-formation started with very different raw materials in the three cases, but it is striking how much Rilke and Yeats had in common finally, in their images of themselves as poets, each with his Tower, and his Epigraph, and his Spirits, and his Rose.

This reaction into irrationalism was common to most of the great writers of the time, and indeed its equivalent is to be found in areas of thought far beyond the borders of literature or of all the arts. It inspired much major imaginative work, which humanism itself could never have inspired. It is humanism's best virtue that it can usefully serve even where it does not directly inspire, by its sense of measure and its largeness and steadiness of vision, but inspiration remains primary. Moreover, the virtues and usefulnesses we associate with humanism are not to be identified with the articles of faith in that creed. At certain times, and this was no doubt one of them, a man might serve those values better by behaviour that involved denying those articles than by reciting them reverently. Indeed, I would admit that von Hügel's humanism did not deserve to be reverently preserved and transmitted—it needed to be rebelled against. It was dull and faded when he inherited it, and if he had been a major creative thinker he would have renewed its spirit much more than he did.

Nevertheless, the question remains whether what Yeats (and Rilke and Blok) enacted was merely the rejection of the outworn, or whether it involved a heavy sacrifice of the still living. It was possible, after all, for T. S. Eliot to reject the impulse to synthesize everything good, and for E. M. Forster to reject the rational and polite, without Yeats's completeness of commitment to 'the poetic' alone. And if both of those writers seem emblems of compromise of a limiting kind, surely

D. H. Lawrence shows how boldly one could go against George Eliot without sacrificing all her heritage. In *The Lost Girl,* Miss Frost embodies George Eliot's values quite nobly, and Alvina appreciates those values quite fully even as she turns away from them and 'loses' herself.

What disturbs me in writers like Yeats is that as they turn away from the values of the past they cut themselves off—they alter the shape and texture of their selves so that the old values have no hold on them. By comparison, even Lawrence remained always potentially able to see the case for reason and restraint and self-sacrifice even while he recommended the opposite. Yeats seems to have cultivated the inability to see what didn't suit him. Ellman, in *The Identity of Yeats,* tells the story of how the poet upset Abinah Bose, when the latter came to see him in 1937, asking Yeats for a message for India, in her distress and unrest.

' "Let 100,000 men of one side meet the other. That is my message to India." ' He then, as Bose describes the scene, 'strode swiftly across the room, took up Sato's sword, and unsheathed it dramatically and shouted, "Conflict, more conflict".'

I cannot see anything there but childish histrionics, and of a kind, considering the situation, in the worst possible taste. But Ellman continues, 'The message sounds savage enough, but can serve more purpose if we put aside the histrionics which made Yeats for the moment oblivious to India and politics and everything but his momentary dramatic rôle. It had its origin in a view of the world as almost incessant strife between opposites, and in a similar view of the poem.' I must object that the whole tendency of Yeats's ideas was to make him *habitually* 'oblivious to India, and politics and everything but his momentary dramatic rôle', and this was no 'for the moment' accident. But I am even more upset by the bland way Ellman interprets the whole scene somehow to Yeats's credit—to dignify his 'view of the world' and his 'similar view of the poem'.

For that is what Ellman's book adds up to, an endorsement of Yeats's way of handling his experience; and since Yeats's experience included deciding about some of the largest possible questions, Ellman's endorsement involves him in some large commitments. Yeats's poetry, he tells us, 'fights its way beyond the frontiers of common apprehension, and brings previously untamed areas of thought and feeling under strong rule. . . . He presents this faith with such power and richness that Eliot's religion, in spite of its honesty and loftiness, is pale and infertile in comparison.' Surely Eliot's religion, even considered just as material for poetry, has a reality and a dignity which Yeats's lacks? Pale and infertile in some sense it may be, but the gaudiness and multitudinousness of Yeats's icons surely add up to a reason why we don't take his religion seriously. Yeats's religion is 'for the song's sake' in important ways, and serious religion cannot be that. Surely however concerned we are with poetry, we must retain a sense of what religion is that makes this difference of quality between Yeats's and Eliot's subject-matter rather important?

Towards the end of Ellman's book he sums up, 'What emerges from a consideration of Yeats's whole poetic career is an impression of its seriousness and importance.' This seems to me true only from a categorically aesthetic point of view—interpreting the word 'aesthetic' fairly largely. 'His sense of decorum never fails him because he knows through long testing the value of everything; and this power to estimate things at their true worth contributes to his talent for general statement.' This is the root of the matter. If Yeats chose to make himself foolish rather than wise, I am disturbed (because I am a literary man) but I have no right to protest. But if I am asked to believe (because I am a literary man) that Yeats's choice somehow did not make him foolish, that it made him *wise*; then I must refuse, with some indignation, I must protest.

It seems to me Yeats did make himself a foolish passionate man; and that this is a considerable price to pay. A foolish man, despite Mr Ellman, does not know the value of everything, or even of most things. I think I appreciate the value of the passionateness Yeats aimed at and in some sense achieved, though I don't see, finally, how a self-respecting man could make the choice he made. In saying that, however, I am conscious that the predispositions of my own temperament affect my judgment. Whereas temperament has surely nothing to do with my feeling that Yeats did make a choice between two crucial alternatives, did turn his back on one thing in order to get another, and that a literary training must not, cannot, mean such a blinding of one eye that we cannot see past what he gained to what he lost.

Of course when I call Yeats foolish I distinguish foolishness from stupidity; the second being the kind of failure of intelligence that seems to come from lack of ability, the first from a perversion of ability; but both are kinds of failure. Yeats was clearly gifted with extraordinary powers of intelligence, but he so used them as to talk a great deal of nonsense. Von Hügel never talked nonsense; and on many subjects he talked a great deal of wonderful sense. On the other hand, set beside Yeats, he seems much of the time only half alive. He has his own kind of diffuse and abstract energy, but never the clean and compact shapeliness, the hot-blooded, clear-eyed pride of movement, which we call vitality; that quality Yeats so much admired and in some measure finally achieved. Von Hügel had made his choice and paid his price, too, as we shall see in the next essay. I think one knows, reading him, that if he had tried to write poetry, it would have been bad.

In many ways, therefore, I accept Yeats's account of the alternatives he had to choose between, as he describes them in the debate between the Soul and the Heart which makes up the seventh section of 'Vacillation'.

The Soul: *Seek out reality, leave things that seem.*
The Heart: *What, be a singer born and lack a theme?*
The Soul: *Isaiah's coal, what more can man desire?*
The Heart: *Struck dumb in the simplicity of fire!*
The Soul: *Look on that fire, salvation walks within.*
The Heart: *What theme had Homer but original sin?*

I think the heart is right, and von Hügel's way would be likely to strike Yeats part-dumb; though what von Hügel stands for is less a simplicity of fire than a complexity of reasons, a morass of duties and prudences. And it would have been a great sacrifice, that partial dumbness. We may take our emblem of all that would have been lost from the thrilling and splendid last stanza of the preceding section.

From man's blood-sodden heart are sprung
Those branches of the night and day
Where the gaudy moon is hung.
What's the meaning of all song?
'Let all things pass away.'

That is a very noble and exciting human gesture, of a kind no culture can afford to lose. I think it implies ultimately a background of more prudent and conventional life, but that background cannot be allowed to inhibit with its claims the freedom of the great foreground figures— *that* cannot be what humanism means.

So I agree with Yeats in much of what he says, and if I disagree with some of his description of the alternatives, this is not of the first importance. In the first section of 'Vacillation' he sets the problem up like this:

Between extremities
Man runs his course;
A brand, or flaming breath,
Comes to destroy
All those antinomies
Of day and night;
The body calls it death,
The heart remorse.
But if these be right
What is joy?

Von Hügel's view of life, as it seems to me, contained quite as many antinomies as Yeats's, and Yeats's choice, joy, was quite as much of a brand or flaming breath, destroying the half it rejected. It seems to me that his was more of a simplification. Though perhaps my idea of the choice differs from Yeats's mostly because each idea expresses the consequence of a personal commitment. Whatever one chooses, one is struck by the bewilderment of further choices opened to one in consequence, and feels that the opposite decision would have made life simpler though poorer. So I can't claim any clear, objectively obvious superiority for my way of seeing the problem. I can't ask that Yeats's way should be rejected. But I *can*—and this surely is of the first importance—claim that the possibility of my choice should always be implicitly there in the language with which the critic discusses Yeats's choice. The critic must be that much of a humanist whatever the poet chooses to be. I have—as humanist—no quarrel—no wholly serious quarrel—with Yeats, only with Ellman. The poet, by the form in which he writes, declares himself an experimenter if not a dissenter. It is only when the critics, the scholars, the teachers, the leaders of the whole literary culture, endorse his dissents, that the humanist need feel himself seriously challenged.

But the contrast between Yeats and von Hügel is interesting in another way. Yeats's ideas, as he often declared, were chosen to make it possible for him to become a certain person—to achieve a certain psychological type. His morality was designed to impose a pattern not so much on his actions, the field of more conventional morality, as on his impulses; and his pattern was not so much one of repression as of release. He tried to make himself over even in the very roots of his nature. One of Ellman's chapters is called 'The Pursuit of Spontaneity', and the paradox is a very serious one.

In this effort of self-formation, Yeats was typical, only going further than most of his contemporaries. For him, as for Blok and Rilke, the idea of becoming a poet—not merely writing verses, but acting, feeling, being, in a specially intense way—was a vocation that justified and indeed energized, extraordinary efforts. But the poet only precedes all other men and in more ordinary measure I think most men of sensibility now follow the same policy.

In any case, von Hügel made equally prodigious efforts of self-formation, but in an opposite direction, in response to *his* vocation, to become a Christian humanist. The two men therefore contrast vividly as psychological types—or more exactly as types of psychological self-formation—as well as ideologically and aesthetically.

The Catholic as psychological type:
von Hügel's pyschology as related to his Catholicism

It is not easy to define pyschology as I am using the word here. But one thing I do *not* mean by it is any parlour-Freudian discussion of the Baron's anal/oral/phallic orientation. My interest lies midway between such specialities and the old-fashioned novelistic psychology of social rôles. It may be profitable, however, to dwell a moment on this second meaning of the word, for the sake of one or two examples who are relevant to our understanding of von Hügel as contrasts. Let us consider W. G. Ward (1812–82) and his son Wilfrid (1856–1916) as psychological types whose psychology had something to do with their social rôles as English Catholics.

W. G. Ward was nicknamed Ideal Ward because of his book *The Ideal of a Christian Church,* of 1844, part of the literature of the Oxford Movement. This book was condemned by Convocation in 1844, and Ward was deprived of his Oxford degrees and his tutorship. In 1845, before Newman himself, he and his new wife became Roman Catholics. His marriage just before had caused something of a scandal, because he was still a Church of England clergyman, and yet he had been the most notable arguer that priests should be celibate. Ward's answer to his critics takes us to the heart of his intellectual personality; since Anglican orders were invalid, he was no priest, and therefore he could marry. This is so revealing because it was quite serious. The bright paradoxicalness seemed only the glitter of naked truth to Ward. In his mind this was a matter of pure logic.

Going over to Rome, he went characteristically to the extreme right wing. He declared he would like a Papal Bull every morning, to tell him how to think. He was an ardent supporter of Manning against Newman for the Archbishopric of Westminster, because Newman was liberal, or—more dangerously still—was not really conservative without being definably liberal. This even though he fully appreciated the superiority of Newman's mind and spirituality;

even though Manning's company—and he became a frequent visitor to the Wards—was a penance to him. And he drew frequent attention to such paradoxes in his own behaviour. A friend of Thomas Huxley at the Metaphysical Society, he one day took him aside and said that as they were on such friendly terms, he did not think it right to let him remain ignorant. Of what? Huxley asked.

' "Well, we Catholics hold that So-and-so and So-and-so" (naming certain of our colleagues whose heresies were of a less deep hue than mine) "are not guilty of absolutely unpardonable error; but your case is different, and I feel it is unfair not to tell you so." '

Huxley replied, he says, 'My dear Dr Ward, if you don't mind, I don't', and seems to have believed that this was a noble directness and simplicity in Ward. But we must surely find a curious failure of feeling in the whole gesture—that is, if Ward meant to be taken seriously. What Huxley's reply suggests is that he was not taken seriously, and that his behaviour as a whole had not led Huxley to expect seriousness from him.

A very forceful personality, and effective within institutions (like the Church in England), he was yet characteristically a disciple in the world of thought, and thus even in the world of power tended to work *through* Manning, or through dogma, or through canon law. He carried other people's principles to their logical consequences—a kind of intellectual N.C.O. Logic was his way of relating to life, to a quite unusual degree. Extremely fat, clumsy with material objects, he was quite uninterested in the agriculture and the natural beauty of the estates he had inherited, but passionately interested in chess, music and dialectic. He was a self-invented man; he cut himself off from his past by becoming a Roman Catholic, just as he cut himself off from his environment by his sensual anaesthesia. His interests were very few and very intense, and he was extremely conscious of his own persona. 'I have the mind of an archangel in the body of a rhinoceros.' The style as much as the content reveals the man; reveals the playfulness at the root of his personality, despite the rigour of his logic and the absoluteness of his seriousness. The impudent complacency of that remark crystallizes a hundred vaguer suggestions of someone playing at being himself, someone executing the gestures of the adult rôle he has chosen with complacent over-incisiveness, an unconsciously mocking exaggeration.

There is a lot more evidence of the same kind—his demand for the subordination of the laity to the clergy, for a purely Catholic education, for a Continental as opposed to a British Catholicism, his distrust of the whole modern world—but the point is surely made. We all recognize that kind of infantilism working itself out in the largest cultural terms, discovering with ever-renewed delight that logic will cut through the most massive-seeming of commonsense adult assurances, being the *enfant terrible* who can yet prove himself more serious than anyone else at the drop of a hat. We recognize it the more easily because we have seen often before this whole syndrome—fatness, infantilism, love of the abstract, cleverness (often at chess, or comic songs, or anagrams, or detective work)—combined with an authoritarian Catholicism. This combination is naturally most to be looked for in converts, and Chesterton is no doubt the most famous British example.

Men who exemplify this pattern may be admirable in many respects, but they are archetypal enemies of 'life'. The sense or senses in which we are using that term will become clearer as the essay proceeds, but let us say that it refers here primarily to mature relationships and personality structures which allow full dignity to the instinctive powers of the self. Such men exemplify the triumph of pure intellect and abstract will over the more instinctive parts of the mind. Von Hügel himself (though no spokesman for 'life', as we shall see) may be our corroborator here; in his letter about Ideal Ward to the latter's son.

'Indeed, it was this state of tension of mind and nerve which struck me from the first as a concomitant, more probably a part-cause, of his special strength and special weakness.

His separate courses at dinner, served in quick succession so as to avoid all delay; his sensitiveness to the vibration of the ground caused by one's approaching the part of the terrace on which, immediately after his dinner, he would be playing chess; his insisting upon getting out and crossing on foot a footbridge, when his carriage forded a shallow brook; and, later on, by the time our friendship had ripened into close intimacy, his suddenly breaking off in the midst of a sentence with an "excuse me, only a ten minutes' nap", and then and there throwing himself on our drawing-room sofa, and, at the end of that time, waking up refreshed and vigorous; all this, with numberless other little symptoms, meant one and the same thing,—an overwrought brain and overstrung nerves.

It was the same mentally. His inability to remain for an instant without definite occupation or amusement for his mind, or to conceive that any living being could so remain; his calling his youngest daughter into his study, with the explanation, "Margaret, *do* attend to poor Fish, amuse the poor dog, he is so dull, so bored!"; his incapacity for imagining that a man could keep simply neutral in his estimate of a stranger ... etc. . . . all this hangs well together, and spells a man who could affirm and who could deny, but who could not suspend, who could revolutionize, but who could hardly reform his judgment. . . .

It used to strike me so strangely to notice in your father, how the more remote a conclusion before him was from the certain premiss, the more anxious and emphatic he would be in insistence on its being "certain if anything is certain", on its "unspeakable importance", on suspense in the matter as "truly alarming". And yet I found he was but following out the natural workings of his own mind. Only by getting a perfectly water- and air-tight vessel of authority could he conceive it possible to keep every particle,— which meant any particle,—of the Faith. The fight with the enemy was on the frontiers, hence a shed or a tree-stump there was in a sense more important than all the treasures of the capital ...

He would, for one thing, always argue as if a particular Definition or Church pronouncement were not only true as far as it went, but as if it were so completely co-extensive with the full truths of which it necessarily gave but *some* negative or positive determination, that it would bear arguing from in any direction and to any distance.'

With such a father, Wilfrid Ward naturally grew up to be a young man. As Chesterton put it, 'It was the paradox of Wilfrid Ward that while he was a man astonishingly young for his years . . . he yet seemed somehow to be the contemporary of the great men whom he had known as a boy.' This is a paradox of logic but not of psychology, for the old-fashioned air is quite parallel with the boyishness in announcing the innocence of one whose development was sheltered from many of the tests and stresses of the adolescence process. Ideal Ward's children did not play at games that could prepare them for adult manhood or womanhood, but at being saints, martyrs, cardinals, resplendent ideals to be aspired after all through life. Wilfrid Ward's friendships, even in manhood, were mostly with older men: the Baron, the Cardinal, the Duke (of Norfolk), etc.; and he was both their pupil and their jester. He was a remarkable mimic. Gladstone 'almost tumbled out of his chair' laughing at Ward's imitation of Manning. Tennyson accused him with comic severity, 'Wilfrid Ward, I'm told you mimic me!' Manning also addressed him as 'Wilfrid Ward', and that mode of address evokes the whole atmosphere of privileged adolescent teasing he seems to have carried with him. In 1900, even, his wife complained of their knowing only people much older than themselves and Ward was then forty-four.

He was a Conservative in politics. He was allied with Lord Hugh Cecil and George Wyndham as the Die-Hards who fought the Parliament Bill of 1911 which took power from the House of Lords. In theological and ecclesiastical matters his characteristic stance is exemplified in his comments on the Baron. He found that von Hügel did not clinch his arguments, did not provide an intellectual basis for Catholicism, was carried away by new views, and had insufficient knowledge of human nature. Above all, the Baron was not controversial enough, not *narrow* enough, to be a Catholic. Ward was not, like his father, an eager reactionary, but he responded to the voice of authority as to something absolute, in intellectual, moral, and spiritual matters. He was no *enfant terrible*; he was not, in the sense his father was, childish; he was boyish—laughing, eager, open, playful, completely amiable, and, when he had to move into the sphere of adult behaviour, prudent, conventional, dull, a pupil.

In Wilfrid Ward and his father, then, we see two psychological types prominently associated with Catholicism in England. And by 'associated with' I mean to imply some kind of causal or genetic connection. The Church has attracted and fostered, even among its intellectuals, and even in such a fiery personality as W. G. Ward, kinds of personal immaturity. It would be easy to cite much more lurid examples from quite other families, but let us conclude with two more examples of the Wards, two more quotations from Maisie Ward's book about her parents. The first is from a letter by Lady Margaret Howard, Mrs Wilfrid Ward's aunt. 'I think of nothing night or day but Father Gurdon's lectures. . . . At the present moment I am occupied with making an exhaustive study of St Thomas in Latin! Whereat much laughter. What are your ideas on the subject of matter and form? I feel rather helpless about it.' The second is part about her, part by her. 'From books she could turn to very vigorous action. She could run six miles in a paper-chase and then dance into the night . . . after she grew up she would say, "I came home so hungry from the dinner last night because I was afraid of eating for fear of losing some of the talk." ' I think we all recognize there a third psychological type or style, a third component of Catholic culture—girlishness; an enthusiastic, energetic, coltish, niceness of mind. It bears the same stamp—of a not unintended immaturity —as the boyishness and the childishness. She does not hope to be on equal terms with St Thomas, the kind of equality a reader achieves with a writer; her dignity lies all in the winsomeness and wholesomeness of her accepted inequality.

It is worth knowing something about these people in order to understand the Baron, for they were all his contemporaries, and in some sense his partners in the (still fairly small-scale) enterprise of English intellectual Catholicism. One thing we shall see is that the Baron's personality was that of a self-responsible, fully-grown man, not that of a boy or of a child. There is a weight of thought and feeling involved in all his characteristic acts, thought and feeling tested and trained by a consciousness of great exemplars, with whom he did hope to be on equal terms. But it is even more worth pointing out that the Baron's psychology could not be revealed by any such method of description. The cultural categories into which one could fit him would plainly not reach to any 'point' about him in which an intelligent reader is interested. The Baron's prose, for instance, unlike Lady Margaret Howard's, demands to be examined and admired on its own terms, as prose. 'The Divine Action will thus stimulate and inform the human action somewhat like the force that drives the blood within the stag's young antlers, or like the energy that pushes the tender sap-full fern-buds up through the hard, heavy ground.' The unforced forcefulness achieved there in the handling of language—and in theology, in philosophy, in personal relationships, in practical politics, he was equally a figure of natural power—that kind of impressiveness cannot be explained by categories of cultural rôle-playing. He was not a type in that sense.

A first sketch of the Baron

To say that may well seem a paradox, since most accounts of the

Baron give us a dozen features more grossly novelistic than any of W. G. Ward's, features of behaviour obviously in some sense intended by their originator to identify him as a 'character'— almost in the Dickensian sense. In his later years, clearly, the Baron came to terms with life by such means. He became an eccentric and a sentimentalist; he offered the world a colourful, gesturing, bumbling figure it could laugh at and love.

Michael de la Bedoyère tells us of his manner in these years. In summer he wore a Panama hat and a cream umbrella, in the winter a top hat with a massive cloak, and black wool gloves, edging his escort off the pavements of Kensington into the traffic as he deafly shouted quite intimate spiritual advice into the other's ear; and putting on the kind of comically hearty performance, with unsuccessful jokes and incorrect slang, one example of which Wilfrid Ward describes as reducing the Metaphysical Society to helpless laughter. This colourfulness was apparently a development of his later middle age. His niece tells us of how his social personality changed from when she first knew him.

'I was already thirty-eight when first my uncle began to teach me. I had known him as a child, but I was afraid of him then, I was afraid first of his deafness and of his ear-trumpet, and next I was afraid of his strangeness. When I saw him at my grandmother's I always hoped I would not have to sit next to him at luncheon. I liked to watch him, but I dreaded to attract his attention. He seemed to me something so different and unordinary, something rather wild, a being belonging to another world.'

But later, to accommodate himself to others, he adopted the comic hearty vocabulary his niece tells us of: 'whole hoggers', 'lumpers', 'meansters', 'my old boot'; his dress and his behaviour grew more and more eccentric; and he had his dogs to sentimentalize over. 'I was much troubled, at the time, with your letter telling of dear, fine Ben's going,' he wrote to Maude Petre, during the war. And in his diary for 1922, 'Puck's vet came in a fine Motor car to see him. He, Puck, has cardial Asthma. The heart, incurable, but the asthma *may* go. Will not hear of his destruction; and is against taking him away even for a little—he would fret too much. . . .' And the next day, 'Waked up by Puck three times in the night, the darling little thing in great distress.' It was above all in these relationships with his dogs that he was able finally to expend the wealth of his unused tenderness.

Established as a 'character', he was exempted from those demands on him which he had found hard to meet, and which had part provoked in him, part derived from, that irritability he blamed himself for so often. In later years, at least, one gathers that that irritability did not express itself very openly, but there is one rather touching and typical example in his message to his niece when her father, a famous musician, was dying. He remembers, and regrets, having once said sharply to her father, some years before, at the beginning of some train trip together, that he must absolutely decline to talk about music on that journey. The later von Hügel, self-insulated, Pickwick-like, exempted from the demands made on normal men, escaped a hundred such tests of his humanity; but he was exposed also to the affectionate (and condescending) ridicule of men even like Wilfrid Ward and Loisy—the men he needed to have take him seriously. He is usually *'ce bon baron'* to his French correspondents; Loisy says, *'Car le bon baron, lorsqu'il se mettait en devoir d'écrire, ne savait pas être bref.'* And Loisy again, quoting, 'How dangerous the Bolchevikism in the air is! If only we could all attain so well-balanced a *sanity,* a *centredness,* an *inclusivity,* so that neither *Prussianism* nor *Bolchevikism* do no more than help us to escape their dangers!' Loisy comments, *'On me pardonnera, je pense, de n'avoir pas corrigé ces touchants barbarismes.'* At such moments, one must admit, the Baron can sound like a latter-day Queen Victoria.

In all these ways the Baron *was* a type, as we used that term about W. G. Ward. But these ways have nothing to do with the quality of life he achieved, in his writing and in his relationships, and they do not begin to define the interest he has for us. They are merely his necessary compromises, his ways of coming to terms with his personal failures. And they amount to turning away from a good deal of himself, that part we called before 'life', experience characterized by the instincts and the senses, the immediate, premental impulses and responses.

The Baron insisted always that he was 'the work of religion', that he had turned away from his natural instinctive self, and made himself over anew; and his language makes it clear that he is referring to a psychological event as well as a spiritual one.

'The fact is that the poor thing that scribbles these lines is the *work of religion.* I weigh my words, Child: I should not be physically alive at this moment, I should be, were I alive at all, a corrupt or at least an incredibly unhappy, violent, bitter, self-occupied destructive soul were it not for religion—for its having come and *saved me from myself*—it, and nothing else.'

In the same passage, he says that religion has no easy entrance into natures that are naturally good—to offer religion to such people might do them harm. But for people like him, religion is life. He recurs to the same theme eleven years later, to someone quite different.

'Let me then go back in my mind to when I was your own age, and try to get on to paper one predominant desire which then came into my own inner life. You see, when I began to try to be good—to serve God—I already, alas, found myself involved in gravely bad habits and inclinations. But this, once I was, by God's grace, awakened to long to be straight and true—to go direct to God and Christ—had one great advantage. I saw young fellows all around me fretting to be *free*, to be their own sole, full masters. They fretted against this and that thing; against this and that person. They thought that if only they could get away from these, they would indeed be free. But I myself *could not feel that to be nearly enough*; I was too little happy in myself to fiddle-faddle at such little things! I wanted, *I had to,* get rid of—not those outside conditions, not those other people and their orders, etc.: but I had, somehow, to be free from *self,* from my poor, shabby, bad, all-spoiling *self*! *There* lay freedom, *there* lay happiness! And I see now at seventy, more clearly again than at seventeen, that I was right there.'

I think we should give full value to phrases like 'I had to get rid of my self'. The entire self, body as well as mind, was just what he wanted to get away from. The relation between self and consciousness in him was sick. But get away to what? In psychologists' terms, I presume, to one of those structures of abstractions derived ultimately from frustrations of the body's desires—to religion, philosophy, work, asceticism. And surely in the Baron's case the plausibility of this diagnosis is remarkably clear;[1] in the marked character of escape, of consolation, of embracing pain and frustration gladly.

'People often ask me what religion is for. What is the use of religion? I do not know how to answer. I simply cannot say

---

[1] Of course, I do not think it conclusive, especially in its evaluative implications.

more than this—that I simply cannot get on without it. I must
have it to moderate me, to water me down, to make me possible.
I am so claimful, so self-occupied, so intense. I want everything
my own way. It is the difficulties and dangers in people that make
them saints. It is almost impossible to me sometimes to stand
people *with* God—without God it would have been impossible.
If I had not had my religion I should have been a blackguard.'

His strictly moral advice to others was harshly ascetic, despite
the geniality and gentleness of his spiritual counsel. He recom-
mended the Stoic rule *abstine et sustine* to his niece; moderate
thyself in things attractive and consoling, persevere, hold out,
in things repulsive and desolating. She should keep beyond her
time of prayer when she is 'dry', and break off when in consolation. Even more striking, perhaps, is an incident reported in his
biography. When his daughter Hildegard was enjoying herself
on holiday in Venice in 1903, he insisted she should come home
just *because* she was enjoying herself. She told her friends there
that this sort of thing often happened—that 'nothing was simple
or spontaneous'; though she loved and admired her father. His
moral doctrine, quite unlike the rest of his psychology of religious
health, harshly divided up the self into mutually hostile halves.

'Without that dividing up of the true self against the false, without
a fear and dread of self that will drive you to God and Christ,
without a taking in hand daily, and ever humbly beginning anew,
but *not in your own strength, but in a despair of self,* which, if true,
means *an utter trust in God and Christ,* so utterly near you day and
night,—religion is fine talk, at least it has not become fully alive;
and without such a life as that, Child,—note what I say—you will
never be happy, you will become feverish, bitter, hard, odious, or
will shrink into a poor surface-thing—although I doubt whether
you could, whether God would let you achieve the latter. . . .'

He carried this asceticism, this love of mortification, even into
his epistemology and his psychology of scholarship. 'One of the
spontaneous activities of the human soul, the Analytic and
Speculative faculty, seems habitually, instinctively to labour at
depersonalizing all it touches, and thus continually both to undermine and discrown the deeply personal work and world of the
experimental forces of the soul. . . . Our intellectual nature is a
storehouse of instruments for the rest, expression, and purification

of our moral-spiritual nature . . . a sobering, purifying, mortifying, vivifying bath and fire.' Thus Christianity itself, he felt, found its cross in science.

It is the ruthlessness of this process of self-renunciation, the energy of this effort of self-formation, that accounts for the quality of life the Baron achieved, and this cannot be described in the terms of the type-psychology we used about the Wards.

The idea of the body

There is, however, another kind of psychology, midway between that and Freudian analysis, whose categories are more likely to lead us to some interesting understanding of von Hügel. This is the kind of philosophical or enlarged Freudianism we find in Norman O. Brown's *Life Against Death* and Herbert Marcuse's *Eros and Civilization*. 'Freud', says Professor Brown, 'takes his place in European intellectual history if we place him at the meeting point between nineteenth-century science and what Whitehead called the Romantic Reaction.' Freud, that is, created a scientific form for and expression of that reaction; which Professor Brown later defines as essentially 'a revulsion against abstraction (in psychoanalytical terms, sublimation) in favour of the concrete sensual organism, the human body'. In the concrete sensual organism are included those immediate intuitive reactions and responses, attractions and repulsions, which give life to our emotional relationships. Those relationships are, in the civilized adult, very much shaped by the abstractions of his society, the systems of thought and value; the moral codes, the philosophical schemes, the scholarly labours, the financial ambitions and anxieties; but life comes only from the body.

If we grant that there is an opposition between these abstractions and the human body, and call Freud—as Professor Brown expounds him—the spokesman for the body; then Baron von Hügel is one of the men best qualified to be the protagonist of the other side, the soul. Not only did he speak for the abstractions—notably, religion and morality—urging men to subordinate their bodies' impulses to them—but in his own life, it seems clear, all the health derived from those abstractions themselves, and none from his body.

But we need to expound Professor Brown's ideas in more detail before we turn to consider von Hügel, because those ideas amount to a very interesting modern version of the old Christian antithesis between the body and the soul, with of course the Christian values reversed. If we can show that the values von Hügel embodied (as well as preached) stand in significantly sharp antithesis to Brown's, we can claim that his 'I am the work of religion' has a very modern meaning as well as its traditional one.

'The special contribution of psychoanalysis is to trace religious and philosophic problems to their roots in the concrete human body,' says Professor Brown; and, later, defining the sexual instinct:

'It is the energy or desire with which the human being pursues pleasure, with the further specification that the pleasure sought is the pleasurable activity of an organ of the human body. . . . Infants are naturally absorbed in themselves and in their own bodies; they are in love with themselves.'

Repression begins with genital organization, and man as we meet him in history, in religion, in art, in philosophy, is essentially the repressed, the neurotic, animal.

'The realm of the unconscious is established in the individual when he refuses to admit into his conscious life a purpose or desire which he has, and in so doing establishes in himself a psychic force opposed to his own idea . . . the essence of repression lies in the refusal of the human being to recognize the realities of his human nature.'

These repressions are the source of the whole cultural life of man; 'substitute-gratifications—a term which applies not only to poetry and religion but also to dreams and neurotic symptoms—contain truth: they are expressions, distorted by repression, of the immortal desires of the human heart'.

Clearly Professor Brown does not deny value to poetry and religion. But he derives their value from sources they themselves are unconscious of—which they often try to deny—in the human body. The chain of explanation which connects the poem or the religious experience with that source sometimes manifestly justifies itself by bringing us into closer and more vivid contact with the poem or the experience itself. Naturally that does not happen all the time; no system of explanation can do that. But a serious problem arises for this system, as for all monisms, when we come to cases in which the chain of explanation is not only very long but very tangled, in which there are *many* seeming paradoxes to be dealt with. Von Hügel, as will become clear, is one of those cases. He answers clearly enough to the pattern of a man transferring his identity to cultural systems, and rejecting his body. But his way of doing so was so extreme and so unhealthy —and his way of dealing with the resultant neuroses was so completely to turn his back on them—that we must surely conclude that he had cut himself off from the body's sources of life. And so if he did achieve life, we must surely conclude that it derived from some other source. Cultural identification must be a source of health almost as potent as personal repression is a source of unhealth.

Man unrepressed would be man without history, says Professor Brown. 'At the biological level, organisms live their lives and have no history because living and dying, that is to say growing older, is in them an inseparable unity. With them, in Shakespeare's beautiful phrase, ripeness is all.' History is in every sense a human invention.

'Man, the discontented animal, unconsciously seeking the life proper to his species, is man in history: repression and the repetition compulsion generate historical time. Repression transforms the timeless instinctual compulsion to repeat into the forward-moving dialectic of neurosis which is history; history is a forward-moving *recherche du temps perdu*, with the repetition-compulsion guaranteeing the historical law of the slow return of the repressed. And conversely, life not repressed—organic life below man and human life if repression were overcome—is not in historical time. If we connect—as Freud did not—the repetition-compulsion with Freud's reiterated theorem that the instinctual processes in the id are timeless, then only repressed life is in time, and unrepressed life would be timeless or in eternity.'

Von Hügel was quite specially devoted to history, and he specially found in it—as he did to some extent in his other 'abstractions', his geology, his philosophy of religion, his moral asceticism, his 'work' in general—an escape from the 'pettily selfish, shouting self'.

The great defenders of man's true innocence and happiness, says Professor Brown, are the psychoanalysts, the mystics, and the artists.

'Modern poetry, like psychoanalysis and Protestant theology, faces the problem of the resurrection of the body. Art and poetry have always been altering our ways of sensing and feeling—that is to say, altering the human body. And Whitehead rightly discerns as the essence of the Romantic Reaction, a revulsion against abstraction . . . [etc.]'

This is most strikingly true of the artists.

'Judged at the bar of the reality-principle, the consolations of art are childish, and they reinforce mankind's wilful refusal to put away childish things. But if man's destiny is to change reality until it conforms to the pleasure-principle, and if man's fate is to fight for instinctual liberation, then art appears, in the words of Rilke, as the *Weltanschauung* of the last goal. Its contradiction of the reality-principle is its social function, as a constant reinforcement of the struggle for instinctual liberation; its childishness is to the professional critic a stumbling block, but to the artist its glory.'

To say that the Baron stands at the opposite extreme from this point of view is only to class him with the majority. But there is something rather more striking, more relevant to Professor Brown's case, in his not being, for all his interest in mysticism, at all a mystic. This probably is due, in a common-sense way, to his distrust of his body. He knew quite well how much 'mystical' experience was hysterical; and how closely connected even the purest mysticism was with a hysterical type; and he knew how sick his own body was. One can guess that he 'could have had' mystical experience all too easily. But he insisted on the control of a broad, clear, steady intelligence; he identified himself with his culture and not with his body. There is also something striking in his insensitiveness to art—the art of his contemporaries, that is, where his preferences seem very much dominated by considerations of their ethical safety. This is striking just because when he talks about literature of the past he says some interesting things. But such art is part of history; pure aesthetic value, much more amoral aesthetic value, he could not handle. It is content that counts, he told his niece, not form. 'And this lack (if it is one) went through all his being', she tells us, 'sheer beauty always left him cold: he needed the beauty of mind; he rejoiced at and regarded the beauty of souls.'

Professor Brown quotes Blake: 'Energy is the only life, and is from the Body . . . Energy is Eternal Delight'—and Rilke: 'The artist is the man who refuses initiation through education into the existing order, remains faithful to his own childhood being, and thus becomes "a human being in the spirit of all times, an artist". Hence the artist tree is distinguished by profounder roots in the dark unconscious.' Professor Marcuse cites Gide, Valéry and Baudelaire. He too makes much of the connection between romantic art and 'the human body', between aesthetics, sensuousness, and sensuality.

Brown and Marcuse make very little use of the novel. But their case is both strengthened in itself and made more applicable to our purposes if we extend it to cover the great novelists, most importantly Tolstoy and Lawrence. In *Anna Karenina* what is wrong with Alexei Karenin but his relation to his 'human body'? (Remembering that this includes his spontaneous emotional life.) What is meant by his clumsiness, his finger-cracking, his swollen veins, his tired eyes, high thin voice, his projecting ears, except that?[1] And the unpleasantnesses of his manner, the mocking tone, the coldness, the stiffness, the legalism, obviously derive from this dislocated relation. The character of his mind, his bureaucratic efficiency, his skill with figures and files and official categories; even the character of his soul, his petty vanity and ambition and self-absorption, his inability to feel anything very much very long; these too derive from his body in a clear and vivid sense. And everything that makes Vronsky a better man for Anna to marry, everything that makes him honourable and simple and lovable, everything that makes him a 'good' man, derives from his simple animal strength and ease and good humour, his broad chest and splendid teeth. Clearly it is his *relation* to his broad chest that matters; not its measurement in inches. But his relation to it is a matter of his spontaneous, instinctive, pre-moral life. All of Vronsky, thoughts, feelings, relationships, is broad and firm and calm as that chest; and it is so because his 'body' is so.

From Lawrence's work we can take Miriam in *Sons and Lovers*.

---

[1] These details are in part a conventional code by which Tolstoy signals to us judgments about the man's inner life. But the wonderful vividness and convincingness of that code is that such physical details are the *natural* manifestations of this inner life condition. We all recognize that this code is not merely conventional: body and soul do interact and mutually express each other in this way. And of the two, the body is always presented as the originating and original entity: Tolstoy's charity of understanding lies largely in his showing us that Karenin *cannot* feel and be any other way than he does.

Here the dislocation takes the more conventional form of revulsion against half of 'bodily' life; the more brutal and coarse elements, sexuality, fighting, self-assertion, and so on. But there is more to Lawrence's analysis. There are times, he makes clear, when it is Paul who rejects the sexual relationship and Miriam who offers it; he rejects it because she offers it against her own more spontaneous feelings, with the wrong kind of voluntariness. It is in fact her 'body' which is wrong—wrong in its relation to the rest of her personality. And if Clara has what Miriam lacks, an untroubled confidence in her own sexuality, her relation to her total instinctive self is just as wrong. Her sense of self is bruised, resentful, haughty, self-punishing, 'difficult', with everyone but Paul. This is expressed in her body, which is heavy, clumsy, sullen, head down; but it also derives from her body—that is, from her most spontaneous feelings and relationships, those unmediated by thought and convention.

Thus we see how the great novelists, as much as the poets Brown and Marcuse cite, acknowledge the power of this scheme of interpretation; which is also a scheme of values. What else can make acceptable the brutal contrasts and tableaux of *Lady Chatterley's Lover* but the assurance that since Sir Clifford cannot give or share life, nothing else he can do or be or suffer really matters. Tolstoy is much more sympathetic to Karenin, and allows him a triumph over Vronsky at Anna's seeming death-bed; but he has to allow Anna, as she recovers, to hate her husband again with a hatred we obviously must acknowledge as natural and inevitable in her—as 'right', even though so completely against Christian logic. His spirituality cows her; it cannot begin to win her, as his wife. His goodness, however sincere, is no real use, has no real value, within those personal and social relationships in which he finds himself. It might seem vulgar jargon to call those 'the human situations', but they do in fact describe the majority of those in which we feel our humanity on trial.

No other novelists deal with the life of 'the body' so fully as Tolstoy and Lawrence, or can show us so much of the health—moral, spiritual, emotional—which belongs to it. But others that have something powerful to say, like Dostoevsky and Proust, derive much of that power from their sense of unhealth. Others, like Joyce in the Bloom passages of *Ulysses,* take a more comic-realistic approach. A novelist like James, in whom there is almost no sense of the body, is a rare exception. (In some striking aspects of his style—its abstractness, its infinite inclusiveness, its circum-locutory inconclusiveness—everything that makes it 'difficult' and 'intellectual'—James resembles von Hügel. There is surely some relation between that similarity and their other similarity, in lack of 'body'.) Modern literature as a whole, Professor Brown is right, is powerfully inspired by this scheme of interpretation and of evaluation of life.

Von Hügel

With this set of ideas in mind, we can return to the consideration of von Hügel himself. But since, clearly, examining him this way we are not going to find him rich in 'life', let us remind ourselves preliminarily, of the kind of life he did have. He was consistently, and notably, 'on the side of life'. In philosophy, in theology, in church politics, he consistently stood for, and fought for, those alternatives which awarded more dignity and more freedom to man using all of his powers. As a spiritual director, he recom-mended breadth, variety, freedom, naturalness—the following of the individual *attrait*. Even in directly personal relations, though here of course he was severely hampered, he was the means of life to others; to his niece, to Evelyn Underhill, to Father Tyrrell. Here is a part of a letter to Tyrrell, 4 December 1902:

'My very dear Friend,
I hardly know exactly *how* or *why*—unless it be in part your, after all not long, silence, I come to have such a strong and abiding, unreasoned and, so far, irrepressible impression that you are in interior trouble and trial—of a specially strong kind or degree: but I know that I *have* this impression. And as, even if (as of course I hope) I am quite wrong, such a spontaneous solicitude can but spring, I think, from deep affection and sympathy; and as its expression, with so much else for me to plan and do, can but appear as what it is,—as a mark of that attachment and deep appreciation which I bear you; why, I think it well worth while to put my own work aside for a bit, and, with *tête reposée*, to write and tell you of my impression. And I feel all the more interiorly pressed to do so, because, at Holy Communion yester-day, two clear pricks of conscience,—one a big one, and one a little one—worked within me and shaped themselves into the resolve of this letter to you [the first being that he had overstressed

some theological difficulty]. . . . I also felt that my last note had been somehow feverish and absolute in tone, and had said more than I meant, or had said it badly. And so I determined to make these two little confessions. And also to tell you,—not, God knows, as measuring myself against you, even if you *are* in darkness, for it may be my turn next!—that, thank God, without having any popular, immediately clear answers ready, without indeed being free from the keen feeling of the difficulties of the position, I *do* feel that, at bottom, and in the long run, all is well. I mean, that it will all be found, in the slow, intermittent, combined and mutually supplementary and corrective devoted-nesses and patient light-awaitings of us all, to have been occasioned by, and to have a place in, that ever-deepening apprehension of the mystery of life and of love, and of the necessity for their continuous, painful deepening within our hearts, which Christianity has indefinitely increased and developed, just because it is life at its most fruitful and most self-conscious point. . . . [After his signature, and one added paragraph, he ends] And now I will sink back into my own work, but with my poor heart prayerfully and affectionately full of you my intensely alive, immensely impulsive and hence astonishingly, most meritoriously and fruitfully balanced Friend!

I was ashamed of the style of my last; I trust this is a little better.'

One wonders, it is true, what criterion of style the Baron can be appealing to, what model he was imitating; but undeniably there it is, style, an intensely individual selection among interesting and dignified and *lively* habits of language. And undeniably there too, through all the strange Gothic ornament and organ ponderous-ness, is a lively human act, a part of a living relationship. This is surely a piece of life being lived at some height of man's powers; something far beyond what we associate with Karenin or Sir Clifford Chatterley. But does this mean that the Baron had some-thing of Vronsky or Mellers in him after all? Clearly not; and the interest of the question is in the clearness of the answer, the purity of the Baron's type, seen from this point of view.

Looking at all we know about the Baron, his work and his life, we find him answering very much to the analysis of Karenin, or of Casaubon (the point about whom is obviously much the same —a man cut off from full participation in human nature). The

Baron was a sick man all his life; or at least for all that part of it of which we know anything. For the first half of it we must rely almost entirely on his own accounts (highly generalized) and for the first eighteen years there is nothing. At eighteen he had an attack of typhoid fever in Vienna which left him for the rest of his life deaf, 'nervous', and subject to a variety of unspecified prostrating diseases. It was also then, and there—his father had just died, and he accompanied the body to Vienna—that he suffered grave moral and spiritual temptation, his recovery from which was his first great conversion experience. Whatever the connections between the two kinds of trouble, bodily and spiritual, he told his niece later that his life between eighteen and thirty had been more of less 'blotted out' by a series of nervous breakdowns. Those twelve years included the first nine years of his marriage.

His letters are full of records of illness and of the consequent limitations on his work and everything else. In 1919, though much better, 'I cannot take to scribbling at all largely (I mean still only letters and notes) without white nights coming promptly upon me and throwing back my full recovery.' And later, 'Even letter-writing must be severely curtailed, and this if only because, if I broke down permanently, I should be exposing myself to deepest melancholy.' And again, '. . . my health *just* allows me, so far (after three weeks' trial), to do one hour and a half of concentrated study a day.' To his niece he wrote, 'My last four or five nights have been, upon the whole, so bad that I dare not yet write directly about your very important and delicate points, since, when I am in such "encompôte" condition, such letter-writing means further bad nights.' And finally, to Miss Petre, as early as 1910, 'I have done so feeling all the time that I was using up every scrap of available energy, and finding myself unable (besides my ever refreshing though tiring Sandow Exercises) to do more than crawl from bench to bench in Kensington Gardens, and requiring again a large amount of dozings in my darkened study.' His sickness was a large part of his personality. Loisy refers to it half the times he mentions the Baron in his *Mémoires*. The Abbé Huvelin deals with it in one of those pieces of advice to the Baron which the latter treasured all his life—he wrote them down, and gave copies to friends at different times. '*Oui, il faut agir. Vous êtes malade; l'activité aura donc en sa forme quelque chose de plus ou moins maladif chez vous. Mais n'ayez pas peur; agissez, aimez; vous avez un besoin infini d'expansion, la contrainte vous tue.*' The Abbé himself was importantly a sick man; what he clearly implies here, however, is that the Baron's sickness was more than physical; but that this too is to be accepted as a part—a large part—of his nature, out of which he must, nevertheless, freely act. It was *as* a sick man that the Baron acted and worked and lived.

He married in 1873 Lady Mary Herbert, a convert and daughter of a convert, described by the Baron's biographer as 'gay, bright, "of the world"', and not understanding her husband's mind or ways. Both were, for opposite reasons, of 'nervous and maladif physiques, with consequent mutual maladjustments'. In later years, while very loyal to each other, they led their own lives. Indeed, they did so, in a more literal manner, at the very beginning. It was not until 1876 that they lived together. For the first three years of their marriage, each stayed mostly with his or her mother, at various hydros. The Baron was at a boarding house in Malvern with his mother, and later was at the Divonne Hydro, seeking treatment for his spine and his 'head-nerves'; at another point his biographer calls it 'seeking a cure for his nerve-frustrated ardour'. Lady Mary seems to have needed mostly 'rest'. Both were on uneasy, highly irritable terms with their mothers, but also with each other. The biography speaks of smugness, self-defence, and over-wrought childish affection in the Baron's letters to Lady Mary. In one of the few quoted he speaks of himself as 'unrestful' and 'over-intense'; but Huvelin has shown him that he is so with everyone, not only with her; and as this is offered her as a consolation, we gather that he has seemed to be particularly irritable with her. Indeed, the glimpses we get of her suggest someone—at least in this relationship—petulant, feeble, hypochondriac. In a later letter Huvelin is quoted as saying, 'When you are at the end of your tether don't try to reason with your dear wife, nor to raise her spirits, nor to calm her—an effective word, followed by a silence during which she will recover herself and return of her own accord, this is what seems to be indicated.' The total picture, glimpsed through the veils of discretion, is of a difficult marriage working itself out in individual headaches and backaches as well as in mutual frustrations and nervous clashes.

This impression is confirmed by the portrait of the Baron drawn by his niece, Gwendolen Plunket Greene. No one could suspect her of disloyalty to her uncle, but when she compares him with her father (Sir Hubert Parry) she remarks a lack of 'nature' in him.

'The world of nature filled my father with joy; and this inspiration in him was not an isolated fact, but joined him into a world of singularly generous warmth and love. Yet beauty was his soul's basis, his very life. He did not only recognize and pursue it, but seemed touched by its mysterious being, quickened by beauty itself; his soul lived and expanded in this sun of love.'

This was just what was not true of her uncle.

'He had not my father's zest and happiness, his almost passionate love of nature and adventure; he could not practice the hardships my father enjoyed, nor rush out as he to meet the exigencies of everyday life.... He was obliged to practice many "self-coddlings" in order to achieve his work. He had no abundance of life, no *joie de vivre*; and though ordered and punctual to a degree in all he did, he was unpractical and vague in a worldly sense.'

He could respond fully to neither art nor nature.

'But here I observed that though natural beauty did not make the *first* appeal to him, nor was his spirit *of* it, as my father's seemed, yet he certainly observed and loved it greatly. . . . And this lack (if it is one) went through all his being; sheer beauty always left him cold: he needed the beauty of mind; he rejoiced at and regarded the beauty of souls.'

All this, we need hardly say, answers perfectly to the Karenin-Casaubon pattern, the pattern of a personality-structure derived not from 'the human body' but from cultural 'abstractions'.

The love of order and punctuality mentioned by his niece—and the anxieties inseparable from that love—were very fully developed in the Baron. We see them again and again in his letters in reference to his use of time, his management of the family finances, his publication of his books, his arrangement of visits, his system of note-taking. It is also manifest in his moral and spiritual teaching. 'Then he so disliked and distrusted hurry and anticipation,' his niece tells us, 'change, excitement and reaction were all his greatest foes; dullness and routine, faithfully accepted, were, he believed, a necessity for the soul's growth.' He made a big distinction between excitement and zest, defining the former as derived from breaking loose, from fragmentariness, from losing our balance and centrality. Perhaps a sufficiently vivid example of the power of this principle in his life is this paragraph from a letter to his niece. 'I think five to seven on the fourteenth will be best for me—have me freshest for you. And Aunt Mary will love to have you to tea at four thirty. I would have mine alone at that time, and we could thus start at five, having satisfied our lower wants.' This is so striking because of the long-standing intimacy and intense affection between him and his niece. It is surely plain that the Baron suffered from all the penalties imposed on the soul badly related to its body; he could breathe and move freely only inside a formidably narrow and rigid cage, and to be with him other people had to enter that cage. At the same time, we should also pay attention to the next paragraph of that letter. 'But this is specially to wish you a very deep and devoted, a very peaceful and *épanoui* birthday. What shall I wish you specially for the coming year—for all the years of your life? I will wish you the ever-increasing practice of just the kind of moderation, alternation, mixedness, which you are already seeing and practic-ing.' Even in that letter the word *épanoui* is not ironical, coming from the Baron, teaching what he taught; it is not even mostly pathetic, coming from that cage he lived in; for he himself *was* *épanoui*. 'Suffering and expansion, what a rich combination!' he exclaimed; and he felt he had in some degree achieved it. That is the paradox we are investigating.

If he had, if he did achieve humanity, relatedness, the power to feel and give joy, then it was as little as possible because of 'bodily' vitality. This despite his being, in his youth, a strikingly handsome man, and always a very impressive one, to the eye and to the ear. A large head, impressively held, fierce dark eyes, stubborn hair, a deep voice and a loud laugh, a brow and a profile, all these seem to put him far from, say, Karenin. But we must amplify and subtilize our understanding of this scheme of ideas, with Lawrence's help. The physique itself is not the point, if we are considering the achievement of 'life'; nor is the forcefulness of the fragmented demands of the ego; nor even is healthiness of the ego's relation to the body, in any ordinary sense. Gerald Crich, Lawrence explicitly insists, was the perfect human animal; Rupert Birkin was pale, thin, flickering, shadowy, often ill, easily neutralized or falsified as a presence. But Birkin was always on the road to health, to life. Gerald was on the road to death. Birkin was always in the act of achieving the right relation to his body and to the spontaneous feelings, desires, relationships, rooted in it. Gerald's healthy handsomeness cannot save him from despair and death, once he has rejected the relationship Birkin offered him; opposite to Karenin in physique as he was, creative love was equally beyond him. The Baron's handsomeness was similarly irrelevant. Paradoxically, his relation to his body could be called less destructive than Gerald's; inasmuch as he identified his self with something quite other, whilst Gerald remained rooted there, in repetitive and sterile exploitations of sense and feeling. The Baron's picturesque presence became a stage property he carried round with him, as disconnected as cardboard. Gerald's was his root and its soil; cramped within rigid limits.[1]

The Baron stood for the denial of the body, almost explicitly. He stood for suffering quite explicitly; he made religion stand for it, and the most unromantic and involuntary and passive suffering. 'Religion has never made me happy. . . . Suffering can expand, it can contract. . . . All deepened life is deepened suffering, deepened dreariness, deepened joy. . . . Dullness, dreariness and loneliness. East winds always blowing; desolation, with certain lucid intervals and dim assurances.' And perhaps most striking of all, most frank: 'I always think it is much harder for a healthy person to be really religious, to find God. When your body is a constant failure you cannot depend on yourself at all, so you turn to God.'

And if religion is inseparable from suffering and sickness, he himself, that very structure and root of his self, is inseparable from religion, as we have seen. In *The Mystical Element in Religion* we are told that St Catherine herself had to drown 'her feverish immediacy, her clamorous, claimful false self, and must lose herself, as a merely natural Individual, in the river and ocean of the Thing, of Law, of that apparently ruthless Determinism which fronts life everywhere, before she could find herself again as a Person, in union with and in presence of an infinite Spirit and Personality'. It is in the Baron's accounts of St Catherine's psychology that we get his most revealing and moving comments on his own. In the light of all we know about him from other sources, both his

[1] Tolstoy and Lawrence perfectly appreciated other ways, including such a way as the Baron's, of seeking and achieving life: Tolstoy more obviously, but Lawrence just as crucially. But in their novels they depict the superiority of the 'body's' way. There is a conflict in Tolstoy's mind, in *Anna Karenina*, but when Lidia Ivanovna represents spirituality, we must all prefer the animality of even Stepan Arkadevitch, much more Anna's. Spirituality seems the more grotesque distortion of human sincerity and dignity, the error most importantly to be avoided. This cast of feeling is implicit, surely, in the literary imagination, and the Baron's case is so interesting because, in order to respond to him sympathetically, we have to go against that feeling.

personal difficulties and his religious preferences, we cannot doubt
that he identified himself strongly with her. Her religion, like his,
was a pure theism, the two poles of which were self and God. For
her, and for him, Christ was not—emotionally—important. Mary
was scarcely mentioned. St Catherine's congenital defect he
declares to have been:

'A great self-engrossment of a downrightly selfish kind; a group-
ing of all things round such a self-adoring *Ego*; a noiseless but
determined elimination from her life and memory of all that
would not or could not, then and there, be drawn and woven into
the organism and functioning of this immensely self-seeking,
infinitely woundable and wounded, endlessly self-doctoring "I"
and "Me": a self intensely, though not sexually, jealous, envious
and exacting, incapable of easy accommodation, of pleasure in
half successes, of humour and brightness, of joyous "once-born"
creatureliness: all this was certainly to be found, in strong
tendency at least, in the untrained parts and periods of her
character and life.'

We recognize there several ideas also to be found in self-
descriptions.

He is very severe on this personality type. St Catherine had no
humour, he says, no wit, she was excessively mental; she was
abnormal.

'For not only is there no trace about her, at any time, of moral
vulgarity of any kind, or of any tendency to it; and this is, of
course, a grand strength; but she seems at all times to have been
greatly lacking in that quite innocent and normal sensuousness,
which appears to form a necessary element of the complete
human personality . . . a person hardly intended for marriage . . .
could not satisfy the less purely mental of the perfectly licit
requirements which make up the many levelled wants of a normal,
or at least ordinary, man's and husband's nature.'

God was never Father or Friend, much less Bridegroom, to her.
At her moments of intensest religious consciousness, she felt
herself *one with* God. Her teaching was abstract and impersonal
Christianity.

Like von Hügel, she was uninterested in evil. 'For, as to the
cause of Evil, she ever restricts herself to finding it in her own
nature, and to fighting it there: hence the personality of Evil,

though nowhere denied, yet rarely if ever concerns her, and never does so directly in her strenuous and practical life.' It was good which absorbed her, and him; when they looked beyond the limits of their selves, they looked for good.

Her characteristic strengths, too, were very much his. Her nature was full of turbulent raw material, he says, but subdued by great powers of mind and will.

'And this very closeness of apposition and width of contrast, and this great strength of mind and will, made all that disordered multiplicity, distraction, and dispersion of her clamorous, many-headed, many-hearted nature, a tyranny impossible and unnecessary to bear. And yet to achieve the actual escape from such a tyranny, the mastering of such a rabble, and the harmonization of such a chaos, meant a constant and immense effort, a practically unbroken grace-getting and self-giving, an ever-growing heroism and indeed sanctity, and, with and through all these things, a corresponding expansion and virile joy. It can thus be said, in all simple truth, that she became a saint because she had to; that she became it, to prevent herself going to pieces: she literally had to save, and actually did save, the fruitful life of reason and of love, by ceaselessly fighting her immensely sensitive, absolute, and claimful self.'

For St Catherine, as for the Baron, religion was the only alternative to psychological-moral chaos; and religion's mark was harmony, the harmony that comes from a person having identified his self with the impersonal.

Someone like St Catherine, and like the Baron, finds life difficult, and 'life'—mature social and personal relationships—very difficult. The easy and obvious things are not easy for them. On the other hand, let us remember that Professor Brown defined man as the neurotic animal. Man is man by virtue of his cultural neuroses—his art, his philosophy, his religion. By such a definition von Hügel was categorically and supremely human. That is a paradox, but it may serve to remind us that man exists, life exists, *in* those joint enterprises—in art, religion, philosophy. 'Life' does not include everything human, or everything we care about.

Culture needs its structures and its abstractions, which include after all literature and music and astronomy as well as armies, computers, and cost accounting. And these things don't get done except by the process of repression, by the renunciation of the body; and they won't get done with any quality unless we can see that renunciation as something other than ugly and sick. As long as sensitive and intelligent people see all real value in the life of the body, the culture will be disaffected, dissatisfied with itself, diseased. The humanist as much as the Catholic must believe in the value of renunciation, the way of the soul.

But there are of course a thousand ways to combine the soul and the body, to follow the way of the soul without destroying the body. Many great men of religion, and many great humanists have been ardent and magnetic personalities, able to participate in life on every level, able to create life in every contact. The Baron was a sick man, and this limited him in many ways, not only the most obvious.

Miss Petre accused him of being cautious and diplomatic, of self-care and of sacrificing individuals to causes; thinking of course of Father Tyrrell. But the Baron was necessarily primarily attached to causes; in fact he was identified with them. This was the structural principle of his personality. He was sincerely *attached* to individuals, like Tyrrell. But he could not be identified with such attachments, he could not place his self there, because that centre of self he had renounced.

But did he not find another? This is the largest of all the questions he faces us with. Considering the completeness, and the cost, of that renunciation, and considering also the richness of life he did achieve, does it make sense to say that that life derived from that one ruined source? Surely we must say that there were other sources of life.

And though, of course, a healthy Christian, like any other healthy person, will have both kinds of centre operative in him, the concrete body and the abstract religion, still there is a sense in which figures like the Baron represent all Christians. For conversion, re-birth, must be, in psychological terms, transferring one's centre from the body to the religious cultural system. As long as the animal body remains a life-centre of even equal importance, there can be only rudimentary religious feelings, in even a very good and honourable man. In a religious man the animal body, and the pride which is its integrative principle, must be radically subdued; it should not of course be ruined, as it was in von Hügel; but it must be dominated by the soul (however uneasy that word makes us today) and the self-dedication which is the soul's integrative principle. Self-dedication of course characterizes all renouncers of the body, humanists as well as religionists. But perhaps we may claim that the Baron's intensity of self-dedication, as well as its formally religious character, mark him off as a religious humanist.

But these are larger questions than we can treat here, where we are concerned to understand one man, and to understand our own understanding of him, our responses to him. Above all we want to understand what value to place upon him, in natural terms. Dedication and soul are not terms synonymous with value, even religious value. Some dedicated souls are morally and spiritually evil, and many are grossly egotistic or habitually wrong-headed. Natural human qualities of understanding, sympathy, patience, energy, are of radical importance in our estimate of even the most religious man. It is because von Hügel was so impressive by those natural measures, at the same time as he so challengingly embodied a Christian psychology, that we find him so interesting. Let us return to the contrast between him and the two Wards. Neither of them were as hampered as he was in their daily life and work by obvious psychological handicaps—failures of body. But neither achieved anything half so impressively on the side of life as he did, in his doctrine, in his personal relationships, in his religious and intellectual politics. And he achieved what he did by means of a classically Christian psychology, a classically religious effort of self-realization.

To remind ourselves a last time of that achievement, let us refer again, both for form and content, to the letter he wrote to Wilfrid Ward about W. G. Ward. We cited at the beginning the paragraphs in which he described the 'state of tension of mind and nerves' which was in Ideal Ward the source of both his strengths and his weaknesses.

'It was the probable root of his strangely large incapacity for entering into minds and trials different from his own [von Hügel cites both Pascal and George Eliot as examples]. And as he never could afford to suspend his own mind and realize a differing one it is no wonder that he was continually addressing so many imaginary *alter egos,* and saw for everyone only his own dangers and his own helps. Hence, what used so long to shock and pain me in him, so clearly zealous as he was for souls, his strange persistence in having everything "out" with everybody, his constant pitching upon the most problematical and provocative points before strangers, or sceptical or scrupulous minds, treating before them, say, of the materiality of hell-fire, or of the interior assent due to non-infallible Church decisions. It was simply that this method would have helped himself.

This was, again, the probable cause of his incapacity for history of all kinds. That 'great empire over the affections' . . . this kind of self-restraint would have been to him intolerable. Hence, too, his fear of the historical spirit: as all suspense must mean negation, and as there was no logical reason why, if one thing were denied, another and another should not be so too, and as the real reason, the varying degrees and kinds of the historical evidence, was practically non-existent for him, an historical mind was to him, if at the same time believing, illogical, dangerous, ignorant of its own necessary consequences.'

This is of course formal writing, but it is also fully alive letter-writing, in every aspect of its form and content. It is full of an idea of its subject; full of detail both bearing this out, and giving us a portrait of him; full of feeling, including some energetic disapproval of him; full of a sense of how the man stood related to other manifestations of Catholicism; full of its own form and function, as direct though formal speech to the man's son and biographer. And beyond and around and through all this is von Hügel's own generous and passionate Catholicism. Test him by the standards he is invoking to measure Ward, and he survives triumphantly. *He* had a capacity for entering into minds and trials different from his own; *he* had a capacity for history; *he* could afford to suspend his own mind and realize a differing one; *he* did not pitch on the most problematical points of doctrine, but on the great central truths, and thus opened religion to others. This too is life, and von Hügel served it, in his way, magnificently.

Von Hügel's major importance for me derived of course from his sponsoring a personality style, a way of handling one's self, which I wanted to believe has dignity, and which my other masters scornfully ignored. In the hands of Tolstoy and Lawrence, I had to realize, the Baron himself would have to seem not only unimpressive but unpleasant. He belongs with Karenin and Lidia Ivanovna. He achieved something larger than we associate with them, but the uncleanness, the unshapeliness, the physical sordidness, which Tolstoy depicts in them so damningly attaches to the Baron too in my imagination, when I allow myself to look at him from that point of view.

And of course I do look at people from that point of view. As a literary man, I draw most of my insights and inspirations, most of my subjects for thought, most of my convictions on moral and spiritual matters, from novels and poems. Few of the sermons I hear begin to compete with the novels I read in moral insight. This fact brings with it several problems for a Christian, but for the moment I want to draw attention only to this, which is not specifically Christian; that the novel-reader who habitually identifies himself with Karenin rather than with Vronsky finds himself in a difficult position.

The whole effect of the novel is to inhibit one from making that identification. Its whole intention is to make one recognize such similarities, such tendencies, only to root them out. (You may say that Tolstoy's intentions are not so clear, and that he does not 'scornfully ignore' Karenin; the question is complicated, but let me say, as a short-cut answer, that the most a reader can feel for Karenin finally is pity, and that this is not much better than scorn, for someone who recognizes himself in the figure.) Perhaps by the time one acknowledges such an identification unequivocally and consciously, the novel's period of greatest potency (to mould you into its image) has passed. The force you can feel it exerting on you even then therefore testifies to the much greater force it exerted before.

It seems to me clear that most men sensitive to literature are influenced, in their efforts of self-formation, by the ideas they find in novels and poems. It is the riskiness and excitement of those ideas that mark off the modern period. If any reader of Fielding had identified himself with Blifil, he would have been upset; but presumably no one did. Perhaps some readers of Jane Austen have identified themselves with Miss Bates rather than with Emma; and I suppose the odd reader of Richardson may have not only recognized his own tendencies in Lovelace, but come to detest and abjure them. But in such cases big moral questions of self-formation are rarely raised, and when they are they are quickly settled by reference to some externally guaranteed moral code. (There could be no real question for Richardson about Lovelace, as there was for Tolstoy about Karenin.) It is only in the modern period, surely, that the novel reader (not to mention the writer) looks for such large and dangerous choices.

The preference, within such choices, has characteristically gone to Vronsky as opposed to Karenin, to the vitality of the body as opposed to the wisdom of the soul. But if the Karenin–von Hügel figure is never depicted with sympathy, with admiration, as a hero, then there are large consequences for the culture which takes its literature seriously. If we don't admire von Hügel, I don't see how we can sincerely admire half the heroes of history and culture. Tolstoy and Lawrence were of course quite ready to reject a half of history and culture. That is usually taken as the result of their hot extremism, but it is more likely that our having it both ways is the result of our cold compromising. Unless we are ready to admire and love von Hügel, I don't see what right we have to a share in any of the great institutions and monuments of human effort. That effect has been, and will be, energized by bodily self-denial; those achievements have been, and will be, the result of repression.

What von Hügel stands for, more exactly, is a certain adjustment of soul to body within the total personality structure, a marriage of soul to body in which the former takes a precedence much more marked than it does in the models modern literature holds up to us. Obviously there can be no question of literally eradicating or completely suppressing either soul or body, though Professor Brown goes quite far towards eliminating the former. But the situation is extreme enough, ideologically, to demand description in these melodramatic terms. The Berkeley students' movement is surely a portent.

I need hardly point out that the body is being preferred to the soul much more stridently at lower levels of literature than we have been dealing with, not to mention the enormous popular religion of pleasure. Our culture as a whole has certainly changed decisively in that direction over the last fifty years. But at the level that concerns us we can turn again to Yeats for an example of the process of self-formation working to opposite effect from von Hügel's. This is a letter Yeats wrote to Robert Gregory in 1910. Gosse had written an insulting letter to Lady Gregory; her son had been angry; Yeats, when told about it, had not shown himself sufficiently indignant, and wrote (though he never sent) this letter of apology:

'My Dear Robert:
I want you to understand that I have no instincts in personal life. I have reasoned them all away and reason acts very slowly and with difficulty and has to exhaust every side of the subject. Above all I have destroyed in myself by analysis instinctive indignation. When I was twenty or a little more I was shocked by the conversation at Henley's. One day I resolved if the conversation was as bad again I would walk out. I did not do so and next day I reasoned over the thing and persuaded myself that I had thought of walking out from vanity and did not do so from fear. As I look back I see occasion after occasion on which I have been prevented from doing what was a natural and sometimes the right thing, either because analysis of the emotion or action of

another or self-distrustful analysis of my own emotion destroyed impulse. I cannot conceive the impulse, unless it were so sudden that I had to act at once, that could urge me into action at all, if it affected personal life. . . . In impersonal and public things—because there this distrust of myself does not come I have impulse. . . . All my moral endeavour for many years has been an attempt to re-create practical instinct in myself. I can only conceive of it as a kind of acting.'

And of course this 'pursuit of spontaneity', even specifically by means of acting, is to be found in many other writers besides Yeats. That last sentence reminds one of Randall Jarrell's remark about Frost. Wondering what Yeats would have thought of Frost, he speculates that he might have said (as Bernhardt is said to have said of Nijinsky), 'I fear, I greatly fear, that I have just seen the greatest actor in the world.' And Joyce portrays himself, as Stephen Dedalus, as being divested of his spontaneous emotions 'as easily as a fruit is divested of its soft ripe peel . . .'. Stephen too associates emotion either with acting or with a psychology opposite to his own. 'He had heard the names of the passions of love and hate pronounced solemnly on the stage and in the pulpit, had found them set forth solemnly in books, and had wondered why his soul was unable to harbour them for any time or to force his lips to utter their names with conviction. A brief anger had often invested him, but he had never been able to make it an abiding passion and had always felt himself passing out of it as if his very body were being divested with ease of some outer skin or peel.'

Clearly this is Yeats's predicament again, and the characteristic predicament of modern man, with his aspiration to perfect spontaneity—the perfect 'body'. The heroes of modern novels nearly always start from an ironic self-consciousness that deprives them of instinct, even though literary criticism often still discusses them according to a quite different scheme of interpretation and evaluation. Critics anxiously chart for us Stephen Dedalus's progress in self-awareness, and triumphantly announce his acquiring 'some irony about himself' or 'some sense of humour about his own experience'; as if progress for such a person could be anything but an escape from self-awareness and irony. Stephen's pride is not an ego-appetite he needs to moderate. It is a policy by which he hopes to recover for his wincing withdrawals the minimal dignity of being voluntary. If that pride ever became a natural mode of self-assertion, a way to act positively on the world outside him, it would be the salvation of his temperament. His failure, and Joyce's failure with the character, is that he does not become proud enough.

For all these writers, and for most readers I know, the pursuit of spontaneity is a major enterprise, perhaps the most important they know, into which they put their major energies of self-creation. Instinct, intuition, blood-knowledge, vitality, these are for us today not things given, but objects of belief, of aspiration, of policy. Whether there is a necessary contradiction between such a policy and a profession of Christianity, is a larger question than we need decide. But that such a contradiction may occur for an individual is clearly enough to be expected. Christianity has, after all, its own directives for people who find themselves in that situation. Von Hügel, as a Christian, could hardly have chosen Joyce's pride or Yeats's histrionics as the way out of his temperamental difficulties. In him, too, 'practical instinct' and 'instinct in practical life' were ruined; but he—to put it in psychological terms—identified himself with the patience of Providence and the enormous justice of God. He made his life out of making that decision over and over again, just as Yeats, in the poem we began with, written twenty-two years after that nobly painful letter to Robert Gregory, makes over again the same decision, to reject the Christian 'temptation' to betray his poetry and his body.

I—though heart might find relief
Did I become a Christian man and choose for my belief
What seems most welcome in the tomb—play a predestined part.

It seems to me that both he and von Hügel got what they bargained for; von Hügel became a good and wise man, Yeats a passionate man and a great poet. Both deserve to be heroes; and both bartered away something valuable in exchange.

But that does not mean that the choice was the same for both. Christianity makes a difference. In *Women in Love*, Birkin tells Ursula she must choose between being a *fleur du mal*, like Gudrun and Gerald, and being a rose of happiness. The freedom of that choice would be hard to define, for Ursula is already, at the time this is put to her, a different kind of person from her sister. Nevertheless, Lawrence convinces us, there is still a choice for her to make, to keep making, and it is the crucial choice for all of us; to commit ourselves either to health or to unhealth, to draw up into our roots and to open up in our faces, either life or death. That we will in fact bear blossoms of one kind or the other, will 'live', vividly, is taken for granted. That is the literary man's version of the choice, in one of its most authoritative formulations. The Christian, I think, cannot see things that way.

If you accept the idea of a Christian psychological type, we may say that that type (which of course only represents Christians) is more the lily than the rose of happiness. And we know that lilies that fester smell far worse than weeds. That is, there is a blanched and waxen purity of sensibility, a spiritual and 'religious' beauty of character, that is hard to harness to the coarser energies and rougher requirements of human life; and when people of this type find normal gratifications of desire *too* difficult, their energies turn away into abnormal directions.

To take the most lurid case, over-refined, over-sensitive adolescents are more likely to have sexual problems.

To take another example, one of the crucial questions for any man is how to respond when he is challenged as a whole, as a being, when someone tells him, 'You are of no account, are you? You can be pushed aside, can't you? I can treat you as I like, can't I?' The natural response is angrily and proudly to assert oneself in counter-action, and this is not necessarily un-Christian, I take it. But in highly intelligent and sensitive people the natural response is not to be counted on to be immediate or complete—as we have seen—and there comes a choice, in what to do about that incompleteness. And then, to set oneself to learn anger and pride, deliberately, that I think *is* un-Christian. At least it must be hard to foster those feelings in oneself, those classic manifestations of the unregenerate self, without undermining one's Christian training. And certainly there is a great tradition of Christian self-formation that urges the believer to accept humiliation, to welcome being of no account. Von Hügel, I think, taught one to welcome that. Lawrence, like Yeats, pointed out that a humiliated man is an ugly human being. Both are right. This is one of those classic Christian dilemmas, which the new Catholicism has yet to tackle, as we shall see. The dominance of soul over body is achieved only with a struggle, and at a price. The Christian is likely to find himself in such dilemmas, at just the depth of 'choice' Lawrence was talking about.

But to become a *fleur du mal* is of course forbidden a Christian. That is not an alternative he is free to contemplate. Correlatively, strength of personality, freedom of self-expression, fulfilment, is not a prime value for him; he does not take it for granted he will bear blossoms, will 'live', vividly, one way or another. The choice for him that is the equivalent of that between the rose of happiness and the *fleur du mal* is between the lily that festers and the lily that withers. Assuming, that is, that he cannot blossom strongly and freely, like the rose of happiness, he must decide to wither, not to fester, as his alternative. That, I take it, is what von Hügel did.

And if the crucial test for the Catholic intellectual is—as I argue in the next essay—whether he can appreciate and respond to the fully expanded personality, in Proust or Yeats, then the equivalent for the literary man is whether he can respect and admire the withered lily, in von Hügel or St Catherine. And let us note that though von Hügel identified himself with his 'causes', the Church, Modernism, etc., he did indeed wither in his self. I mean that he lived through the experience of withering, of diminishing the self, over and over again, all his life. This is something different from that process by which a man transfers his ego to his cause and enforces his self through that. There are plenty of examples of the latter among Catholic intellectuals, but what von Hügel exemplifies is something different.

Von Hügel's cannot be called the Catholic way except in a very abstract sense, because the Church includes every psychological type and ways for all of them. On the other hand, his is a way with a well-defined tradition in the Church, as the next essay shows. Perhaps it is worth distinguishing here between the Devout Humanism to which he assimilated himself and the Christian Humanism we associate with Erasmus and More, and with the platonizings of Pico della Mirandola and Ficino. (I follow Brémond here, in his *Histoire du Sentiment Réligieux en France.*)

Christian Humanism was speculative rather than practical, and aristocratic rather than popular; it sought the True and the Beautiful before the Good, and addressed itself to the élite rather than to the crowd. Devout Humanism, on the other hand, was before all else a school of personal holiness, though one inspired by a sense of the dignity of man. It was opposed to the Protestant Reformation's idea of disgraced, degraded man, and to the similar ideas propagated by Occamite Catholicism; which were current in the early stages of the Counter-Reformation. Such ideas of man made God's laws appear as arbitrary commands, human intelligence as reasoning in a void, and ethics as nominalism. Faith then was seen as the enemy of reason, and the supernatural of the natural. This Reign of Terror in religion, with the consequent scepticism in philosophy and rigorism in morals, is most often identified with the name of the Jansenists; and the Devout Humanists were in historical fact the principal objects of the Jansenists' disapproval and reforming zeal. The two groups represent opposite extremes of Catholic belief about human dignity.

Brémond (a friend of von Hügel) gives many examples of this Occamite and Jansenist Catholicism, and of its evil effects on the artistic and imaginative world of sixteenth- and seventeenth-century Europe—he cites Michelangelo and Vittoria Colonna as its victims. But in the next essay it is from modern Catholic literature that I take my examples of an anti-humanist, anti-Devout Humanist, sensibility. That sensibility has recurred again and again, throughout Catholic history. So has its opposite.

Perhaps in the case of such a persistent and extreme antithesis, there must be something in both extremes of value to Catholicism. Von Hügel, for all his moderateness, represents an extreme of his own kind—of reconciliation between the religious and the secular. But that does not mean he is un-Catholic. In *The Spirituality of the New Testament and the Fathers*, Louis Bouyer puts the problem this way:

'Between the love of the world as the divine creation and the hatred of the world as the instrument of the devil, it seems that Christian spirituality can neither settle down in any compromise nor make a choice. Synesius of Ptolemais represents, perhaps, a type of bishop who is too amiable, too human; Tertullian, for his part, is a type of priest whom we can easily find completely odious. The fact remains that both the one and the other incarnate something that cannot be complacently assumed as maintained in a stable equilibrium with the opposite element.'

Von Hügel obviously belongs with Synesius of Ptolemais, and most modern Catholic writers with Tertullian. It is worth noting that in this contrast von Hügel stands for something almost the opposite of what he stood for in the contrast between him and Yeats. There he stood for the claims of religion to limit and subdue the proud autonomy of literature; here he stands for the claims of literature to evade and mollify the harsh dominance of religion. Von Hügel's is a central position. It offers us the best chance, I think, of sharing in the virtues of both extremes; though it suffers, of course, from not offering the excitements of extremism.

One last point. Von Hügel's humanism is a very peaceable and pacifist and passive attitude to life. Its emphasis is more on how to accept injustices than on how to right them. Clearly it will not do for those who see the world as a battleground—and that includes many of my heroes. On the other hand, it is possible for people of very unpeaceable temperament to accept its discipline in literary and artistic matters. If we interpret the discipline of humanism to mean an insistence on variety of response, on plurality of sympathy (taking stringency and passion for granted) we may say that Orwell accepted it. Art, after all, can only flourish between battles. During war the Muses may or may not be silent, but they receive little sincere devotion. And surely this is true of other kinds of war besides the literal kind—political or personal embattlement, or religious militancy of the kind I go on to discuss.

Two kinds of Catholic sensibility

von Hügel and the modern Catholic novel

Baron von Hügel was not, of course, primarily a literary man, but it is legitimate to discuss him nowadays in the same way as one discusses novelists and poets, for two sorts of reason. First because he was a powerful sensibility, with interesting patterns of preference in modes of thought and feeling, and second because he was so literary in his expression. To expand the second point a little, he was literary both in that he did, in his odd way, write remarkably well, and in that so much of what survives of his work does so by its verbal life. His systems of ideas, as distinct from the language in which they are expressed, I am not competent to judge, but it seems that there is a consensus of opinion against them. That is, the larger theologians, philosophers, Biblical scholars, since his death, do not seem to have awarded his work any living importance. But as a writer—on religious and philosophical subjects—time has not dimmed him.

For instance, in this passage from a letter to his niece, the idea still lives; and it does so verbally, it is brought to life by the gaiety and wit of its literary movement, the vigour and muscularity of its literary form.

'You see, my Gwen, how vulgar, lumpy, material, appear great lumps of camphor in a drawer; and how ethereal seems the camphor smell all about in the drawer. How delicious, too, is the sense of bounding health, as one races along some down on a balmy spring morning; and how utterly vulgar, rather improper indeed, is the solid breakfast, are the processes of digestion that went before! Yet the camphor lumps, and the porridge, and its digestion, they had their share, had they not? in the ethereal camphor scent, in the bounding along upon that sunlit down? And a person who would both enjoy camphor scent and disdain camphor lumps; a person who would revel in that liberal open air and contemn porridge and digestion: such a person would be ungrateful, would she not?—would have an unreal, a superfine refinement? The institutional, the Church is, in religion, especially in Christianity, the camphor lump, the porridge, etc.; and the "detached" believers would have no camphor scent, no open air, bounding liberty, had there not been, from ancient times, those concrete, "heavy", "clumsy", "oppressive" things—lumps, porridge, Church.

Obviously what gives this life is not something limitedly literary, not a belletristic exquisiteness; but it is a vigorous move-ment of thought, explaining and persuading, which expresses itself completely in a range of literary devices. Those devices are completely adapted to their function. The more one knows about the recipient of the letter, the more one appreciates the choice of, for instance, 'the sense of bounding health' and 'liberal open air' and 'ungrateful'. One takes for granted the idea of 'vulgarity', as what he started from, what she in effect gave him to work with; but one admires what he made of it, with the one transition to 'lumps', for instance. In this extended, but perfectly ordinary, sense of the word 'literary', the Baron was, and indeed is, a literary figure.

The same qualities are present, though in a more heavily solemn mixture, and more eccentric, more Victorian-Gothic in style, in this passage from a letter to Father Tyrrell.

'I go on feeling, with that persistent, dull, unsought-out sort of impression which life has made me think is generally well-founded (at least for my own case), that it is somehow, just now, of extreme importance to the fullness and fruitfulness of your whole work and being, that you should not fly on, but should circle round—should bear with, should strengthen up, and be strengthened in return, by those who, with limits and poverties innumerable, love and sacrifice themselves with you and for you. You are born to be daringly, deeply independent: just because of that, do not let any over-swiftness, any unlimitedness, any impatience with that dearest and greatest of the disguises under which God works in man—I mean love of friction and our poor bovine, humble slownesses, of a goodly dose of stupidity—get into or anywhere find lodgment in that amazingly rapid nature of yours. Bagehot is helping me finely to articulate this sense in myself; it is the sense of creatureliness, I am sure. And so I want you to stick to the *Rinnovamento* group, and to wait upon their little failings, if they have them, as they, in turn, would wait upon yours. And further developments would stand over—would wait with our great patient, waiting God.'

Here the Baron is persuading much more than explaining, and his way of exerting personal pressure is characteristically tentative, circumlocutory, abstract, almost impersonal. He intellectualizes and etherealizes his counsel, making it a manifestation of some impersonal 'life' wisdom, so that it merges almost imperceptibly at the end of the paragraph into the patience of God—without von Hügel himself assuming any shade of omniscience or even ordinary knowingness. That being the shape of his meaning, the slow diffusely incantatory rhythms, and the recurrent, hidden variations on the main image (of movements) are magnificently at its service. This is the work of a very considerable stylist.

But we have to show not only that he was literary, but also that he was a significant sensibility; and perhaps the first thing to do is to discuss why that has been tacitly denied, why he has been so long ignored. At the time of his death (1925) he had a big reputation; not as a stylist—this aspect of his work was usually dismissed as 'Germanic'—but as a philosopher and theologian. He was particularly the favourite of non-Catholics. Father d'Arcy said that year that one could hardly pick up any book on mysticism by an Anglican, Nonconformist, or even rationalist, that did not echo the Baron's opinions and manner. Bishop Gore and Archbishop Temple made much use of his theology in their own work. But within his own church, the attitude to him was less enthusiastic, and this proved the more influential on later opinion. The coolness was due not only to his association with the Modernist movement—for which he nearly suffered official censure—but to his pervading liberalism, in every aspect of religious thought and feeling, his desire to learn from the other forms of Christianity, and the other religions, and non-religious kinds of moral and spiritual truth, his attempt to build a catholic wisdom larger than Catholicism itself. This seemed dangerous to the more conservative, and dull to the more advanced, after 1925 Liberalism, in most spheres of life, was old-fashioned, and not only among Roman Catholics. Many forces in the intellectual world converged to swing sympathy away from everything von Hügel believed in. It seemed—to the most intelligent—a time for choosing sides, and Rome's whole virtue lay in her defiant irreconcilability with even the best of the modern secular world. 'In a frank supernaturalism, in a tight clericalism, not in a pleasant secularization, lies the sole hope of the church,' wrote Santayana.

Santayana could claim, as convincingly as anyone, to be a detached and intelligent observer, so we might quote a little more of his essay on 'Modernism and Christianity'. This was published in *Winds of Doctrine* in 1913, and prefigures what T. S. Eliot was to say twenty years later with more immediate authority and influence.

'In more recent times we have heard of liberal Catholicism, the attitude assumed by some generous but divided minds, too much attached to their traditional religion to abandon it, but too weak and too hopeful not to glow also with enthusiasm for modern liberty and progress. Had those minds been, I will not say intelligently Catholic but radically Christian, they would have felt that this liberty was simply liberty to be damned, and this progress not an advance towards the true good of man, but a lapse into endless and heathen wanderings. For Christianity, in its essence and origin, was an urgent summons to repent and come out of just such a worldly life as modern liberty and progress hold up as an ideal to the nations. In the Roman empire, as in the promised land of liberalism, each man sought to get and enjoy as much as he could, and supported a ponderous government neutral as to religion and moral traditions, but favourable to the accumulation of riches; so that a certain enlightenment and cosmopolitanism were made possible, and private passions and tastes could be gratified without encountering persecution or public obloquy, though not without a general relaxation of society and a vulgarizing of arts and manners. That something so self-indulgent and worldly as this ideal of liberalism could have been thought compatible with Christianity, the first initiation into which, in baptism, involves renouncing the world, might well astonish us, had we not been rendered deaf to moral discords by the very din which from our birth they have been making in our ears.'

In von Hügel's terms, it was Christianity as a sect, not as a church, that Santayana was assuming. But obviously this is not a quarrel about terms only, and equally obviously it is Santayana's attitude and feeling which is the more akin of the two to the stringent Catholic minds who followed them both. Von Hügel's attitude and feeling has seemed very milk-and-watery in comparison.

Amongst Anglicans, or at least amongst some, this swing of opinion, away from liberalism, was less marked less early. England was an old-fashioned country, and Anglicanism an old-fashioned religion, between the wars; so it was there that von Hügel retained his reputation longest. In 1937, in an introduction to *Von Hügel and Tyrrell*, Canon Lilley described the two as having introduced an 'interconfessional *English* theology'. They saw religion as the deepest kind of life, and faith as a venture of the total human spirit. This has 'an irresistible appeal to the characteristically English type of mind and its habitual outlook upon things of the spirit'. Von Hügel himself was severe on the inadequacies of that kind of sentimental nationalism; though one should perhaps grant that his sensibility did aim at that mild bright sunniness associated with the cult of England in the decade before the war. There is no need, however, to point out how double-edged such a recommendation must have been in the general intellectual atmosphere of 1937.

Ten years before, in 1927, an Anglican who was to prove very influential on contemporary sensibility had assigned von Hügel to the pre-war years. T. S. Eliot wrote a review of the Baron's *Selected Letters* for *The Dial,* called 'An Emotional Unity'. He praised the man ('a rather grand personality') at the expense of his work, and his heart ('his *instinct* was orthodox') at the expense of his brain. 'He and his interests are, in some important respects, out of date.' We have a different attitude to science now, and a different attitude to religion. He belongs to the past. This was only two years after the Baron's death, but of course it was true enough, once granted Eliot's power to *change* our attitudes to science and religion. Modernism, which he largely identified the Baron with, was a movement with which Eliot had little sympathy; modernists, it seemed to him, were men trying to reconcile two irreconcilable modes of feeling within themselves—instead of defiantly espousing the one (derived from traditional faith) and totally rejecting the other (derived from modern positivism). But Eliot's real sympathy perhaps lay more with *them*—men like Loisy—than with the Baron. 'Von Hügel, a much simpler soul, escaped all these torments because of his emotional unity.' It is clear that Eliot knew very little about the Baron, and his article, though it intends to be generous, is in fact condescending; liberalism, even more than the modernist movement, was uncontrollably antipathetic to Eliot.

His feelings were exact, but his ideas were often vague. And his mysticism is no longer the order of the day. He belongs to a past epoch, a period of intellectual indistinctness, in which he moved among a host of half Christians and quarter Christians. The present age seems to me much more of an age of black and white, without shadows. Mysticism—even the particular Christian mysticism studied by von Hügel—is not the issue of our time. We are able to quote with approval that remark of Bossuet of which Professor Babbitt has reminded us; 'true mysticism is so rare and unessential and false mysticism is so common and dangerous that one cannot oppose it too firmly.' We demand of religion some kind of *intellectual* satisfaction—both private and social—or we do not want it at all.

It is interesting that Eliot should quote Bossuet on mysticism, for von Hügel, too, often referred to the Bossuet-Fénelon confrontation on that issue, but in order to show how much more impressive was Fénelon's performance. To quote Bossuet via *Babbitt,* to remind us of *Babbitt*'s preference for 'intellectual satisfaction' over 'mysticism', is to give away one's case. The whole article shows Eliot at his weakest, but at the same time—as was so often the way with him—at his most characteristically positive. We must, however, be grateful for such a clear demonstration of the sense in which von Hügel was out-of-date even at the moment (1927) and in the area (Anglicanism) of his apparent apotheosis.

It was to be forty years before the atmosphere could be said to be favourable to him again—if indeed that is true even of today. Of course Eliot's pronouncement did not immediately or by itself prevent other people from continuing to take an interest in the Baron; but the character of that interest became, as time passed, more and more pietistic, desultory and backwatery. Apart from one American edition of *Letters to his Niece*, he has been reprinted, since 1930, only in the form of 'selections'. There have been four of these (counting one in 1928); none of them Catholic in origin; and the selections are usually of a paragraph or two at a time, or sometimes a sentence or two—certainly not of a whole essay. The editors, understandably, speak of the Baron as a growing force in the world of thought. 'Since his death his influence has continued to widen and deepen, and at a greater pace, especially in Britain and America. It seems likely to continue steadily for some years to come.' This is the comment of P. Franklin Chambers, whose *Baron von Hügel; Man of God* came out in 1945, and was reprinted in 1946 and 1947, and is now available in paperback. This is certainly evidence of a kind of popularity; and the Baron is, even in these brief quotations, impressive; but it was not by means of such selections that influence *could* widen or deepen in the world of thought in 1945. A part of the general reaction against liberalism was a deep distrust of the easily accessible, the exoteric, in ideas. Von Hügel has been the favourite of non-specialists; a Catholic disapproved among Catholics, a philosopher unknown among philosophers, a theologian ignored among theologians—that has been a disastrous reputation to have since 1925.

For instance, when his biography came out, in 1951, by Michael de la Bedoyère, the publishers cited praise of the Baron by Dean Inge, Evelyn Underhill (calling him the 'sanest of our spiritual teachers') and Middleton Murry (saying 'of this ideal Catholicism we may say that, if ever it were to become actual, the road would be straight and smooth . . .' etc.). None of the three were Roman Catholics, and all were in some sense intellectual casualties of the war Eliot (amongst others) led against liberalism; none of them were, by 1951, major directors of opinion. The biographer himself took a rather indulgent tone towards his subject: the Baron was a very good man, and a very learned scholar, but a rather simple soul. That tone had been set, among Catholics, as early as 1936, in an article by Archbishop Goodier, which literally calls him a 'simple child' in crucial theological matters. Anyone who has read von Hügel carefully knows that such an attitude cannot be taken at its face value. The Baron's was not a simple mind. All such phrases can mean is that their speakers did not find in von Hügel something they were looking for, and that its absence seemed to them to justify their dismissing what they did find. What they dismissed—with relief—was the Baron's summons to a universal charity towards every kind of moral and spiritual effort, his wonderful openness, suppleness, subtlety, the example he offers of a mind in love with every kind of human good. What was missing was a readiness for harsh rigorism, a 'Jansenist' suspicion of many forms of human expansion, a 'Manichean' division of society, and all life, into the black and the white; all those features that characterized the accredited Catholic sensibility of the time.

In strictly literary matters we cannot say that von Hügel fell out of date with his death, in 1925, but only because he had already been out of date for the twenty years preceding. Not only Lytton Strachey and D. H. Lawrence, but such professional Catholics as Francis Thompson and G. K. Chesterton, remained outside his range. He seems never to have mentioned either of the latter, though his friend, Wilfrid Ward, welcomed Chesterton on to *The Dublin Review* and into his home immediately he appeared as a writer, and before he was received into the church. He was the writer Ward had been waiting for. But the Baron stayed aloof. Dickens and George Eliot were his novelists, and one can guess that Chesterton's paradoxes and debating skills and inability to grow up must have seemed to him a poor performance for a 'Catholic writer'. The same thing done more seriously, by his older friend, 'Ideal' Ward, had failed to satisfy him. As for those other writers who, coming after Chesterton, worked out a sensibility both sharply contemporary and sharply Catholic, one cannot even guess the Baron's response. He lived in another world. But his interest is that one can say he *lives* in that world; for it is still there, still habitable by others, and an alternative to the one we have been offered as categorically Catholic.

In other words, von Hügel, since his death, has been quietly put away. His reputation has been assassinated by silence; that is, by being quietly mentioned as one of a very quiet company. But the way in which this has been done (see Eliot's article, for instance) should itself rouse our suspicions and prepare us to find him interesting. He was the last belated representative of the great liberal movement of thought and sensibility, and since we have lived through, and come to the end of, the reaction against that movement, we naturally look back to what came before. Since he was also a man of remarkable gifts, intellectual, literary, and religious, we must also find him impressive. We can use him in seeking an alternative to the modern 'Catholic sensibility'. His combination of the highest standards with the broadest sympathies is just what we have been starved of. The readiness to see the good in everything but also to demand the best, by purely human standards, is what modern Catholic writers have not shown. But we must begin to discuss this modern sensibility.

A neat historical coincidence helps us measure the distance that separates von Hügel from the modern Catholic writer. The niece to whom he wrote his most famous series of letters, Gwendolen

Plunket Greene, had three children, Richard, David and Olivia, about whose upbringing she consulted the Baron. They all became, as a family, close friends of Evelyn Waugh at Oxford. He tells us in *A Little Learning* that he fell in love with the whole family, including the mother, and focused this affection on Olivia as the only appropriate member. The children appear in his account of them as not unlike sympathetic characters in his early novels—tall, elegant, languid, eccentric, amusing, crazy. It is a sharp contrast to read the Baron's account of one of them, on his visit to Richard at Oxford. 'Such a fine, large, clean, straight lad. . . . I was a bit surprised to hear a "No" to all my games questions—cricket, football— . . .'. Place Evelyn Waugh beside Richard in your imagination, and you could not wish for a neater vignette of the split between the generations after the War.

This split affected more than personality styles. It affected attitudes to religion, as Eliot said, and it affected literary modes, as he and Evelyn Waugh demonstrated. It affected profoundly the whole concept of 'the Catholic writer' which became, for that generation and the next, a very important cultural image. By virtue of that split, everything the Baron stood for, as a sensibility, became unavailable to Catholic writers who refused to restrict themselves to rectory or vicarage audiences.

Like most new concepts, this was an old one transferred from its place of origin, and transformed by being given more intellectual glamour. J. L. Prévost dates the Catholic Novel from 1858, when Barbey d'Aurevilly brought out a new 'Catholic' edition of his pre-conversion novel, *Une Vieille Maîtresse,* with a preface (not published till 1865) on the problems of Catholic writers. M. Prévost distinguishes three main currents in the novel, which all begin from Barbey d'Aurevilly. The first, the traditional and Balzacian, represented by René Bazin and Henri Bordeaux, has not been of major importance in the twentieth century. The second, the mystical and prophetic, can best be identified by the name of Léon Bloy; the third, concerned with the psychology of sin, is most associated with François Mauriac; and both these currents are to be observed in the work of Bernanos, who is perhaps the most extreme case of 'Catholic sensibility'. These two currents of sensibility *have* been of major importance in the twentieth century, and have had younger representatives in France (Julien Green), in Germany (Gertrud von le Fort), and England (Graham Greene).

F

In the nineteenth century this Catholic sensibility was quite recognizably and even crudely a species of Romanticism. These novelists' work usually belonged within the Romantic sub-species, Satanic melodrama; rhetorical in language, violent in action, bitter and extremist in spirit. *'J'attends les Cosaques et le Saint-Esprit,'* Bloy wrote at the end of *Au Seuil de l'Apocalypse.* These writers were explicitly in rebellion against the modern world, against industrial and scientific progress, and implicitly against the human condition. To quote Bloy again, *'L'exposition, c'est l'adoration du très Saint-Sacrement de la matière, les quarante heures de tous les cochons de la volupté ou du bien-être qui s'appellent le 19e siècle. Une pareille fête date l'ère de la fin de toute pensée, de toute âme, de toute forte spiritualité.'*

In the twentieth century this sensibility has expressed itself with more sophistication—that is, with our kinds of sophistication. The relationship remains close, however. Bloy was Barbey d'Aurevilly's secretary and disciple, and Bernanos acknowledged his overwhelming debt to Bloy. What 'Catholic writer' means today can be suggested by reciting a few names from current French, British and American fiction. Mauriac and Green in France, J. F. Powers and Flannery O'Connor in America, Greene and Waugh in England—with Muriel Spark and William Golding as post-war epigoni. And what these names most importantly connote, taken together, is surely an anti-humanist sensibility; in these writers' novels, human achievements and modes of being are consistently and triumphantly shown to be inadequate, egotistic, evil, just in being themselves, in being human. Under stress all natural goodness breaks down; only grace-assisted goodness is valid, and grace-assisted badness is perhaps even better. But the attack on human nature is even more radical than the disparagement of human achievement. *'Je hais l'instinct sexuel,'* says Julien Green, and his attitude to the artistic instinct is almost equally hostile. *'Un homme qui tremble devant le péché n'écrira jamais de romans.'*

We might take one or two examples from Bernanos' *Le Journal d'un Curé de Campagne,* one of the more powerful and authentic of these books, authentically about spiritual and moral experience, and authentically modern in sensibility. The pictures of family life (at the Château) and of childhood innocence (Séraphita) operate as—amongst other things but prominently—exposures of humanly comfortable myths of natural goodness. The same is true of the pictures of the countryside and of village life; *this* is what these things are *really* like, Bernanos is saying, not those nineteenth-century bourgeois idylls you have been cosseting your mind with. Even the pleasures of bodily health—eating, drinking, sleeping—are morally undermined for the reader by the relentless detailing of the Curé's bodily miseries. Then the central action works by lining up a number of accusers of life, whose rhetoric— sometimes purely verbal and sometimes partly active—the Curé innocently transcribes into his journal. Le Curé de Torcy, Mlle Chantal, the two doctors, Séraphita, M. Olivier, these are ruthless enemies both of all idealism, including most ordinary heroics, and of all comfortable, middle of the road, contentment. Not only do they denounce humanity for the Curé, they each in turn, inde- pendently, single him out as one of themselves. They are hard in their superiority to life's comforts, including its moral comforts, including, for some of them, the virtues themselves. But they recognize in the little Curé, soft to the point of amorphousness, dispossessed of every scrap of natural dignity, their natural ally and equal. In M. Olivier's speeches, which are climactic, we even see the sickly and tearful Curé, *by virtue of* his human humilia- tion, associated with, assimilated into, the stark bronzed valour of the Foreign Legionary; because the two are equally the enemy of the comfortable, life-loving bourgeois. Of the other vividly- drawn characters, Mlle Louise and Louis Dufréty represent ordinary human weakness, and they are beneath contempt. The Curé feels a physical revulsion from their touch. They are figures of vanity, not of pride. They value the things of this world. And all the while the reader is being disturbed in his normal dignity and decency of self-relation by being made to feel the Curé's corrosive self-pity and self-contempt. The book in fact enacts a humiliation of the central character, which accumulates in the sympathetic reader's mind an angry resentment against ordinary comfortable people and events, just for being ordinary and comfortable; a resentment which is intensified and complicated by the hero's self-hatred, but sanctified and lifted above criticism by seeming inseparable from true Christianity; and which is exultantly redeemed by the triumph of an erected and angry pride in other people, who acknowledge and receive among them the humiliated one. Thus the sympathetic reader gets it both ways.

It would be too much to say that all this is categorically 'Catholic writer' in feeling, but the attack on every kind of human complacency and natural comfort surely is. It would be easy enough to demonstrate the same kind of thing in the work of the other writers mentioned, or in, say, 'The Cocktail Party'.

That von Hügel stood at an opposite pole of Catholic sensibility from this is equally easy to demonstrate. 'God is the God of Nature as well as of Grace,' he told his niece. 'He provides the meal and the yeast.' And as he expands this, we see it amounts to a condemnation of Bernanos.

'Those who most exalt the power and need of grace do so usually by most depreciating nature. God thus gets glorified in direct proportion as man gets vilified. The more holy I find God, the more wicked I feel myself to be. This is touching and real, and almost irresistible to vehement natures, but it is dangerous and excessive.'

In an essay he put it more formally.

'Man's personality, the instrument of all his fuller and deeper apprehensions, is constituted by the presence and harmonization of a whole mass of energies and intimations belonging to different levels and values; and not one of these can (in the long run and for mankind at large) be left aside or left unchecked by the others, without grave drawback to the personality. Religion is indeed the deepest of energisings and intimations within man's entirety, but it is not the only one; and though through Religion alone God becomes definitely revealed to man as Self-conscious Spirit, as an Object, as *the* Object, of direct, explicit adoration, yet those other energies and intimations are also willed by God and come from Him, and (in the long run and for mankind at large) are necessary to man's health and balance even in religion itself.'

Although in Bernanos' case we discussed a novel, and in von Hügel's an essay, it makes sense to say that the latter contradicts the former. Von Hügel insists on the validity and the importance of all life's values—including the value of happiness, of comfort, of moral well-being; and on our duty, *as children of religion*, to care about and work for the perfection of those values. His and Bernanos' are sharply opposed statements of sensibility, mutually hostile attitudes to life, and if the first is commonly identified with 'the Catholic writer' there is good reason to remind ourselves of the second.

Perhaps the most vivid and large-scale instance of the Baron's feeling for Nature-*and*-Grace is the education he gave his niece as a preparation for and accompaniment to her religious instruction. Together they read (meticulously) Caesar, Cicero, Lucretius, Virgil, Tacitus, Horace, Livy, Pliny, Herodotus, Hesiod, Thucydides. Their main interest was of course in the general cultural value of these books, and he sent her accompanying volumes on history, on statuary, on Greek coins, geography, etc.; but at the same time he sent her quite copious details on editions, and instructions on reading methods and on note-taking. The books were to be treated as objects of study. It was a discipline he subjected her to; and its purpose was to counteract her religious enthusiasm. The merely religious woman, he told her, is so often 'a bore'. What he was afraid of for her, it is easy to see, was some over-emotional espousal of religion in rejection of the rest of life, and espousal of Catholicism in rejection of Anglicanism and England. It was partly because of that threat of hysteria and negation that he warned her always *against* entering the church. They studied the religious classics in the same way, though at the same time he was sending her devotional books to be read in quite a different way; to be 'absorbed', in complete quiescence of the critical faculty, dwelling on whatever satisfied her and turning away from whatever did not as unselfconsciously as possible, like a browsing cow. While in English literature they went together from Caedmon to Bradley on Shakespeare—'a *glorious* book'. Only by knowing that she loved all these things fully at the same moment as she loved God more could he be sure that she loved God rightly.

The way this coloured his whole view of the history of Catholicism is evident in this passage from the Essays.

'The Church Father Lactantius and the Popes St Gregory the Great and Alexander II were no less certain of, and no less zealous for, Superhuman Religion—for the supreme truth of Christianity and of Catholicism, than were the Church Father Augustine or the Popes St Pius V and Paul IV. But the former combined, with this all-pervading and all-crowning faith, a keen sense for the natural virtues, as the inviolable prerequisites, concomitants and consequences of the Supernatural Life; for the elements of truth and goodness present in all men and in all religions; for the essentially free character of the act and habit of faith; and for the irreplaceable persuasiveness of love; whereas the latter were all but exclusively engrossed in the specifically religious virtues, in the completest religion, in this religion's scholastic and juridical formulation, and in the influence and utility of pressure, fear, commands, obedience.'

Von Hügel himself is surely the type of the modern Catholic with a 'keen sense for the natural virtues' and 'for the elements of truth and goodness present in all men and in all religions'. Perhaps even more striking is his keen sense for 'the essentially free character of the act and habit of faith', and for 'the irreplaceable persuasiveness of love'. On the whole, we must say that the modern Catholic writer has not shown any marked sense of those last—a vengeful scepticism about anyone's ability to love or to believe anything much long has been more his note. It has been left to the spokesmen for psycho-analysis (Erik Erikson is a good example) to stand for love in message and manner.

Now this is surely an anomaly so extreme as to make its point— that something is wrong with 'Catholic sensibility'—as soon as it is pointed out. Christianity is a gospel of charity. When its spokesmen must be identified with attitudes so much the reverse of charitable, something is badly wrong. It is surely as simple as that. The situation is such that the simplest terms will do to analyse it. We can take Erikson's *Childhood and Society* and ask how many modern Catholic books are inspired by anything like so impressive a spirit of love, working within an elaborate intellectual discipline? Romano Guardini and von Hügel himself are the first two names that occur to me; and they are the two writers on whom one has to rely in general. But the names of the imaginative writers occur only because they so strikingly do not meet the challenge, so fail to understand its relevance.

Von Hügel used Troeltsch's distinction between 'church' and 'sect' and 'group of mystics', as the three forms of religious organization. The 'sect' he identified with the 'world-fleeing elements' in Neo-Platonism and Buddhism, and monasticism in Catholicism, as well as with the more obvious Protestant sects. Thus Tertullian, Kierkegaard, Valdes, are typical sect figures. Of the 'church', Roman Catholicism is the supreme example, and this is its ultimate superiority over its rivals.

'Only the two movements of World-flight and of World-seeking, of the Civilising of Spirituality, and of the Spiritualising of

Civilisation: only This world and That world, each stimulating the other, although in different ways, from different sources and with different ends: only these two movements together form man's complete supernaturalised spiritual life. But if so, then the Church's large and leisurely occupation with Art, Philosophy, the State was not and is not, in itself, a corruption, but a normal expansion of one of the two necessary halves of the Church's own complete nature and end. And this again means that the Sect-type in fact represents, at its best, half of the whole truth, whereas the Church, at its best, represents both halves of the same whole truth. . . .'

It is an almost unique distinction in von Hügel, that he could give a phrase like 'the civilising of spirituality' a respectable firmness and fullness of meaning. His mind could stand so firmly and so fully both inside and outside Christianity.

This went along with a characteristic stress on ease, simplicity, spontaneity, in the spiritual life; which did not mitigate a marked austerity in purely moral questions. Morally, he divided the self up into mutually antagonistic halves, and held that for the Christian there must be an unceasing struggle against his lower self; renunciation, self-punishment, self-hatred in that sense, were simple goods to him. But the spiritual and devotional life is a life of love, and follows love's laws. One must follow the natural inclinations of one's spirit. 'Drop things,' he told his niece; 'always keep on dropping and dropping. My religion, my illness, suffering and life have taught me that.' And in another place, 'Do not suppress pleasures, but let them flop. Pleasure is like the fringe of your dress, the afterness of an act. Ignore them, let them flop, never work directly for them.' And to Juliet Mansel, 'We will not strain after this, I will never push you; reactions are ever near us, and how dangerous they are!'

In both these ways, he followed his master and his saint, the Abbé Huvelin. Huvelin says:

'*Il ne faut pas faire comme le lion s'irritant contre le moucheron. Il faut haïr nos défauts, non d'une haine dépitée et trouble, mais d'une haine tranquille. Il faut avoir la patience de les voir, et d'en tirer parti; il faut en tirer l'humilité.*'

That is very much the voice of St François de Sales, and through Huvelin, but also directly, von Hügel drew on the spiritual tradition that included St François de Sales, Fénelon, Père de Caussade. In fact, von Hügel's sensibility is largely the sensibility he found in these men, and appropriated to himself: in substitution for that chaos of appetites, irritabilities, frustrations, and miseries, which he found in himself 'by nature'. Here is his own description of that sensibility or temperament, *à propos* of Fénelon.

'It is the combination of a rarely light (not frivolous)—a light and elastic open temperament with an earnest will and gently concentrated determination. People as determined and as ardent as he, usually are, or become, heavy, rigoristic. And again, people as light and elastic as he, usually are, or become, frivolous and corrupt. By that combination—the earnestness without rigorism —he always strikes me as belonging, in his measure, to that minority of Christian teachers who have reached closest to that same combination in Our Lord Himself—to have caught up a few drops of that genial rain, that royally generous west wind, that gently drops and brightly blows through the virile sunshine of His love. St Francis is another, and, of course, a much greater instance of that delightful paradox. The future of religion, indeed even already its present propagation in our poor old world, lie in it.'

It is St Francis of Assisi von Hügel refers to there, but St François de Sales was probably closer to Fénelon in this way, and certainly to von Hügel. The three men may be said to have shared this sensibility, which is the sensibility of a movement, indeed of more than one movement, within Christianity. The tradition of spirituality in sixteenth- and seventeenth-century France which Brémond calls Devout Humanism, and of which St François was the great master, developed this Christian temperament, perhaps more notably than any other tradition. St François, Fénelon, and von Hügel, while different enough in initial endowment, were all men of marked introspective and introactive powers, and their individualities were largely transformed by those tactics of self-management which they held in common. St François is described by Brémond as a dove who made himself into a serpent; a naturally weak character, timid, withdrawn, and unresistant, bullied by his tutor when a child, by his valet when a man, by his brother all his life; he made himself, for those who met him in the life of religion, like Ste Chantal, a severe and sometimes imperious director of conscience. The Baron was perhaps nearer to being a serpent who had made himself into a dove. Loud-voiced, stiff-necked, impetuous and irritable in his first reactions, he learned to distrust his own nature quite radically, and made himself cautious, meticulous, self-reserving. Both were (as was Fénelon) great directors of conscience by letter, especially of women, and especially of people in the world. All three were great men of the world themselves—men of exquisite manners—great psychologists of the religious affections, and great men of letters. And their main spiritual teachings are all in the same key, fall within the same compass, between the same gentle discretion and the same energetic severity. All emotions about the self, even angers against one's faults and aspirations to more virtue, are foolish and dangerous; yield, elude, evade one's faults; divert the spirit from its trouble and pain, its sins and angers. At the same time, be ruthless with yourself, as in this advice of St François to Chantal. 'Cut, sever your friendships, do not amuse yourself by untying them. Scissors and knife are necessary. No, the knots are fine, intricate, tangled . . . your nails too short to take hold of them. Only the sharp knife will do it. The cords are of no value. Do not spare them.' Change the idiom, and this could be von Hügel's, both for what is said and for the manner of its saying, the combination of personal immediacy and impersonal coolness. Von Hügel was formed in that school, which we can call, extending the reference of Brémond's term a little, Devout Humanism. Of course, if we can legitimately identify this sensibility, this temperament, with the tradition of Devout Humanism, we cannot identify it with Christianity as a whole. Von Hügel's claim—that Fénelon's temperament was specially close to Christ's—is important mostly as an act of faith, not as an objective observation. He is declaring his own allegiance, his own intention, his own programme of self-realization. But such acts are of vital importance, even in the world of pure thought, and taken as such an act, von Hügel's claim is perfectly legitimate. His preference is none the less fully Catholicism, for being a kind of Catholicism. It is certainly no less fully Catholic than that kind—quite as much a matter of individual temperament—which we have learned to identify with 'the Catholic writer'. In fact, the Church historically has endorsed Devout Humanism and condemned Jansenism.

As an example of how von Hügel's sensibility led him to act, how it expressed itself in practical religious advice, let us cite this letter (dated Epiphany, 1921) to Juliet Mansel. He advises her to go to Holy Communion, even though she is ill, and even though she has been out of touch with all forms of religious life.

'And then follows the week of humble, gentle practice of your resolutions, with little peaceful turnings to Christ to help you keep them or to forgive you when you fail in them.

You will thus (and thus alone) get a unity and drama, a reality and awakeness, a depth, steadiness and tenderness into your life which nothing else ever can or will of itself supply. All will spring up afresh, green and delightful. Your very expression, certainly your health, will gain a repose and a zest delicious to behold. I noticed close to your door, immediately on the other side of the Cathedral, St Andrew's Church; look, Dearie, there, at the Notice Board, and if there is Holy Communion marked there for twelve o'clock or so on Sundays, do you slip out, without telling anyone, especially without listening to your *raison raisonnante*— slip out as you used to do to help others in the War—and get your Holy Communion then.

When I come on Monday I will not say, nor expect, one word about this whole matter. Only let me say here now that simply *nothing* you could ever do will give me so complete a joy as if you thus give the secondary part of you the slip and if you thus restart, more deliberately and circumspectly than ever, your building up of interior unity in the daily watch and ward against the false self.

At the Fishmongers I often admire the way in which they slit up soles from head to tail—even the slimmest sole. Such division leaves these fishes truly broken up. Yes, because they *are* but fishes—*soles*, not *souls*. For as to souls, human souls, these, wonderful to relate, do not even begin to attain to their true unity, indeed they are not really awake, until they are divided up—until the spirit within them begins to discriminate itself against the petty self.

In the Scottish rivers the salmon will leap and leap, and only after much leaping will they succeed in jumping up and into the higher reaches. Jump, Child, jump: *I* jump with you, look, we both manage it!

Loving old Fatherly one.'

Through the odd, old-fashioned, cumbersome manner, the mind can be seen at work, really lively and really impressive. Let us note that Juliet Mansel was an Anglican, as were several of those who came to the Baron for direction. The formal limits of creed and communion were things he over-stepped easily—without ever impeaching their validity. Note too the elaborate manners of his method; the things he will say in a letter, but not face to face, nor indeed refer to face to face even after having said them in a letter; as with St François and Fénelon, with von Hügel the concept of manners applied to the whole range of behaviour, into the most intimate spiritual experience. Note above all that it is health as a whole the Baron is concerned with—'Your very expression, certainly your health, will gain a repose and a zest delicious to behold'—and he acknowledges no conflict between the demands of nature and those of supernature in measuring health. What he does acknowledge, implicitly, is religion's responsibility to nurture natural forms of moral and spiritual health—to care about and for quality there as much as non-religious thinkers care. While von Hügel is its spokesman, one need not feel that religion prefers a vulgar heartiness, or even a merely communal seriousness, in the non-religious life of the spirit. The Baron took every discrimination in quality, however personal, with full seriousness.

Perhaps the Baron's voice may seem old-fashioned today not only in the sense that it has been long displaced by younger and hostile voices, but in the more essential sense that the melo-dramatic cast of twentieth-century history, the mounting fever of crisis modern man has lived through, has made inappropriate such a peaceful and unembattled piety. Those sharper, angrier, more anguished voices, which we have called collectively 'the modern Catholic writer', are perhaps speaking for and to our experience as the Baron is not, are perhaps the only appropriate way to talk, after the concentration camps and the bombs and the brutalities. But to say this is surely to over-simplify the problem of appropriateness. Melodramatic troubles can be said to demand, more than other troubles, unmelodramatic responses. Moreover, the responses we are considering are works of literature, and if we look at the strains and falsifications of language, of feeling, of art, in the work of those Catholic writers, their literary failures, which are at least close to being failures in Catholic feeling, then we must reject their claims to be the necessary and natural voice of the times. There are men of talent amongst them, and works of merit have been produced, but nowadays it is the weaknesses of even those works which strike the attention. We have to look out for, however unconsciously we do so, a new Catholic sensibility; and von Hügel can be a useful touchstone and perhaps a guide in our search.

For he is surely a fine practical theologian of that grace which delivers man not from guilt, but from shame; ascribing guilt to our consciousness of particular things done or omitted, the results of pride or passion, and shame to our consciousness of general states of being (non-being and half-being), the results of weaknesses and failures in our humanity. The legalistic and activist cast of Catholic moral consciousness has tended to leave these states, so important in our spiritual life, out of account. They are difficult to speak of in confession. It is therefore particularly the job of Catholic culture and the Catholic writer to investigate these areas of experience, and to complement the executive efficiency of the Church militant with the suppler and more complex sympathies of the literary imagination.

Catholic moral theology often seems to assume a perfectly working animal ego in the natural man—a mass of healthy appetites needing only to be checked and uplifted by Christianity. There is little religious interest in the internal workings of that ego. It's what you do with what you've got that interests the priest. But our spiritual life consists quite largely in what we do about what we haven't got—the complex and powerful movements of mind set off by those lacks. Von Hügel turned the full force of his mind on to that area of the spiritual life.

In his later years especially, the Baron came to concentrate on these problems. 'It may even be questioned whether a man's apprehensions of the human which are in the most close contact and in the most constant contrast with the same man's apprehensions of the Superhuman, are indeed Evil, Suffering, Sin. I believe those closest and most constant concomitants of the superhuman intimations to be, in actual fact, the feeling of Weakness, Instability, Dependence.' In his essays and in his letters, von Hügel talks about these feelings of weakness, this natural shame, from a religious point of view. He shows *how* failures in humanity (in feeling, in forcefulness, in steadiness of purpose) are, and are not, failures in religion; and how successes as a human being are, and are not, successes as a son of God. The attention he directs on to this problem acts as the kind of sympathy, the kind of spiritual balm, these wounds need. Whereas modern Catholic writers on the whole have implied that human successes are religiously uninteresting, if not dangerous; that the awakened man will so see through worldly values that he would rather triumph, in the world, by brutal means than by gentle—that only religious sanctions can tame him. And they have treated our wounds, our human failures, not with balms but harsh astringents. Bernanos, for instance, exults in the human humiliation of his Curé; Graham Greene insists on the drabness and dreariness of human nature; tenderness to humanity is the last feeling one can hope to find convincingly expressed in a Catholic novel. Perhaps the Catholic writer in effect confuses shame with guilt and poverty of endowment with poverty of performance. The figures they offer as representatives of the human race are usually unlikeable; *that* is their shame, and their responsibility, about which they are expected to do something religious. In "The Cocktail Party" for instance, the plight of Edward and Lavinia is clearly the plight of two unpleasant people, who should not be married to each other, who are inadequate human beings. That plight is given a merely spurious dignity by being associated with supernatural standards and religious vocations, and by their being made to represent average level happiness and dignity. The play does not try to understand their human failure, much less to love them; that is largely why it outrages our feelings.

We have nowadays a new movement in Catholic opinion, and the rudiments of a new Catholic sensibility. This is partly in reaction against what we have been calling 'modern', and in so far it must be towards von Hügel. It is in some sense liberal. It is closer to Modernism than anyone has dared to be since the condemnation of Modernism. In *The Council, Reform and Reunion*, Hans Küng lists Catholic steps towards positive fulfilment of the valid demands of the Protestant reformers; Catholic appreciation of the religious motives in the Protestant Reformation: growing regard for the Scriptures; development of the liturgy into a people's liturgy; an understanding of the universal priesthood; adaptation of the church to other cultures; purification of the Papacy from politics; reform of the Curia; etc. This is roughly the programme of the Baron's kind of Modernism. He worked quite actively for all these aims, except the third, the reform of the liturgy; and there he was a pioneer advocate of frequent Communions, and opponent of Mariolatry. He was in fact a pioneer of ecumenicism and *aggiornamento*. It was just for being so that Eliot found him out of date. Now a cycle of religious tendency seems to have been completed, and 'liberalism' in some sense is again the programme of the future.

Karl Rahner, in *The Christian Commitment,* reverses the Baron's terms, and says that the Church must become increasingly, in modern times, a sect as opposed to a church. But the actual policies he wants seem to be deeply in sympathy with the Baron's. The fulfilment of once having been fully a church (in the Middle Ages) must be considered a cultural accident, not a religious achievement, and Catholics must not aim or yearn back to that. The modern diaspora is a 'must', something to be accepted and not to be fought, and so is the whole of the modern world. Catholicism will necessarily become more and more a minority culture, a sect. But it must just therefore struggle to avoid a ghetto mentality. (What Rahner means by ghetto is close to what von Hügel means by sect.) And in non-religious matters Christians must participate in the secular culture, and value its triumphs as triumphs. This is very much in the spirit of von Hügel.

Let us take as a last example, the matter of personal honesty. In *Generation of the Third Eye: Young Catholic Leaders view Their Church,* sympathizers with the new movement in America were asked to give some personal account of their experience in the Church. They found, the introduction says, that Catholics have no tradition of 'taking a hard look at ourselves, at least outside of the confessional'. Honesty is the word most of the contributors recur to; they were asked to give an honest personal account of their Catholicism, and they found they had severe problems which derived just from their religious training. This simple but devastating charge could come with surprise only to men who had never before stepped outside the church intellectually and imaginatively; but for Catholics—this is the point—that has been very hard. Von Hügel is the great patron of those who do; he is the patron of all personal honesty among Roman Catholics, particularly in intellectual and religious matters. He understood how specially difficult it is for a Catholic to be personally honest in such areas, what a special kind of honesty that must be, how much at odds with ordinary honesty in some ways, and how difficult to combine with ordinary honesty.

'Also because, especially since the Renaissance, perfect truthfulness, in view of the new exigencies in matters of history and of sensitive interest in subject-matters of no direct religious significance, is, I believe, the most delicately difficult of all the virtues for the average institutional religionist.'

He is, by the same token, one of the great patrons of the Catholic intellectual. He says, at the beginning of *The Mystical Element in Religion*:

' "Where my heart lies, let my brain lie also": man is not, however much we may try and behave as though he were, a mere sum-total of so many separable water-tight compartments; he can no more fruitfully delegate his brains and his interest in the intellectual analysis and synthesis of religion, than he can commission others to do his religious feeling or willing, his spiritual growth and combat, for him.'

He had a rare sense, one especially rare among Catholics, of the moral dignity of the intellectual function. Men differ no more in intellect than in other things, he pointed out. To be very clever made one no more abnormal than to be very gifted in strength or wealth or something else. The religion natural to intellectuals was then just as fully religion as that natural to 'the Irish washerwoman'.

'Both at the beginning, then, and throughout, and even at the end of the soul's life, the intellectual element is necessary, and this above all for the planting fully and finally, in the very depths of the personality, the Cross, the sole means to the soul's true Incoronation.'

And so it could only be right, from every moral and spiritual point of view, to follow up the natural impulses of the intellect, however critical—though of course in the manner appropriate to the subject being investigated, which in religious matters is different from what it is in scientific matters.

In so far, then, as this new movement is led by intellectuals, and inspired by a demand for more honesty and liberality of sympathy, it promises a return to the spirit of von Hügel. Of course, the modern Catholic writers were intellectual too. But their love for the Church clearly did not derive from its being a place for the free exercise of their natural function as intellectuals; one might even say it was much more for the Church as a place for the mortification of that function, for the dishonouring of nature and freedom.

But it is not yet clear that there is a whole new Catholic sensibility, either achieved in literature or adumbrated in theology. The new movement has so far markedly emphasized the *community* of Christians, and *communal* action as the life of the Church. It is the liturgical assembly which is the Mystical Body of Christ, says Father Bouyer, and everything else in the Church is there for the sake of that; the liturgy of the Mass enacts and reconstitutes the Risen Life, by and for bishop, priest, and people, and everything else is subordinate to that. That 'everything else' includes the hierarchy, the Curia, canon law, scholasticism, and so on. But it also includes the devotional life of the individual Christian. The emphasis is strongly on communal and liturgical devotions; individual devotions are usually stigmatized as sentimental, imaginative, or 'mystical' in a bad sense. The whole Counter-Reformation Church, the source of so many of these practices, is suspect; it is the Early Church which the new movement wants to take as a model. Consequently one whole half of Christian life, the more personal and private, has received little attention and half of Catholic sensibility has remained unrenewed.

Von Hügel belonged to the Counter-Reformation traditions in the Church rather than any other, at least in his spirituality, his Christian temperament. Devout Humanism, which began in sixteenth- and seventeenth-century France, is essentially a tradition of private devotions. And of course none of the wiser leaders of the new movement deny the value of, the continuing need for, such traditions. But they are in effect suspicious of them, and they have much less themselves to offer, in that area, of the individual Christian life. The language and the concepts of self-interrogation, of contemplation and meditation, of personal relations, are what they were. Küng and Rahner and Congar keep much of the vocabulary of the modern Catholic writer, and take their examples from them. Rahner speaks of the follower of Christ as a displaced person, marked with the sign of contradiction, and a man with his centre of gravity displaced outside himself. This, if taken seriously, describes the Christian psychology of, in fiction, Bernanos' Curé, or, in real life, Simone Weil. One suspects it is not to be taken seriously, for such feelings don't seem like cardinal features of the psychology of one of the 'people of God', a member of the liturgical assembly, a unit, in human terms, of a group life. In any case, it is at the opposite extreme from the 'light, open, elastic temperament' which von Hügel claimed as specially Christ-like, and the 'royally generous' West Wind blowing through the 'virile sunshine' of God's love. And the exciting thing about von Hügel's language is that it opens out a door into the open air, out from that dark grim prison of 'Catholic' anti-humanism which has outlasted many movements—a prison still far from broken open.

The new Catholicism is still in danger of inheriting from the old a syndrome of anti-humanist attitudes, that range from one extreme of brutal moral and theological abasement of the individual to the other extreme of cheerful childlikeness in group activities. That syndrome is anti-humanist in its hostility towards, or at least its nervousness about, the splendours of the expanded human personality. That is, in all but the specifically religious manifestations of that ideal; of course, it is not nervous about the jovial priest, or the community-song-leader; but the splendours of the expanded human personality include such oddities as *A La Recherche du Temps Perdu.* The intensely private and peculiar, the subtlest and most passionate discriminations, imaginations, attachments, and repulsions, all these are part of man's emotional-spiritual life. They all have to be taken seriously, and taken generously, by those who are called to be the arbiters of that life. There is no substitute for this in even the healthiest of group-activities.

The most impressive manifestations of the new Catholicism so far have all been categorically communal; the changes in the liturgy, the ecumenical negotiations, and, in America, clerical participation in the Civil Rights movement. No one can feel anything less than enthusiasm for all of these. But unless the Church can find an equally new approach to the individual's emotional-moral life, we shall not feel sure that its sensibility has been renewed. We shall not be sure that being a Catholic does not still involve not being a humanist, not really loving human achievement and natural being fully. The more powerful the community principle, and the more radical the calling of the People of God, the more we shall need independence and privacy, need to stand outside the Church at the same moment as inside; or our talk of avoiding a cultural ghetto will be an empty gesture.

The Baron's sensibility would reassure us against these dangers. The temperament of Devout Humanism, if we would recognize it as fully and centrally Catholic, could be our instinctual chart to a renewal of Catholic feeling. We need von Hügel's instinctive

G

love of life and reverence for the splendours of the human personality, his readiness to trust that critical impulse which is the most faithful servant of those splendours, his readiness to demand the best in natural things, to care about and for that best. The sensibility which combines that with the severest moral asceticism and the most total gift of self to God, and which moves from one to the other easily and spontaneously—that is a Catholic sensibility with much to offer us today.

But since writing that essay, I have realized much more how far out of sympathy with von Hügel the new Catholicism is. Liberalism is *not* the programme of the future; a much more rigorous and rigid attitude is being prescribed; especially now I live in England (the essay was written in America) I see how much the liveliest new Catholic thought is drawing on Marxism. Now Marxism has never been kind to liberals, and the interfertilization of the modern world's two great totalitarian faiths—though much to be welcomed in other ways—amounts to something of a threat to the liberal and the literary man. Von Hügel is as useless, as irrelevant, to the new Catholicism's purposes as to the old kind's, and I can't hope to find my allies there to help build a Catholic liberal humanism. The new men make being a Christian into belonging to an organization—though belonging heart and soul, of course, and to a revolutionary organization, and one dedicated to changing human nature, by means of changing social institutions and policies and attitudes. I need not say that I am describing their ideas in cartoon form, and I am not implying that this is all they mean by Christianity. But it is an activist, somewhat secular, and above all communal religion they want.

I take Brian Wicker's *Culture and Liturgy* to be a good statement of the kind of new Catholicism I mean. (Its spokesmen write for *Slant* and *The New Blackfriars*, and could be called New Left Catholics.) I should say immediately that I find this idea of Christianity very impressive and challenging and promising. But there is no place (as yet) within this map of Christianity for anyone following the psychological pattern and programme we saw in von Hügel. Where is the Devout Humanist to place himself in relation to these new ideas, insights, duties? Neither his intensely private relation to God, nor his passiveness towards the political world, nor even his kind of respect for man, has any honoured function there.

The new Catholicism is explicitly the enemy of religious individualism. '. . . God chose to rescue man from this calamity [of the fall]
in a communal, not an individualistic, way. This he did by creating a
chosen people . . .' Mr Wicker reminds us. And this opposition
between individualism and something organic—and a progressive
development in history—puts the new Catholicism into a very helpful
perspective. De Lubac says in *Catholicism*, 'The attempt to rescue the
Church from "individualism" began again in the Catholic school of
theology in Tübingen upwards of a century ago. In 1819 the pros-
pectus of its official organ, *Theologische Quartalschrift*, says, "The central
fact is the revelation of the plan realized by God in humanity: this plan
is one organic whole with a progressive development in history." '
Obviously this idea of Christianity and the Church has a lot in common
with those other ideas of an organic society and organic culture which
also began in the German universities at the beginning of the nineteenth
century, and which had such an important career in the arts (and in
political philosophy) in all the countries of Europe during that century.
It is just because the two sets of ideas have a common origin that Mr
Wicker is able to harmonize his two themes so well, integrate his two
concepts, culture and liturgy.

But as a Devout Humanist, *après la lettre*, von Hügel participated to
some degree in both the baroque and the bourgeois modes of Catholicism—two of the new movement's chief enemies. Let us define
baroque as referring primarily to a very elaborate, ceremonial, and even
operatic style of presenting the liturgy, and the whole public life of the
Church; and bourgeois as referring to an individualism of piety which
leaves the realms of politics, economics, sociology, quite out of religion's purview, with the status of facts of nature, never to be changed.
As for the first, Devout Humanism was a school of personal, not
liturgical holiness, and its heroes are often the villains of the new
movement. St François de Sales, when he was made bishop, took a
pious resolution always to say his beads when he was *required* to attend
a public Mass. Piety to him was something that called him to withdraw
from the public celebration of the liturgy into private devotions. This
is a story today's reformers tell to show the worst of the evils they are
fighting. And though von Hügel was a Modernist, he was no precursor
of liturgical reform. Much of his devotional counsel consists of
devices for sliding around and through official procedures, quite like
St François' beads—rather than of proposals for changing those
procedures. And the bourgeois mode of religion is likely to go along
with the baroque, individualism of political responsibility with
pompousness of ecclesiastical style—a pompousness characteristically
combined with symbols of suffering and humiliation, the Way of the
Cross, the crown of thorns, the flagellation, the crucifixion. As Mr
Wicker says, it is in a Church only partially involved in the life of

society that devotion to the suffering Christ and to the Sacred Heart is likely to arise, and that, complementarily, the Church will present itself to the world in a worldly, courtly and ceremonial style. Where the Church renounces the struggle to create a society that embodies its own values, it naturally offers symbols of the value of renunciation and suffering, and naturally ornaments those symbols with specifically worldly splendour, as in jewel-encrusted Sacred Hearts. Because such a Church has no real faith in the risen Christ, as still living and present in the liturgical assembly, and as a power able to act on the world. And it seems to me that von Hügel probably could be convicted of telling us not of a risen and triumphant Christ, but of a suffering and dying one.

In these respects (and many others) the new Catholicism has things to tell us which cut across von Hügel's teaching, and which are in many ways more important. But not in the way that matters most to me here. I speak throughout this book as the representative of literature— literature in its relations with a larger than literary belief—in the first half of the book Catholicism, in the second half Communism. I am looking for the scheme of ideas that will allow a literary man to do full justice to both a totalitarian faith and a free imagination. With that point of view, I find von Hügel's humanism promises more than the new Catholicism, despite its 'individualist' taint. After all, we *are* always individuals as well as members of a culture, and as individuals we suffer pains and guilts and shames which we must find some answer to, some symbolic representation of, in the Church. Moreover, individualism is as dangerous a thing in devotional matters as in aesthetic and economic matters, but it is not simply bad in any of them. Individualism is an expression of individuality, and individuality cannot be wished away. It is as highly individuated beings that we write poems and novels, for instance. Some significant degree of individualism must be not just allowed, but encouraged, and admired.

I need hardly say that I realize the dangers of going to extremes in either direction. An extreme individualism of sensibility is just what I have been protesting against in my comments on Yeats. The regimented and rigidified imagination of the Catholic or Communist writer is no worse than the over-distended and overweening, soaring and veering imagination of the totally free writer. Modern poetry, especially that part influenced by symbolism, and represented well enough by Yeats, Rilke, and Blok, had often opted out of modern culture—that is, out of fully responsible participation in it. That is why Professor Brown claims it as his ally. (A special kind of responsibility, of course, these poets undertake more fully than other people, but it is at the cost of many more ordinary kinds.) On the other hand, the corporate and ideological sensibility which the new Catholicism seems to stand for is not a practical alternative. In the arts, at least, to turn away from individualism is to turn away from vitality—not that the two are to be identified, but that there can be no vitality without a really free licence to individuality. (And by individuality I mean Proust and Nabokov, I mean accepting them as masters and models.) I think this is shown by the case discussed in the next essay; though it is the old Catholicism and not the new which limits Mr Powers' freedom, the relevant fact is that it is an authoritative corporate sensibility, which suspects any individualism as 'spiritual pride' or 'moral irresponsibility'.

The significant alternative is surely a humanism in which every value is included, every interest is given a place, and thus individualism is held in check, but at the same time the laws holding everything together are so gentle, the loyalties so unmilitant, that freedom is effectively built into the system. One must frankly admit that this gentleness is from another point of view feebleness, that the whole system is unwieldy and lymphatic—has little of the animal heat and animal grace of other attitudes to life. It is characteristically people like von Hügel and George Eliot one thinks of as representing it. But this system is a framework, a setting for a variety of temperaments, some very different from von Hügel's. His temperament only marks the limits, gives the laws to the others—the gentle and liberal laws appropriate to this idea of culture.

'Liberal' is of course a bad word to most people today—a label to be equated with 'Bloomsbury' and 'civilization'. Mr Wicker, for instance, has contrasted liberalism with socialism, and argued that the former is a radically inadequate politics, in the largest sense of politics. He defines liberalism by making E. M. Forster its representative and spokesman, particularly in 'What I Believe' and 'The Challenge of Our Times'. And he expresses respect for it by agreeing with Lionel Trilling on Forster's great political virtue—that he is not 'eschatological', that he fixes all his attention, including his hopes and his affection, on humanity as it is here and now.

Forster and Trilling are names I would accept as representing what I mean by liberal humanism in the twentieth century as much as von Hügel and George Eliot in the nineteenth. I chose the names I did partly because they are less familiar in this context, and partly because in the twentieth century liberalism has been on the defensive, and has been narrowed down; von Hügel stands for a *larger* world-view than Forster does. And as for Mr Wicker's main point, I would be ready to admit that liberalism by itself is a very inadequate politics, and for the reason he gives. That is, that liberalism often resolves the tension between the world of personal relations and the impersonal by taking only the first fully seriously. However, I think one might argue that socialism, as he describes it, is a dangerously idealistic business, and to be a good politics would require a liberal component, as he defines liberalism; but above all, the criteria of value, and hence the valuableness of policies, in literary matters are different from what they are in politics. For instance, E. M. Forster and Lionel Trilling are immensely more distinguished as literary men than they are as political thinkers.

I think the new Catholicism, like most Marxism, has an *idea* of culture, which is barely distinguishable from a purpose for it, and which is too energetic, too forward-moving, to be helpful when we want to interpret the multiform phenomena that serve such disparate and divergent interests—for instance, in the arts, the writer's need for freedom and his need for roots. Ideally and theoretically, there is nothing irreconcilable about such a conflict. Seen in the right theoretical perspective, Mr Wicker often tells us, all these interests fit together naturally. But that only proves the weakness of theoretical-ness; for such conflicts, for the individual artist or politician, have occurred all through history and have been cruelly destructive. So what a theory of culture should set out to do, I think, is not to attain a point of view from which all conflicts of principle are resolved—just because it can do that so easily by rising unhelpfully far above the individual conflicts. It should set out to engage with, helpfully, just as many of these individual conflicts as it can link, however loosely, together. Of course this is a liberal idea of cultural theory, aiming less at clarity and moral energy than at inclusiveness and moral complexity.

But surely inclusiveness *should* be the prime virtue of such a theory, when it is to be interpreted by the adherents of a totalitarian faith, ready to make simplifying decisions? Catholicism, like Communism, has all too often been an alternative to liberalism and humanism—it was when you saw through the latter that you turned to the former. That is just as inadequate as a 'Bloomsbury' choosing of the other alternative, and it is a combining of the best of both which is the only adequate aim. Von Hügel and Guardini are uniquely important to radical Catholics because they are our one dependable guarantee that we need not sacrifice our non-radical values, honesty of thought, delicacy of feeling, etc., which we may symbolically associate with literature.

Of course they don't solve our problems for us. Von Hügel was important to me at the time of my conversion because I felt he had worked out a way to combine those values (his version of them) with Catholicism. But I soon saw I should have to work out for myself a way to combine all von Hügel had to teach me with what D. H. Lawrence made out of 'literary values'. Lawrence, who meant as much to me as von Hügel himself, belongs with Yeats as an example of extreme indi-vidualism. He stands as far from humanism in one direction as, say, Mauriac's Catholicism does in the other. And if von Hügel could help me with Mauriac, he had nothing to say about Lawrence—he didn't know the point from which Lawrence would attack him, he hadn't circumscribed it. Nor has any spokesman for Catholicism I found.

This was a task I had to work at myself. It was the most vivid case within my own experience of an anomaly that must often occur in the lives of literary people who are also church-members. I mean that Lawrence has taught me more than anyone else about moral and spiritual matters all the time I've been a member of the Church, and most of it has been in direct contradiction to most Church teaching I've heard. I haven't, in practice, felt myself torn between opposite imperatives, but I have, in theory, felt very puzzled to explain why I wasn't so torn. It is now fifteen years since I was received into the Church, and I suppose this book is as much as I'm ever likely to achieve in the way of explaining that. I am not torn apart because both sets of imperatives submit themselves to interpretation (and reconciliation) by something else—my beliefs, my self-discipline, my learned temperament, as liberal humanist. That sentence, which I hope the book as a whole puts some meaning into, is as much as I shall be able to do towards 'combining' Lawrence with von Hügel.

Von Hügel, like Fénelon and St François de Sales, built up in himself the temperament of Devout Humanism, a way of taking things, a way of believing what he believed, a way of feeling what he felt, a framework that structured his whole mind. Lawrence, like Yeats, built up in himself a very opposite temperament, which we could label Individualist Spontaneity. The literary man today, the interpreter of and commentator on literature, must be attuned to this second possibility, cannot afford to be hostile to it. (I certainly was, early on, and radically impatient and rebellious it made me, in ways I shall no doubt never now outgrow.) But, especially if he is committed to a larger than literary faith, he needs to be attuned to other things, too. He needs to be able to respond to a variety of things in a variety of ways, and to make those ways interact rather than to systematize them. That is the temperament of liberal humanism, and it seems to me a lot more promising for literature than the temperament of the new Marxist Catholicism—which we could perhaps label Ideological Radicalism.

It is worth reminding ourselves of the one great champion of Catholic liberal humanism since von Hügel's death, Romano Guardini. Among his books, *The World and the Person, Freedom, Grace, and Destiny,* and *The End of the Modern World,* are particularly full of proofs of his richness of temperament and sensibility. For instance, in the section entitled 'Euphoria and the Perfect', in the second, he moves between natural and supernatural categories with just the ease von Hügel demonstrated, praising natural and supernatural beauty with equal conviction.

'Another form of this graciousness is discovered in what may be called the moment of perfect peace. . . . The tensions which are part of life are not removed—that might bring boredom and satiety—but they have reached a harmony, full of meaning and yet delicately flexible, with the promise of an ultimate fulfilment.

This condition finds its symbol in the twilight of very clear days. Seen in it, objects seem to enjoy the full range of their essential form and at the same time they become transparent, letting us glimpse through them some ultimate and unique reality.'

These symbols of Guardini's can be symbolic for us of his interest in harmony, peace, and universal justice. Like von Hügel, he gives us an image of a religious man as a mind responding with perfect intelligence and freedom to everything in the universe.

'The condition we have been analysing cannot be brought on through pressure. It is not to be confused with the peaceful harmony that comes from a healthy way of life or a long process of self-discipline. This is related to the moment of perfect peace as planning is related to encounter, or work to creation, or a juridical process to the act of grace. . . .

Closely linked with this impression of grace is that characteristic feeling, stirred from time to time by a perfect natural scene, by a natural scene whose proportions fit in harmoniously with our own, personal feelings and do not swamp them with its immensity, sublimity, and depth.'

And we find examples of the same kind of thing in art, Guardini tells us; certain kinds of art. We will find this graciousness not in the work of a Grünewald or a Michelangelo, but in a Mozart or a Raphael. Such art takes force for granted and shows how it rises from its interior source to express itself in released loveliness and radiant happiness. This idea of the release of loveliness, important in the original Greek word for grace, is retained in the Italian '*grazia*' and the French '*grâce*'.

If this had been a major voice, a dominant strain, in Catholic sensibility in this century, we should not have had the phenomenon of the 'Catholic' writer to deal with, and J. F. Powers would have written a quite different novel.

J. F. Powers and Catholic writing

J. F. Powers' work does not fit into the more obvious and brightly lit categories of contemporaneity. It has the quiet quality of a private discovery, a private taste, remote from the market-place clamour of 'Is the novel dead?' and 'Alienation in the modern novel'. Powers merely writes his fiction, and what he writes has therefore a calm timelessness, even a classic quality, in a limited but real sense. It is moreover calm and pure in another sense; in the intensity of workmanship put into it—the authenticity of the observation, the objectivity of the imagination. All this was perhaps true also of his short stories, but the scale of *Morte d'Urban* makes us see him as a much more sizeable talent, a feature of the literary scene deserving careful consideration.

The novel is much more peculiarly his, peculiarly him, than the stories were. In certain ways, it is quite unlike anything else in American literature. Discussing *Dead Souls* with some students, *Morte d'Urban* was the only American fiction I could think of that dealt with a huge official hierarchy—the semi-official aspects of its social and cultural life—in that spirit of quite poetic exasperation. America, and for that matter England, has just not had that subject to offer its writers—except that of course it doesn't have it any more now than before, only that Powers found it out. More exactly, then, America and Britain have not effectively offered their writers that subject.

But the analogy between Gogol and Powers will bear developing a little further. Both are concerned with the evil-breeding niceties of status and distinction within the hierarchy—the cracks and crevices within which meanness, resentment and contention crawl—and with the inhumanities inherent in its system of thought; compare the central device of buying and selling dead souls with what is perhaps the central device of *Morte d'Urban*—the business administration language about the religious life. But both authors are more in sympathy and at ease within the hierarchy than without; the outside world is full of freaks and monsters. Nozdrev and Pliushkin in *Dead Souls,* Billy Cosgrove and Mrs Thwaites in *Morte d'Urban*, are more fearful figures than anybody inside the hierarchies, and the energy with which they are presented is in part the energy of horrified amazement. (The *ways* they are presented are also quite similar—compare Mrs Thwaites with Korobochka.) The outside worlds, of Russia and America, are places of bounding vitality, brought to life by their authors' enthusiasm; and the inside worlds are dry, dusty, dead; but the authors' imaginative experience resides in the inside world, and the outside is embraced with a somewhat theatrical and theoretical rhetoric.[1] Figures like Billy and Sobakevitch, however much vitality they represent, really horrify their creators, surely. Chichikov, while a parody of humanity, incapable of a full range of feelings, does not. Nor does Father Urban, though his creator makes the same point against him (the Belleisle episode is the *locus classicus*). Indeed, it is clear that the two novelists *like* these two main targets of their criticism, in many ways. They like them because they are, after all their awfulness, gentle, decent, limited people, inadequate to the full responsibilities of being human, but incapable of really destructive violence or treachery. Urban and Chichikov are quick, clever, alert-minded people, very quick at picking up and applying the techniques of success their society is teaching; *too* quick, for both their long-run and their short-run success as human beings; but not in the least wicked, and with less, not more, than the normal share of animal appetitive assertiveness.

The two heroes are so similar because they are the agents of similar purposes; they exemplify wonderfully both what society's techniques of success are, and how wrong they are, while, at the same time, being fundamentally harmless, even nice, they save us from the dangerous and exhausting extremes of indignation. They are at the same time our antagonists and our protagonists

[1] This embrace is very tentative in *Morte d'Urban*. Perhaps it is most palpable in the invoking of an antithesis to the Order's mean-spiritedness—that large, vigorous, masculine spirit of successful big business—that world where big, exciting things happen, and big exciting emotions are felt, as well as the world of big, beautiful cars and houses. That Billy, who represents big business, should be so unambiguously bad, and that Sally, who ought to represent another aspect of the big outside world, should be so quickly disposed of and so feebly rendered, surely weakens the book. The general design demands that these representatives of the free life should be vividly attractive to the reader, to fill out the theme's full range of dangerous tensions.

in the comedy of society's constant betrayal of humanity, both victor and victim in one.

Both novels are fundamentally picaresque, and though figures from early episodes recur later, this is largely a formal, pattern-making device. Essentially, the interest moves on all the time, from one character-sketch to the next, from one kind of social oddity to the next, from one part of the country to the next. Urban and Chichikov are travelling men. And they are so at the behest of their authors' general purposes, more than at the behest of their own individuality, their inner integrity. Their inner independence and integrity (meaning what Tolstoy gives to Anna Karenina) is largely subordinated to their function as mask and pawn. Their creators are discoursing on a variety of topics, and using them in a variety of ways to do so.

It is a coincidence that the general character of the Mid-West as landscape should generally resemble that of Gogol's Russian steppe, but two more specific aspects of that resemblance in the novels are probably not coincidence. The first is that sense of 'the provinces' that exudes from those huge bare expanses, the sense of banishment, of being far from the centres of life, close to huge meaningless matter itself. This is complementary to the sense of 'the provinces' exuding from the towns and communities Urban and Chichikov find there, but in the landscapes there is a dignity and a dimension and a dangerousness. This sense is one of the things that marks Powers off from other Anglo-American writers most obviously. You find an attempt at it in the consciously Russianizing authors of the twenties, like Sherwood Anderson, but in Powers it is not in the least imitative or self-conscious or rhetorical. It belongs naturally and inevitably to his subject, to his sense of a huge and highly centralized hierarchical organiza-tion, the fringes of which are very conscious of their distance, in every sense, from the centre.

The second resemblance, which is related, is that Urban and Chichikov both see this landscape with alien, townsman's, eyes. (This is one of the main values of Urban's name.) In so doing, they extend into another dimension, they perfect their function as focus of the novel's comic vision, their rôle as product of their society, too perfectly adapted to their social function and out of relation to all wild, free nature. Their creators are able to outreach them, to invoke for us that rich beauty and size which their heroes cannot deal with; though, as I have suggested, the books'

vision is not long at ease out there, and quickly returns to identification, and implicit sympathy, with the characters' vision. We
laugh with, as much as at, Urban, as he trudges out past the city
limits of Duesterhaus, and fantasies his own death from a pack of
starving dogs. When we get a glimpse of 'wild' human life, as in
the teen-agers of '24 Hours in a Strange Diocese', the glimpse
leaves us feeling quite as appalled as Urban. ' "Drag?" said the
driver, in whose face there was a hint of human intelligence, as
there is in a shark's.'

These resemblances between Powers's work and Gogol's, which
are interesting in themselves, will be more seriously interesting if
they help us to locate the essential character of his talent and
achievement. They should help us see, for instance, how unlike he
is to Evelyn Waugh, with whom he is most often compared.
When Waugh is writing at the top of his talent, as in *Decline and
Fall* and *Put Out More Flags,* the two writers have practically
nothing in common. They are both Catholic novelists: but that
phrase becomes quite unusable as a practical criticism category
when it yokes together such incompatibilities. Nor does that other
sense of the phrase, when 'Catholic novelist' means the likenesses
between Graham Greene, Mauriac, Bernanos, etc. apply—without
serious modification—to Powers. And yet I think there is a sense
of 'Catholic novelist' which applies to his work very interestingly;
but this I must return to later. Rather than Waugh, a neo-
Catholic writer, it is Joyce, a post-Catholic, whom Powers
resembles. And this resemblance has something to do with their
common Catholicism—with their parish experiences—and even
(indirectly) with this third sense of 'Catholic novelist'. I assume,
that is, though it could hardly be proved, that the grey and gritty
spiritual atmosphere of so much Catholic fiction has something
to do with the writers' specially Catholic experience of a spirituality both harsh and drab, because bureaucratized; and that that
quality in Stephen Dedalus's emotional life, even outside the
Church, owes something to Joyce's Catholic experience. It is
still Gogol whom Powers resembles more, but Gogol was a
professing religious novelist. And if Urban is more like Chichikov
than Bloom, as a representative of his creator, is it not because
Joyce had refused to be a professing religious novelist—and so
could exorcize the spectre of man's inexorable calling and effectively love mediocre humanity with a fullness a Catholic novelist
must often find impossible?

But to follow that argument involves using some large abstract concepts for which we must first work out some more concrete referents. Let us return to the comparison with Gogol and consider one of the striking differences between the two writers. Powers is much quieter in his effects, more elliptical and under-stated, and relies more on our recognition of little things we have seen and heard, which have evoked little feelings in us, of irrita-tion and exasperation and amusement. Though those effects are there in Gogol (both writers work within the same comic range) we surely remember more, and respond to more, in him, those wild poetic conceptions—the nose and the overcoat, for instance, —and that wild poetic language, in the evocations of Russia, etc. Powers has some fairly extreme comic effects, things which verge on comic routines, like the golf-ball knock-out and the strip-tease scene at Belleisle, but these are obviously quite different. They are closer to the comedy of Kingsley Amis. As in Amis's work, there is in *Morte d'Urban* an uneasy relationship between these broadly comic routines and the close careful recording of above-all-ordinary experience. Amis exploits that uneasiness, exaggerates it, makes the reader ask, 'How can he ask me to take *this* as seriously as *that*?'—ask it so often that this questioning becomes a big part of the reader-writer relationship. Powers does the reverse; he smoothes away the roughnesses of the transitions as best he can, and bases himself firmly on moral realism, with only unobtrusive excursions into the land of farce and fantasy. Whereas in *Dead Souls* the mode of farce and fantasy is at least as important as the other, and we move from one to the other under Gogol's guidance with no sense of crossing frontiers. In *Morte d'Urban* we do have that sense sometimes; for instance, when we read the sentences from Theodore Roosevelt that obliquely recall Urban's misadventures. This is in effect a private joke direct from author to reader, and for the moment the figure of Urban is obviously being manipulated; we are made aware that someone else is there behind him, the author; and we don't know what our relation to him should be, brought thus face to face. Gogol too is a notably enigmatic writer. Compared with Tolstoy and Lawrence, neither Gogol nor Powers speak in their 'own' voice—which means, I suppose, the central tone of self-committing seriousness. But Gogol has a voice for directly addressing the reader, the voice of fantasy and exuberance. Powers remains hidden, and this is to be an important datum in our argument.

Now let us abandon all comparisons and contrasts, and try to define directly the character of his achievement. Powers is an artist of language, in quite a special sense. He has as fine an ear as any novelist ever had, he has great skill, within his range, in playing one kind of language against another, and he has so great an interest in language as to swamp, from time to time, all other interests, and to flood his artistic control.

He catches a dozen official and commercial jargons; let us just cite the longhair record store, '¡Panache Ltd.!', and the television programme résumés, and the Poinsettia Smorgasbord, held in the Greenwich Village Room of the General Diggles Hotel. He often simply plays with language, as when Billy is driving too fast, and 'A squad car zoomed out of ambush and came into contention'. Or more richly, 'Nuns could coo their way out of such difficulties, or, that failing, would often fight, and sometimes cardinals would ride forth in their behalf.' Sometimes it is closer to conventional wit, as when Father Urban, finding exceptional merit for the Novitiate, 'had overshot the mark on occasion—two of his recruits had proved to be homosexual and one homicidal'. But most often there is a sharp sense of spoken language employed, some hidden effect of ambiguity or innuendo exploited, as when Urban 'employed Brother Harold (who'd reached the point in the chapel where he needed to get away and think, before going on) . . .'. The book is full of *free* verbal wit of this kind, gay, spontaneous, generated by the language itself—odd phrasings, odd contrasts, things heard and read—almost independent of the characters and events. Let us take one last example, from the chapter richest of all in this free writing, '24 Hours in a Strange Diocese'.

'Then he got in, started the motor, which had a plummy sound he loved, shifted himself into a slouch, and, with his head resting easily to one side as if he were dreaming, he—there was not other word for it—tooled toward the outskirts of town.

The little snub-nosed Barracuda was five months old, had wire wheels, leather upholstery, and so on, and it certainly made a man feel good to drive it. At a stoplight, though, when a girl in a white MG paused alongside him, a girl wearing sunglasses and nothing else—so it appeared from where he was sitting—and with a crisp blue dog beside her, Father Urban experienced a heavy moment, a moment of regret and longing. He wished the little Barracuda were black or white instead of bright red, which just wasn't right for him, and he wished he had a crisp blue dog beside him. So he put on his sunglasses. When he hit open country, he threw away his cigar and gave the little thoroughbred its head.'

The word 'tooled' concentrates and crystallizes the whole activity of wit in the first sentence, while the next paragraph is full of verbal tricks at the service of intelligence and affection quite equally. The feeling of the phrasing shifts and ripples, a verbal equivalent of the play of light on a glittering sea.

But it is naturally enough in dialogue that this gift for spoken language shows itself best. We might notice, to begin with, those marvellous imitations of Father Urban in action as a public speaker; the extract before the Overture, the speech to the Poinsettia Club, the sermon at the retreat, the sermon for Phil's funeral. This is pure and naked mimicry, differing from realistic recording (of the novelist's kind) only in that all the points about the thing imitated are rendered with dangerous sharpness. But differing from ordinary satire in that *all* the points are rendered, that the rhetoric is allowed to remain eloquent and energetic. The imitation is scrupulously fair. It is only malicious in that it is mimicry.

Nine-tenths of the characterization is done by such mimicries, from Mr Bean, defending outdoor advertisements, and Billy, playing old favourites at the piano, to Father Louis, who is known to us almost exclusively for his phrase about a 'second rate outfit'. Father Wilfrid, one of the most fully developed characters, is made real to us in a number of ways, but surely by any count the most important of those ways must be verbal mimicry. From 'that's your pocket gopher' and 'winter snuck up on us' to his elaborate instructions to Jack about returning the pants to Father Chmielewski, Powers has worked out a dozen patterns of speech which render Wilfrid's mode of being.

Let us note that our first example comes to us through the Powwow minutes, for Powers' delight in language makes him vary the modes of reporting as well as the matter reported.

Rector: In my opinion, our water is something that could be— well, talked up.

Fr Urban: You don't mean it's therapeutic, do you?

Rector: For all I know it is. But I was talking about the way it tastes. Our water *tastes* good.

Fr Urban: Has it been tested for purity?

Rector: Yes, and it's right up there. The iron content is very low—for this part of the country. The main thing, though, is that it tastes so good. I don't know but what I prefer it to the water at the Novitiate. But be that as it may.

No pattern of speech could represent more vividly—but with no cost to plausibility and moderateness and other intentions—the innate and unconscious shiftiness of Wilfrid's mind. The stinginess of that mind comes out in his dealings with the decorators, which comes to us through his own anecdotes. The bossiness is most vividly dramatized in the interrogation section of the Father Chmielewski affair, where the questions are italicized and not set off by the normal punctuation devices. While other aspects of that mind are given to us in conjunction with Father Urban's exasperated reactions, implicit or explicit—Wilfrid's fellow-feeling for animals, his aspirations as a photographer. And the key-motif of his character is given in another mimicry—the speech about the little red squirrel, who, given the chance, will castrate a grey squirrel. 'I've often wondered what would happen if a *great* red squirrel came around the house. I don't know but what I'd put my money on the little fella.'

The verbal mimicry of Wilfrid is the most ingeniously varied, perhaps because he is Urban's major antagonist, but there are a dozen other figures built up by the same means; Mr Studley, Zimmerman, Paul, Monsignor Renton, Dickie Thwaites. All of these are heard rather than seen; the only character who is mostly *seen* is Sally, and that is perhaps because she has no equally vivid speech-pattern, and is in fact not a successfully rendered character.

Naturally the people and events are also presented in ways other than the purely verbal. But these are usually closely tied in to the verbal. Take the kinds of specialized knowledge employed. There is much inside knowledge of the political and social procedures of the Roman Church; of the geography of Chicago and of the railways of the Mid-West; of house-repairs; of fishing; of golf. A lot of this knowledge is quite straightforwardly at the *service* of the purely verbal effects—some of it is merely jargon to colour dialogue—and the rest is filling out conceptions which are sketched in at least as fully by the language. And a similar kind of subordinate technique is the description of social manœuvres. The way Billy announces his gifts to the Clementines, the way the

Bishop offers Urban a parish which is not St Monica's, the way Monsignor Renton gets between Urban and Phil when the latter says he will build; these are personal styles of gesture in just the same sense as the personal styles of language into which they blend. Powers takes great pleasure in the description of such manœuvres, and shows great expertise in the shaping of them. But his interest in them is just an extension of his interest in language, or to put it the other way, his interest in language is much the most concentrated mode of his social observation.

Then one of the formally unifying devices of the book is almost purely verbal. That is the playful contrast of modern with chivalric language, which is first announced in the title. This is made the focus of attention only in Jack's writing about Sir Launcelot and the Catholic Knights of the Round Table. But it occurs, fragmentarily, throughout the book. In the sentence about the nuns, for instance, in the fantasy of Mrs Thwaites as a chivalric queen, in the Belleisle castle, in the golf-match; where Urban, his driver drawn, is involved in an ordeal by combat, and the Reverend Doctor Percy, Hillsop Memorial Presbyterian Church, Minneapolis, has the function of a crone crying, 'Woe! Woe!' This use of language is largely playful. It does not carry the weight of comment such language sometimes does in *Ulysses*. But it is nevertheless a major formal device.

Of course the language is often much more than playful. The comment it conveys is perhaps most typically exasperation, with varying degrees of explicitness and complexity. In the Overture, for instance, Urban gets the Clementines to send Billy the firewood only after he has said, 'I happen to know that the Dalmatians are making a play for this man.' Immediately following this sentence, we see him guiding Billy round the Novitiate, where he meets his former antagonists.

' "We have more than we can use", said one.
"You're welcome to more", said the other.

Father Urban, moving on, guided Billy to Our Lady's Grotto. They knelt for a moment in prayer. Then they drank from the spring.'

There are a lot of things going on there, of course, a lot of claims on our response, but one of them is the tension between 'making a play for this man', and 'knelt for a moment in prayer'. That tension is pretty taut, and makes for a pretty energetic indignation.

A few pages later on Paul 'fences' with the traffic, at one corner giving way to a truck driver who 'calls his bluff', but at the next corner 'he was himself again, cutting the Rolls through a soft surf of pedestrians'. In the general picture of Paul we are getting this exaggeration conveys a (controlled) exasperation. This is developed by the talk of Billy's electric trains, always being made to crash into each other—'It was almost as if he expected them to save themselves.' Then comes the incident of the pedestrian who refuses to scare, and stands in front of Paul, challenging him to run him down. ' "Ever see anything like that, Fahdah?" "Oh well", said Father Urban, and fell silent.' This is a common pattern of the anger in Powers' work. He makes us see, through his protagonist's eyes, something that makes us furious, and then deflects our indignation on to the protagonist, for not doing enough about it—and by implication, of course, on to ourselves who would do no more; a 'Judge not that ye be not judged' pattern of literary response.

But sometimes the comment Powers is making cannot be limited to the description 'angry'. It includes too much fascinated attentiveness and appreciation. For instance, the major theme of moral and spiritual vulgarity—expressed primarily in language. Father Boniface talks of 'beefing up the Order', but Father Urban knows it will come to nothing with men of Father Boniface's stamp 'calling the shots'. He claims he preaches 'a pretty clean mission', and 'keeps the razzmatazz to a minimum'. When retreatants come to the Hill, we are told 'the word must have gone out "Buy Clementine" '. As for the nuns of St Monica's, Father Urban 'occasionally threw the boss a $10 bill—"Buy yourself some cigars, Sister." They all loved him.'

This tone is not simply angry, but the fascination all this vulgarity has for Powers derives from his deepest moral concern in the book, the miscegenation of the transcendent with the all-too-human, of religious values with worldly ones, which means *mostly* the values of commercial America. There is therefore an indignation and revulsion deeper than anger diffused in many of the verbal devices of this kind. Father Urban suspects that Brother Henry envies him—'the ground crewman's envy for the man who actually did the flying'. He is sure the big dealers, 'the priests or nuns who could make or break a pamphlet', will not be fooled by Father Boniface's new cover. Monsignor Renton, Father Louis, Urban's friends, the men with sharp, intelligent, impatient minds, all use this tough, pool-room and locker-room vocabulary, with images drawn from sports, the army, politics, above all salesmanship. Powers was much influenced by the New Critics, and it is in the imagery of his fiction that his major interests are most clearly and forcefully expressed.

Morte d'Urban is therefore a triumph of language. But sometimes this triumph is at the cost of other things. Indeed, in the important matter of the author's voice, the cost may be said to be paid by the language itself. Since its patterns fail to cohere and interact in the way we expect from fictional language, we do not cherish and value each passing effect as also a part of the total meaning—as we do with Jane Austen's language. We relax our attention a little, we let ourselves be entertained, we are a little disengaged and disappointed. For who is telling this story, forming these sentences, formulating these comments? Clearly it is not the author himself. This voice keeps giving itself away.

'Mrs Burns, however, had no reservations about Father Urban. If he in any way fell short of the ideal (and of course he did), Mrs Burns didn't know it.'

And later,

'Father Urban, however, by the power of his example, and, of course by God's grace, had caused Johnny to question not the lives of the saints but his own life as a parish priest.'

Clearly, in these cases the narrative voice is mimicking Father Urban's, and in a satirical though fairly quiet way.

At other times it is clear that the point of view is Father Urban's, without there being either any mimicry of his language or any criticism of his thought. We follow his eyes and his thoughts; we trust his vision. He even *enacts* the author's comment at times.

'They were descending to the lower level of the LaSalle Street Station. "I told him I wouldn't change places with him for a million bucks."

Father Urban deliberately missed his cue but let it appear that he was concentrating on the steps.
"That's what I told him."
"What'd he say to that, Paul?"
"I *meant* it, Fahdah."

"I'm sure you did, Paul. Was anyone with him at the time?"
"Some guy. I don't know."

Father Urban had thought so. He had an idea there was always someone else present when Billy and Paul put on their little show.

The grey Rolls was parked under a "No Parking" sign. Paul opened the rear door for Father Urban and pushed the bag in after him. When Paul was seated behind the wheel, Father Urban leaned forward, opened the glass partition, and stuck a Dunhill Monte Cristo Colorado Maduro No. 1 in the slot between the chauffeur's head and ear. As usual, Paul made too much of it. He was accustomed to Billy, though, and Billy was a stickler for gratitude. Of course, where Billy was concerned, there was much to be grateful for.'

These are then two rôles played by the 'narrative voice'. There is no narrator, properly speaking, because the voice is only a number of such rôles, without any integrating, self-identifying central tone. But these two rôles are consistent enough with one another. Our problem begins when we find other rôles which are not.

The book begins with a piece of sheer ventriloquism—no vestige of a speaker—and then plunges into one of the most puzzling of all its sentences.

'It had been a lucky day for the Order of St Clement the day Mr Billy Cosgrove entered the sacristy of a suburban church after Mass and shook the hand of Father Urban. Billy, a powerful-looking man in his late fifties, hairy of wrist and sunburned (from golf and sailing, Father Urban would discover), had warmly praised the sermon—in which Father Urban had roared and whispered and crooned about Francis of Assisi and Ignatius of Loyola and Clement of Blois and Louis of France and Edward of England and Charles of the Holy Roman Empire—it was he who, you might say, owned and operated Europe but who, in the end, desired only the society of monks—it was he who rehearsed his own funeral, lay down in his coffin, joined in the prayers for the repose of his soul, mingled his tears with those of his attendants—it was he who rose from his coffin in good health, retired to his chambers, and was seized by a fever from which he very soon died . . . and the wonder was that Father Urban could go on in this high he-who manner without minimizing in the least the importance of becoming a penny-ante benefactor of the Order of St Clement.'

Obviously this language is full of comment and point of view; but whose? Who says Father Urban 'roared and whispered and crooned', and who says 'the wonder of it was . . .'? The only obvious answer is that this is Father Urban's own professional appraisal of his own performance, comically distancing himself from it, being tough after the event. And that would of course be consistent enough with the idea of the voice we have been building up. But it is not a convincing answer. That is not one of Father Urban's sentences; it is too formally literary, both in its general structure, and in its tone of mockery. One could more easily accept it as the voice of a like-but-unlike friend (a more literary Monsignor Renton) except that this tone quickly disappears and recurs only in the most unsystematic way.

We could ask more of the same kind of question—who narrates the final episode, in which Father Urban is seen from such a distance?—but the problem is not so much that the voice changes from passage to passage, but that it wobbles within a passage; that when we have worked out what it is doing on a given page, we find verbal effects which are inconsistent with that idea. 'Father Placidus (Hartigan) had everything, and he had it in spades.'[1] This is an admirable sentence for Powers' general purposes, an admirable example of *his* language game. But in this particular context, where the voice is re-creating Urban's youthful enthusiasm with only very distant comment, that second clause is surely out of place; it would, heard by that speaker, destroy that enthusiasm; it is satiric in effect. This phrasing surely 'came to' the author, and demanded to be written down. But it is not a simple lapse; it is a specifiable and demonstrable instance of something generally there in the voice, a vagueness, a looseness, a lack of control, through that whole passage of 'Grey Days'. A little down the same page we find,

'When they stepped out of the machine to stretch their legs, the muddiest ponds sparkled like jewels for Father Placidus, the

[1] A parallel case is the last phrase in this quotation. 'All that remained of the great days and the great teams were photographs and memories. Father Placidus, in his ball cap and sweat shirt, blowing his whistle, Father Placidus, in his choir robe, waving his ivory wand, Father Placidus at the piano, at the pipe organ, at the altar, and in the pulpit at the kill.'

grass grew greener for him, and nuts of all kinds fell from the trees at the sound of his coming.'

Did Urban think like this at the time, or in looking back? Surely not; surely this is another kind of language that 'came to' the author. At the end of this passage we find,

'He would not say that life had dealt harshly with these men because of their treatment of him. Not a-tall. "Revenge is mine." And rightly so, for all the crimes of men are crimes against Him, and would be seen as such but for ignorance. Nevertheless, in view of these casualties, it was sobering to think what might befall Father Boniface now that he'd joined the select little group of people who'd made life unnecessarily difficult for Father Urban, and Wilf, if he didn't watch himself, would soon be joining that group.'

Again it is surely clear that the first words are Urban's echoing somewhere in his mind; and equally clear that the last are not. The words at the end are somebody else's, however plausibly the thought may be attributed to him (though I am not convinced of that); but whose then are the words?

When Father Urban came to the Clementine Chapter to push through his golf-course proposal, 'he also said *hello-hello!* to a number of dim bulbs whose existence he'd always tried to overlook in the past'. Clearly neither he nor any friend says this, which implies a sour and brutal commenter. But three pages later we read, 'At this two or three notorious suckholes (among them Brother Henry) nodded', which seems to be a mimicry (with satiric exaggeration) of Urban's own language. We will take one last example from a later chapter.

'He spent most of the day in his room, in a Morris chair, in the company of the great historians from the library downstairs, but sometimes he could be seen moving slowly about the grounds, under the great oaks, reading his office, and wearing his cassock— he had decided against slopping around in slacks while there.'

This comes in the middle of the passage in which the voice is clearly describing what Father Urban saw. Suddenly we see *him* 'moving slowly about the grounds'. Is this seen through his own eyes? If so, to whom is he saying it? If to himself, what is the satiric point of the phrasing, and are we to read the whole narrative as a self-directed reminiscence? None of these questions has a satisfactory answer, but they lead us to our general proposition, that the voice is diffuse, chameleonic, chaotic.

This is quite striking by itself, in a writer as aware of form, of unity, of craftsmanship, as Mr Powers. But it becomes more important when we see in it a clue to something dissatisfying in the handling of the central character. Some of the riper vulgarities attributed to Urban ('Buy yourself some cigars, Sister') seem scarcely to fit the quick-minded man we meet at, say, the Zimmermans'—a mind very quick and quite educated in matters of taste. We begin to wonder just how stupid and vulgar he is meant to be.

How *are* we to feel about Father Urban? Of course, we are to like him; not only as the moral hero of the encounter with Billy and the defence of Katie, nor only as the comic hero of the rise of St Clement's and the golf game against the Bishop. Let us take these for granted; there is no problem there. We like him in a more immediate and intimate sense in a passage like this.

'Father Urban drove Jack to the Hill—"No, I won't come in, thanks"—and then drove himself back to Great Plains, slowly, enjoying the landscape in the moonlight. The hills, under snow, the trees casting shadows, had an enchanted look, the look of night in the north in the movies, and the sky was all broken out with stars. Once, at a bend in the road, the headlights slipped up on some white rabbits playing in a field. Father Urban hadn't realized that rabbits had such fun. The world was really a beautiful place. He rolled along enjoying it all, oblivious of himself, until he entered the city limits of Great Plains. He was sorry that he'd have only two or three more days with the car, which he'd come to depend on, and he was going to miss the deep satisfaction there was in doing the work of a parish priest—his daily Mass meant even more to him at St Monica's. He had done well there in the last five weeks. Could he have done better? He did not think so. His record would speak for itself.'

In such a passage the foolish complacency at the end surely strikes us as merely fallible, as merely filling out the humanness we have been invited to like so warmly. The whole of '24 Hours in a Strange Diocese', from which we quoted the passage about the Barracuda, is activated by this warm, humorous identification with Father Urban. Fallible but full-sized—no Don Camillo— Father Urban represents our humanity.

It is a fairly cognate act of identification which activates 'A Grand Place, This'. We see things exactly as Urban does, and we sympathize with him, though we are not called on for such direct acts of fondness towards him.

'The station agent, writing at his desk, seemed unaware of him. An old dog, lying behind the counter woke up and gave him a look that said, Can't you see he's working on his report?

"I'd like to call a taxi, if I can," said Father Urban, giving the town the benefit of a doubt, and then he waited.

Presently the agent got up and came to the counter. He pushed the telephone at Father Urban and tossed him a thin directory. "Cost you a dime to call", he said.

The dog opened its eyes, as if it wanted to see how Father Urban would take the bad news.'

And later, when he reaches St Clement's,

'In a field, at some distance from him, a muffled figure was moving slowly through the dead grass and weeds, through the haze. Father Urban coughed. The figure, that of a man, rounded on him. When Father Urban saw the gun, a rifle, he feared for his life, thinking this was some half-witted yokel—who, having been given hunting privileges, and having killed a stranger, would get off scot-free at the inquest.'

We see and feel what Urban does, and though our appreciation is enriched by our awareness of the sensibility through which the experience travelled to us—'he feared for his life' and 'some half-witted yokel'—the point is not one *about* that sensibility, much less *against* it, because that sensibility is not significantly differentiated from our own. This is a friend of ours, describing something alien to us, too.

Out of all these different kinds of liking, we could construct an image of Father Urban's total career as our protagonist, which would show him developing from ordinary careless decency at the beginning to moral awareness, sobriety, and even activity at the end. But the 'plot' scarcely fits that image; the episode at Belleisle, in which his early self is what matters, comes after the heroic act with Billy. More important, there are so many passages throughout the book which the image does not account for at all. Father Urban is after all the main representative of that worldliness in religious matters which rouses the author's deepest indignation and disgust. Many episodes have as their main point the delineation of the moral flaws in him, with a force that makes that delineation an accusation. The warm liking, understanding, and sympathy is nowhere to be found at such moments; and they occur throughout the book. This critical point of view is implicit on the whole figure of Jack, and Urban's treatment of him, and contrast with him. Jack is first described to us as 'an older man for whom, in a way, he had a lot of respect'. The acidness of that phrasing is taken up again a few lines later. 'Now and then Father Urban threw him an engagement, but he didn't like to do it. Jack didn't generate much heat from the pulpit, and . . .'. As Urban leaves the room he looks back and 'thought how well poor Jack, with his glasses off, went with the pictures'. Pictures we have previously heard described as 'large, pious oils (copies of Renaissance masterpieces, executed by a now departed Clementine) in which everybody seemed to be going blind'. The comment made here on Urban is as scathing as his own condescension, for Jack is endorsed by the book as representing moral and spiritual values of the purest and most selfless kind. When he and Urban are sent to Duesterhaus together, their attitudes are contrasted significantly. 'Jack's attitude was the right one, of course, but it must come easier for someone like him. What did *he* have to lose?' The effect of this is doubled by its casualness and by the completeness with which it overturns Christian values. The 'natural' understandableness and indeed truthfulness of the remark is not denied, of course; but the event undercuts and undermines it, and the anecdote as a whole has a sharply 'supernatural' point.

Seeing Father Urban's career through the book from this point of view, one might build the image of a worldly priest, given a second chance by being removed from the world to the Hill, but, merely resentful of his banishment and irritated by his companions, resuming a worldly career until struck down by the golf-ball, and ending his days in an appropriate grey haze. But this is even less satisfactory than the first image. It fits certain passages—Urban with Jack, Urban as the friend of Monsignor Renton and Father Louis and Father Placidus—but it does not fit, satisfactorily, even Urban with Wilf; where, I would suggest, the reader cannot feel anything but identified with Urban. He is not the worldly priest, he is our protagonist. We have reacted exactly as he has to Wilf's behaviour; we have no room in which to turn round on him.

Urban's relation to Wilf is for me the most perfectly realized and intensely interesting part of the book. But in it, as I said, Urban is not so centrally 'the likeable human', and certainly not 'the worldly priest' but 'the impatient intelligence'. It is this rôle of his which wins the writer's and the reader's deepest identification with him, and their richest blend of responses—from condemnation (self-condemnation) to delight (self-delight). This Father Urban has no 'career' through the book of even the broken kind the other two images provide, but it is possible to see the narrative as a series (not really 'organized' at all) of encounters designed for him. That is, it is remarkable how many silly, foolish and stupid people appear in the narrative, and perform their foolishness almost gratuitously; Ray Bean, for instance, Mr Studley, Dickie Thwaites, the curates of Ostergothenburg, Chester Henn, and so on. Characters with more serious functions, moreover, come forward from time to time with some striking foolishness, at which we can only drop our jaws and stare; Jack, of course, and Billy, but even so sharp a mind as Monsignor Renton has his monologue on the world shortage of oil. It makes sense to see the book as an anthology of imbecilisms, and Father Urban as our protagonist in dealing with them, the intelligent man in Boeotia.

There are, then, three fairly distinct images of Father Urban and of his 'career'. Though distinct, they are not, in the abstract, incompatible. But in the book they do not make one, because each represents a different basic attitude, as well as interest, in the author's mind. Thus different episodes have not so much different as separate atmospheres, and there is a lack of continuity and inner development through the whole. Perhaps the best way to demonstrate that would be to discuss two passages in which Urban's personality is awarded some independence of interest, some three-dimensionality. First, the description of his early life and how he came to become a Clementine. Second, the dream of how he might have lived had he not become one, and the whole encounter with Sally. Neither of these is really satisfactory, and (both cause and consequence) the image of Urban in the book as a whole remains fragmentary.

The reminiscence is about the town in which Urban grew up, and the people he knew, rather than about him. We are told that his father was greenskeeper at the country club, but we get no sense of who his father was, or his mother, or how he felt towards them. This is significant because we in some sense want to know these things; the different rôles he plays in the book leave us with a feeling of ambiguity and vagueness, a need to pin something down. Was he ever an affectionate person? Was he a happy child and adolescent? What were his characterizing attachments and irritations? These are things we rather positively don't know. Then we are told of his association with Monsignor Morez, but we are not told why he should have thus destined himself for the church so early. Was he a very sensitive boy? Did he recoil from the vulgar, go-getting world then? Had he an important religious life then? These questions are in the air, and the author seems, in this section, to be aware of them; but he cannot answer them. The figure of Father Placidus accounts for Urban's becoming a Clementine, but it does not account for his becoming a priest.

The daydream has equally the air of fictional guesswork. The questions are faced directly and fully enough, but the answers are not convincing. It is a caricature we get at the moment we needed a portrait. The idea implicit in much of the imagery, of the seducing lure of the big business world, is here made explicit —and made cruder. Urban would have been in heavy machinery— 'some kind of business you could breathe in'—and would have got presents from 'dictators of the better sort'. There is an open imitation of *Ulysses,* and a series of private jokes with the reader, which mark the author's uneasiness. We hear someone mimicking Urban, his private voice, and, quite unlike the mimicry of his public voice, we hear the effort put into it, we feel the distance between the model and his mimic. And the whole episode of which this is the centre is unconvincing. Sally is an unrealized character. The sexuality of the encounter and the challenge is unrealized. And when she puts the climactic accusation to him, 'I mean you're an operator—a trained operator like Mrs Leeson, and an operator in your heart—and I don't think you've a friend in the world', then I think the reader feels let down. For one thing, the logic of their conversation *should* make the climax an accusation of Urban for being a priest, not for being a poor human being. For another, his inability to answer makes this a crucial indictment, while it is too cliché in language and thought for that function. And above all, this is not what is interestingly wrong with Father Urban. So that again, in handling Urban as a whole, the author betrays an uncertainty, a clumsiness, which derives, I suggest, from the ambiguity of his purposes for the character, which derives in turn from the ambiguity within his attitude towards him.

Having explained my reading of the book, I should like to return to my remarks about 'the Catholic novelist', and ask what connections may be drawn between the two. Powers is of course a Catholic novelist in two senses he has himself referred to; that he deals in Catholic material, and that he is 'philosophically' Catholic. The first goes without saying, and the second has perhaps been sufficiently illustrated by that contrast between Urban and Jack. Jack is better than Urban; because Jack lives by Christian values and Urban by worldly ones; it is as simple and ruthless as that. But I am interested in a different sense of 'Catholic writing', which refers to a literary tradition, and is therefore closer to considerations of literary success; which determines the sorts of intelligence (and stupidity), generosity (and meanness), energy (and feebleness), a writer can aim at and achieve.

The ending of *Morte d'Urban*, for instance, is a piece of Catholic writing in this sense. That grey accumulation of defeat and decay, that atmosphere of hope and energy being buried in the (humanly) meagre and meaningless, is something we recognize from other Catholic writers. Graham Greene, William Golding, T. S. Eliot, Mauriac, the defeat of human virtue and talent is a major Catholic theme; the malignancy of the human environment—which extends into the human psyche itself—rendered as suffocating dullness and pettiness. This is the obverse of that other rendering, found in, say, Flannery O'Connor and Bernanos, which dramatizes its savagery and horror. And what we find at the end of the book has of course been present intermittently throughout; the atmosphere of the whole Clementine Order, and especially of Duesterhaus, is full of that petty negativism and constriction. The blow from the golf-ball and the headaches which follow from that are, after all the subtleties have been taken into consideration, quite simply a judgment on Urban—a punishment for his freedom, administered by the more serious part of the author's mind. A punishment to the more unregenerate part of that mind, and to the reader, for the pleasure we have both taken in that freedom. The author has allowed us escapes from the serious and Catholic mode of feeling, by means of the first and third images of Father Urban, but at the end of the book we must realize that these have been only holidays. We have freely and gaily liked Father Urban as a human being, and we have vividly and complexly sympathized with him as a smart man among fools, but we are not allowed to finish the book without realizing that these were superficial responses, and that the truly serious response undercuts them—and is neither vivid, free, nor gay.

Let us take just one more example, from within the book, of this kind of Catholic writing; the end of 'A Couple of Nights Before Christmas'. The hiding of the bambino brings the hostility between Wilf and Urban to boiling point, and the comedy changes character, becomes more painful, in a way more serious, but in another way less so, because we become more aware of the pettiness of the issue and the feelings involved. The egotism in both men is stripped ugly naked, but also pitiably small, so that we turn away from it in boredom and revulsion as well as in disapproval. The significance of the Christmas tree and the Christmas phrases echoing in Father Urban's mind make this pettiness the more disturbing; and Jack's mediation and example have the same effect. But let us note that neither the tree nor Jack's example effectively are an alternative, as something for us to contemplate. They allude, remotely, to what men ought to be; but their effective reference is to what they ought *not* to be. This very skilful piece of writing is classically in the Catholic literary tradition I mean.

But the main point I would like to argue is that Powers's ambiguity about Urban, from which so much else derives, is also related to his being a Catholic writer. For Powers, the official language of Catholicism, about the priesthood, about the Church's mission, about men's salvation, about the spiritual life, has an absoluteness and an enormousness of reference which deprives him of full creative freedom. He is not free to like Urban as much as his creative instinct urges him to, because Urban is, after all, simply wrong; the writer has to switch back on to another track of feeling, in order to be—even within the comic mode—serious about him. He is not free to use Urban as the protagonist of his own intellectual impatience, because it is simply wrong to be impatient, and simply twice as wrong for a priest. Of course, Powers *gives* himself the freedom to like Urban in these ways, for twenty pages at a time, but it is always a holiday, and a severer truth is always awaiting his return to seriousness—a truth of a separate kind, which displaces and diminishes the other. We cannot say that Urban should have two hundred pages of freedom rather than twenty. But we can say that he should have the full span of freedom which the creative instinct would award him, unbullied by that (in this context) external reference of official Catholic language. Father Urban needs the same measure of freedom—in the kind appropriate to him—as Bloom has, as Basil Seal has, as Chichikov has.

There are other factors at work in the weakness of Urban as a whole character. The difference between him and Bloom, for instance, is more a matter of Joyce's quite genial omnivorousness of interest than of his unity of tone about Bloom. But then isn't Joyce's omnivorousness exactly what he bought in exchange for his Catholicism? Isn't that undiscriminating embrace, of all the low variousness of life, exactly what Stephen Dedalus chose, in preference to the high vocation the Jesuit rector offered him? In any case, Powers' Catholicism is one important source of his ambiguity towards Urban, and that ambiguity is certainly the source of the uncertainties in the voice, and of the weaknesses in the form.

The form of *Morte d'Urban* is much to be admired, in many ways; it is very faithful to the shape of what Powers has to say, and it is very skilful. But what Powers has to say is desultory and intermittent, in the ways we have described, and so the unity of subject and purpose, that vital principle of formal shapeliness, is missing. The skill has to work externally. A great deal of the effect of climax is achieved simply by the change into Latin in 'One of Our Best Men'. And a good deal of the effect of total shapeliness is achieved by the use of chivalric romance language. Both of these devices have comparatively little to do with any inner thematic development. What they do express that is thematic is the author's (comic) yearning for a noble language—and mode of experience—which would be uncontaminated by modern vulgarisms. But the expression of this thematic concern is placed where it is purely as a matter of design, independently of character and even development. Some illusion of unity and inner development is given by skilful interweaving of figures and references and plot lines from different episodes. The Thwaites used to own St Clement's Hill, Mrs Thwaites is one of Urban's projects, Dickie has two or three small parts to play, and Sally one big one; as a family they tie together a number of episodes that are thematically quite various. Mr Studley turns up at St Clement's, and at the very end at the Novitiate; the matter of the railway passes recurs; so does Rex. These things give us both a feeling of artistic pattern, and the sense of a self-consistent world out there, with the real world's blend of randomness and design. But they are external in that they don't derive from or correspond to any substantial development in Urban and what he represents, or in our understanding of that. His circumstances change more than he does; he is changed to fit them; he becomes *less* real, less substantial, in consequence of those changes. And *one* source of all these difficulties is surely the author's inability to integrate all his feelings about his protagonist, an inability that derives from his being a Catholic writer.

Morte d'Urban remains, nevertheless, an interesting and impressive book, not only in itself, but as a stage in Mr Powers's development, and as a stage in Catholic writing. If the Catholic-writing problems cannot be said to be solved in his novel, they are treated with much more real success than in his more 'perfect' and tightly organized short stories.

The Lord's Day, The Forks, The Valiant Woman, Dawn, The Devil was the Joker, Zeal, The Presence of Grace, these seem to me completely typical Catholic short stories. Which means that in them the reader is constantly cheated, constantly checked in his sympathies by the reflection that one must be charitable, constantly forced back upon himself and made to relish the ignominy, the indignity, the selfishness, the inadequacy, of being what he is, human. In *Zeal,* for instance, one finds the intelligent and likeable Bishop being oppressed, imposed on, by the tiresome and unpleasant Father Early; unable to defend himself because where native timidity and sensitiveness would be reinforced by anger, in steps the injunction against anger, the injunction of poverty of spirit; so that he ends by accepting a human defeat because he is 'superhumanly' forbidden to fight back. That is the pattern also of *The Forks, The Lord's Day,* and *The Valiant Woman*; it defines the moment when reluctant submission becomes acquiescent, when natural defeat is swallowed up in 'supernatural' victory. But what we are shown and made to feel is the defeat, not the victory.

And what makes us most reluctant to respond to this pattern is that it seems to be a mere mortification. The good is not renounced in favour of something better, but in favour of renunciation. The act of giving up is the final end and focus of the whole exercise. We are drawn on by Mr Powers, drawn into the acts of sympathy and identification which we will later be asked to renounce, by his own liveliest preferences. His talent, as we know, is for the perfect detail, the thing seen or said which is so authentic we acknowledge to ourselves, 'That is exactly right. This is perfectly real.' We hear and feel Father Early, we suffer him just as acutely as the Bishop does. The Bishop *is* but a characterless membrane of sensibility, to be impinged on, to suffer. He is Mr Powers, imagining himself a Bishop sitting next to Father Early. But the point of the story is that Father Early *is* zealous. The Bishop is in some sense wrong, which is to say that the reader was wrong to prefer him.[1]

In *The Forks* the Monsignor has not even Father Early's grace of spirit, and Father Eudex has not even a positive obedience open to him; he can only suffer in silence. In *The Lord's Day* the nun's mind—and the reader's—is affronted as brutally as if she were physically shouldered aside by the rankly coarse priest. She staggers and stands still again, her eyes down; and the reader does the same. It is a humiliation of the better, and a humiliation of nature. We are made to like and admire Father Eudex—who works with the janitor, who gives his overshoes to the picket, who wants to give money to the strikers—in order to later feel his inadequacy. And we are made to see things the way he sees them—the natural way, bright with life—in order later to feel its wrongness. We, with him, see the Monsignor go to his cherished car; 'He gave the left fender an amorous chuck and eased into the front seat. Then they drove off, the car and he, to see the world, to explore each other further on the honeymoon.' This is of course very malicious, but it is even more very witty and attractive; and we cannot renounce the malice without renouncing the wit, which is, in literary terms, merely mortifying nature.

Catholicism, then, encumbers its writers with considerable difficulties. These difficulties can all be said to be of their own making—which only means that solutions to them exist, not that those solutions are available to or attractive to each individual case. Thus the choice to be a 'Catholic writer' is itself a voluntary one. You can be merely a Catholic and merely a writer without failing in either vocation. And you can be (or perhaps could be)

[1] If the story were an intellectual or a theological exercise, this would be a crude misreading. But it is a story, dealing in natural truths and natural feelings. Mr Powers excludes the supernatural: all we see of the Bishop's victory over himself is a few lines of dialogue in which he is doing what he did not want to do.

a Catholic writer without being a 'Catholic writer'; Chaucer and
Dante were. To be a 'Catholic novelist' of the kind I have been
discussing means following a tradition established perhaps a
hundred years ago, if we count Barbey d'Aurevilly as its
originator, and introduced into Anglo-American fiction only in
this century. It is quite possible to imagine a much better Catholic
literary tradition. But it is not so possible to find such an alternative, really current and available; and meanwhile we must
presumably use the word Catholic for what we have. Mr Powers,
struggling, however consciously, against its limitations and
disadvantages in *Morte d'Urban*, seems to me its brightest hope.

Of course, if we return our minds to the climate of opinion we began
by discussing, exemplified in Ellman, we see that a Catholic writer like
Powers could not begin to achieve true artistic freedom, according
to the crucial modern definitions of that freedom. Yeats, and others,
demanded for literature the right to feel itself radically different from,
and insubordinate to, all other modes of discourse, including those of
religion. Literature is always about something else, and means something else, even when it uses the same terms as, say, religion; it has
its own meanings for terms like eternity and salvation; and these are
the true meanings.

'Literature differs from explanatory and scientific writing in being
wrought about a mood, or a community of moods, as the body is
wrought about an invisible soul; and if it uses argument, theory,
erudition, observation, and seems to grow hot in assertion or denial,
it does so merely to make us partakers at the banquet of the moods. It
seems to me that . . . argument, theory, erudition, observation, are
merely what Blake calls "little devils who fight for themselves", illusions
of our visible passing life, who must be made serve the moods, or we
have no part in eternity.'

This is a large charter of freedom for literature, a large bill of rights,
and surely most modern charters are versions of this one. Surely, too,
no Catholic writer could sign this. Of course one can keep distinct in
one's mind some meanings of 'eternity' which belong to the realm of
literature, and others that belong to religion. But if that statement of
Yeats is to have its intended significance, to endorse it is to promise

I

to devote one's life-energies to the meanings that belong to literature. If one is ever to draw the line, if one is *ever* to draw back and turn to religion's meanings as more important, if one admits the possibility of a conflict between the two and of the preference then going to religion, then I think one's endorsement of Yeats's charter betrays its intention.

It is just as striking to realize what sympathetic exegesis (implicit endorsement) this enormous charter does receive from the contemporary literary world, in the person of Yeats's critics. 'To hold certain ideas as "beliefs" would give them a sort of autonomy,' says Ellman, 'the mind, whose independence Yeats demanded, would become subservient to them, instead of their being necessary expressions of it.' And later he observes that Yeats's idea of moods, 'made forceful asseveration possible to a man whose point of view was flexible. They admitted the poet to a world which the scientist, the banker, the clergyman, and the philosopher, clutching like dolls their substitute-realities, were forbidden to enter.' This language is typical of the climate of belief of the modern literary world, and into it the Catholic writer is surely forbidden to enter—by the first sentence quoted, for instance. As even the secular humanist is by the second.

Of the two problems here, that created by the great symbolist writers themselves, and that created by the scholarly critical writers around them, the first is in some ways the more acute, because the young writer and reader is necessarily so sensitive to the dicta of his great masters. But this is less insidious than the second, because a scholarly-critical climate of opinion necessarily presents itself as merely there, the background, the facts from which we all start. Yeats at least some of the time felt he had made a dangerous choice, and allows us, even while we read and admire him, to make the opposite one. Ellman implies that, for a writer, there was no choice; and the difference between writer and reader is surely one of degree only—and that a degree of imaginative power, and consequently a difference the reader must be striving to overcome.

Frank Kermode, in *The Romantic Image,* is more ambiguous than Ellman. He contrasts Yeats with Arnold on this issue, of a choice between religion and poetry. Arnold, he says, ceased being a poet just in order to save his soul. 'Yeats understood his own guilt and felt conscious of damnation; he did not walk out of his dream, but simply extended it to include everything, and went on being a poet till he died.' This presents the issue clearly enough—dramatically indeed—but the terms have somehow lost their natural weight and substantiality, their meaning. I see no evidence that Yeats felt conscious of *damnation,* or that Kermode is thinking of the full consequence of those words when he uses them. In the climate of modern literature, it seems, such an issue cannot be taken seriously.

On the other hand, to react away from this anarchic aestheticism, back to any of the cultural theories of art (among which belong both the Soviet theory and the approach the new Catholicism offers), is no real use to the Catholic literary man or indeed anyone else. Such theories only nurture a really lively feeling for literature when, as in Dr Leavis's case, they are held in implicit tension with a quite contrary impulse to admire the intensely individual and rebellious. (I argue this case more fully in *The Problem of Boston.*) Unless that contrary tendency is built in —as I hope some equivalent is into this idea of a humanism—every cultural theory of literature must nurture a dull sensibility and a feeble art.

Such theories do not explicitly offer to prescribe to either the creative artist or the man of taste, but they have that effect. Every systematic statement of what art is offers the materials for a systematic statement of what art ought to be; as Bowman puts it in his book on Belinsky. Madame de Staël moved in a decade from a study of literature-and-society (*De la littérature considérée dans ses rapports avec les institutions sociales*, 1800) to the formulation of a programme for literature in her own society and time (*De l'Allemagne*, 1810). Any cultural theory of art will be aesthetically illiberal unless it contains and includes its opposite, individualism. Thus I am not surprised to find Mr Wicker attributing Orwell's individualist principles to a mistaken aesthetic. Orwell's insistence that the artist must reject all party lines and maintain a *personal* artistic integrity Mr Wicker attributes to a belief that art records—whereas the truth, he tells us, is that art imitates. However that may be, I can see why Orwell's sharply various and inconsistent taste—for Henry Miller, for instance—had to be explained away by Mr Wicker; and I can see why I range myself more with Orwell.

Orwell saw very clearly the conflict between cultural responsibility and the individualism of the modern artist, and the need for both tendencies to be powerfully affirmed at the source of any lively modern sensibility. Orwell was not interested in the kind of humanism I have been outlining, but the taste he so vividly and persuasively reported is a good example of the kind that would derive from that theoretical position. His temperament, too, is a good example of the range of temperaments unlike von Hügel's own which can express themselves within the limits of liberal humanism, which obey its discipline, and which draw their vitality from its nurture.

In the world of Catholic literature, on the other hand, the writer's vitality and individualism figure most often only as the means of covert bullying, the writer identifying himself with a creed and enforcing himself and it together. No doubt any rigid creed and massive institutional power is an attractive object of identification for the bully; and there is also a heartiness, a promise that we are the people who know how to really *enjoy* life (unlike those niggardly Nonconformists and greyfaced atheists) recurrent in Catholic sensibility in different periods and places.

Gide wrote in his diary in 1925, 'In the presence of Claudel, I am conscious of what I lack; he dominates me; he oppresses me; he has more base and surface, more health, money, genius, power, children, faith, etc., than I have. I can only think of piping down.' Surely no one who has read Claudel can doubt that he had this effect because he wanted to. And other people's accounts of Claudel show that Gide's reaction was far from eccentric. Jacques Rivière said that Claudel always 'wants to force our innermost consent. He is determined, in spite of ourselves, to wrench us from doubt and dilettantism.'

Twenty years before, in 1905, Gide had written in his diary, 'As a young man, Claudel looked like a nail; now he looks like a sledge-hammer. Not a very high forehead, but rather wide; face without subtlety as though carved with a chisel; bull neck continued by the straight line of the head, through which passion can rush and flood the brain . . .'. Claudel could see nothing in Descartes, hated Stendhal and Flaubert, referred to Zola as 'that disgusting Zola', but found Coventry Patmore a great religious poet; Gide continues, 'He gives me the impression of a solidified cyclone. When he talks, it seems as though something were released inside him; he proceeds by a series of sudden assertions and maintains a hostile tone even if you agree with him.'

Guardini says that according to Catholicism *logos* precedes *ethos,* that knowing and feeling correctly is more important than acting vigor-ously to Catholics—that when Faust says, 'In the beginning was Action' he announces the major modern heresy. But in this confronta-tion of Gide with Claudel, it is surely the former who has given the precedence to logos, and the latter to ethos; do not the two personali-ties express that precedence pretty clearly, in structure and texture? Moreover, I think this would hold true of most confrontations of liberal humanists with Catholic writers. The latter are the activists, the bullies, the would-be commissars. That heresy, with its huge emotional consequences, is a fate that hangs over all adherents of a totalitarian faith. For Bernanos, the greatest villains were literary intellectuals (M. Ouine is said to be a portrait of Gide himself), and the greatest sin 'curiosity', and the mark of Satan on his villains is their laughter. For both Claudel and Bernanos another mark of Satan was irony. Laughter, irony, curiosity, literariness, when these are what you hate most in life, you are possessed by the spirit of violence, the spirit of destruction.

Martin Turnell remarks, in *Modern Literature and Christian Faith,* (on which I am drawing in these paragraphs) on how large a rôle is played by violence in the work of Claudel, Mauriac, and Greene—as in the work of Bernanos and Bloy, we might add. Violent death usually follows violent passion for all lovers, saintly or sinning, in Claudel's plays. In the realm of personal relations, Claudel's God is an angry God, and this is true of most other Catholic writers. And in

Mauriac's novels, religion is the destructive element, the source of conflicts, between the Church and the world, between the love of God and love of his creatures, between the individual and his family or environment or community.

In the work of these writers God and religion destroy life, and it is surely not too much to say that the effect of these plays and novels is angrily and proudly to participate in that destruction. The writers are always on the side of those characters who hate the world—who don't belong in it. The sinners differ from the saints in the object of their loves, but both belong together in radical opposition to the bourgeois, the property-owners, who are at ease in life. The Catholic-writer syndrome is surely one of the most transparent of all masks for a hateful revenge on life and all who enjoy it; one of the evillest, most distorting of self-disguises.

The Communist-writer idea is different, but carries its own hostility to the fully expanded human personality; its own vengefulness against life. That Catholic hatred of the bourgeois was the inspiration of some unsavoury attempts at a joining of hands between Catholics and Communists, united in a common zest for destruction. And in so far as the new Catholicism continues this attack on the property-owner, it will continue the old anti-humanism. Sometimes even Rahner and Küng sound as if what they are offering us is a theological equivalent of Bergman movies—some fashionable and high-falutin gratification of our impulse to smash things. Surely the one type a modern intellectual cannot afford to have as his enemy is the bourgeois. That hatred is both too easy and too risky. The energies it draws on come too easily—our traditions include no severe scrutiny of those motives—and go too far—we know already of too much that is rotten in our civilization, and we can't afford to energize our knowledge with this hatred.

I used Proust before as an example of what the fully expanded personality could be. His cork-lined room is an emblem of psychological sickness, one must admit, but then 'health', in the arts particularly, is not a touchstone to be too hastily applied. There is a sense in which every great artist has been sick, and every man of sensibility must have abandoned some of the crudest, and most effective, defences against sickness. The literary man always needs, in Virginia Woolf's phrase, a room of one's own. There is a sense in which all individualism is a mark of disease. But if you declare war on individualism you declare war on literature. It seems to me this is proved by the literary history of Soviet Russia. And I suspect the new Catholicism of unconsciously hostile intentions. The humanism I am describing would fight against the anarchy of Yeats but for the privacy of Proust.

Perhaps the difference for a humanist between Yeats and Nabokov, and their two kinds of anarchy, is even more interesting. Nabokov too refuses any kind of humanist co-operation in maintaining cultural values, and his attacks on crucial moral standards are much more disturbing than Yeats's. But because Nabokov is a decadent—that is, because he implicitly admits his non-centrality, his disqualifying wilfulness and destructiveness—he does not subvert the structure of humanism as Yeats does. One cannot, that is, imagine a critic of *Lolita* implying that Humbert Humbert is merely 'sensitive', or that Nabokov's values are the only ones 'for a writer'.

Nabokov is in some sense a symbolist, and therefore belongs, on the humanist's map of things, with Yeats (and with Rilke and Pasternak) in the opposite direction from Powers and Sholokhov, who exemplify the literary mind self-subordinated to a totalitarian faith. The central humanist position I hope to have sketched out in the first three essays, on von Hügel. But I hope also to show humanist taste in action in my comments on these non-humanist authors; for the essence of humanism is the belief that one must recognize differences of ideology as serious divisions and yet achieve what union is possible, in sympathy, appreciation, response, across those divisions. And I want to distinguish this humanist taste from what it might mistakenly be thought to be—from all vulgarized approximations to it—and therefore most sharply of all from such taste as might make the same theoretical declarations. And so in discussing Nabokov and Sholokhov, who for opposite reasons offend humanists, the balance of my stress is on appreciation, on overcoming initial resistances, on deepening response. Whereas in Pasternak, so general a favourite with the same readers, I mostly point out reasons for resistance, in restraint of enthusiastic response. I largely take for granted, therefore—our political and moral consciences need no alerting to them—the things that offend humanist feeling in Sholokhov's Marxism and Nabokov's symbolism. I can only hope this does not make my argument in this part of the book seem inconsistent with what it was before.

But before we turn to Nabokov, and later Pasternak, perhaps we should offer some definition of symbolism, since that will be so important a concept in our discussion. Kermode in *The Romantic Image* offers us two useful definitions; of romanticism and of symbolism. Romantic he says he uses as 'applicable to the literature of one epoch, beginning in the late years of the eighteenth century and not yet finished, and as referring to the high valuation placed during this period upon the image-making powers of the mind at the expense of its rational powers, and to the substitution of organicist for mechanistic modes of thinking about works of art'. All the writers we are concerned with are then romantic (or rather romanticism is the major artistic mode of the period in which they worked) and some are symbolist.

Some characteristics of symbolism are, 'The work of art itself is symbol, "aesthetic monad"; utterly original and not in the old sense "imitated"; "concrete", yet fluid and suggestive; a means to truth, a truth unrelated to, and more exalted than, that of positivist science, or any observation depending upon the discursive reason; out of the flux of life, and therefore, under one aspect, dead; yet uniquely alive because of its participation in a higher order of existence, and because it is analogous not to a machine but to an organism; co-extensive in matter and form; resistant to explanation; largely independent of intention, and of any form of ethical utility; and itself emblematized in certain recurring images, of which, as the next chapter shows, the Dancer is the most perfect.'

Perhaps it is even more relevant to our interest in *Lolita* to note Kermode's assertion that the symbolist artist's morality is quite different from that of other men; that the truth that the artist sees both isolates him from other men and risks his immortal soul (an idea glimpsed in Joyce and Pater, expounded fully in Thomas Mann); that the modern idea of art derives from a rapprochement between the poet and the occulist.

Nabokov is not in any complete sense a symbolist—it was always rare for a novelist to be, and by now the period of complete symbolism is apparently over—but he, like nearly every important modern writer, is so in part; quite enough to make him a rebel against humanism. And in opposition to him we can set the Tolstoy of *What is Art?*, who represents that humanism in its crudest authoritative form, expressing its demands on literature with a vigour we have to listen to but also finally have to dissent from. He forces us to redefine our creed.

The morality of *Lolita*

People talk of the art of the future, meaning by art of the future some especially refined new art which they imagine will be developed out of that exclusive art of one class which is now considered the highest art. But no such new art of the future can or will be found.

Tolstoy, *What is Art?*, 1896

But the art of the twentieth century has been, by and large, of the kind Tolstoy declared would not—must not—happen. Nearly all our really brilliant literature, in Europe and America, has been of that kind and not of the kind *he* prescribed. And though there are many varieties within the huge body of modern art, the type Tolstoy would have most abominated, the type he was most talking about, is near enough epitomized in *Lolita*. This can be made clear in a direct way by referring to his descriptions of the literature he dislikes, and indirectly from those descriptions of what literature *should* be which occupy most of the space of *What is Art?*. He defined that 'art of the future' which he announced *would* come by making it the opposite of all we find in Nabokov's work, which he can be said to have foretold quite accurately, by negation and by retrospect. And this is not such a paradox, nor such a wanton conjunction of the radically unrelated, as it may seem. Nabokov stands in immediate and intimate relationship to the Symbolist tradition Tolstoy was denouncing, which replaced Tolstoy's own tradition in Russian literature. He belongs to that branch of the tradition sometimes called Decadent; Sologub's *The Petty Demon,* for instance, has a good deal in common with *Lolita,* though it is (at least in translation) incomparably less interesting.

The especial refinement of Nabokov's art is clear enough, both in the exquisite rendering of his effects, and in the trickiness of those effects' whole genre—the highly sophisticated taste they express, which so energetically avoids every suspicion of the ordinary, of the obvious, of the morally or intellectually banal. Who can compare with Nabokov for this refinement, among the writers who have appeared since *What is Art?* was published? Not Lawrence, or Joyce, or Mann. For equal refinement we would have to go to a minor writer, or to other Russians, to other developers of that 'exclusive art of one class', to Balanchine or to Stravinsky. Those three have between them contributed much of the most elegant art, of the most sophisticated taste, to the contemporary Western world; and behind them Fabergé, Diaghilev, the Impressionist collections, all pre-1917 St Petersburg still stands as a glittering emblem.

As Mirsky says in *Contemporary Russian Literature*, 'Russian Symbolism is a part of the general cultural upheaval which changed the face of Russian civilization between 1890 and 1910. . . . In 1890 the sole function of art in Russian was to "express ideas"; in 1915 Russian society was aesthetically one of the most cultivated and experienced in Europe.'[1] And since 1917 the benefits of that aesthetic refinement have spread far beyond the frontiers of Russia. The ballet of Balanchine, the music of Stravinsky, the novels of Nabokov, this is the best of that art of the connoisseur Tolstoy rejected in favour of an art of the common man; the art of the future, in which 'Only those productions will be esteemed art which transmit feelings drawing men together in brotherly union, or such universal feelings as can unite all men.' There *are* modern ballets, symphonies, novels, which serve that ideal with some success, notably in Soviet Russia, but nothing could go more against it than the theatrical and luxurious art of the three great expatriates, in which the instincts of the virtuoso and the impresario are disciplined only by the taste of a cosmopolitan intellectual. And of the three it is Nabokov and *Lolita* who present the most four-square target to the aim of Tolstoy's destructive analysis.

'We think the feelings experienced by people of our day and our class are very important and varied; but in reality almost all the feelings of people of our class amount to but three very insignificant and simple feelings—the feeling of pride, the feeling of sexual desire, and the feeling of weariness of life. These three

[1] This pronouncement raises many questions like 'What is meant by civilization here?,' 'What is meant by society?' I think the reader can work out answers to these questions which leave the sentences intact.

feelings, with their off-shoots, form almost the sole subject-matter of the art of the rich classes.'

These categories do not fit Nabokov's subject-matter *descriptively* —for instance, it is not a hero's weariness of life he treats, but the pain and horror inherent in all life—but *diagnostically* they do fit. Seen from Tolstoy's point of view, that is, *Lolita* clearly would seem to anyone to fit those categories with variations, to be recognizably a development from the art which fitted them exactly. Tolstoy mentions, as contemporary examples of the sexual theme, Rémy de Gourmont's *Les Chevaux de Diomède* ('every page contains lust-kindling descriptions'), Pierre Louÿs' *Aphrodite*, and Huysmans' *Certains*. 'They are all the productions of people suffering from erotic mania.' Humbert Humbert's nympholepsy clearly would seem to Tolstoy a recognizable development of that 'normal' erotic mania.

Of the three conditions he thought necessary to successful art, individuality of feeling, clarity of expression, and sincerity, the last was much the most important to Tolstoy. 'Sincere' in some sense of course applies to *Lolita*, but it is in a sophisticated and tricky sense, while the way Tolstoy used the term made its simpler senses determinative. This condition, he says, 'is always complied with in peasant art, and this explains why such art always acts so powerfully; but it is a condition almost entirely absent from our upper-class art, which is continually produced by artists actuated by personal aims of covetousness or vanity'. With this kind of sincerity *Lolita* is not sincere. That folk-tale anonymity of the author, that austere elimination of all personal cleverness, is at the opposite extreme from the novel's art. Nor is it *clear*; *Lolita* obviously belongs to the 'involved, affected, and obscure' genres typical of upper-class art. This art, Tolstoy said, because it came out of unbelief, had long ceased to aim at communicating with all men. It restricted itself to an 'exclusive' audience, with whom it could communicate by 'allusions comprehensible only to the initiated'. This method had reached its climax (at the date of *What is Art?*) in the work of the decadents. 'It has finally come to this: that not only are haziness, mysteriousness, obscurity, and exclusiveness (shutting out the masses) elevated to the rank of a merit and a condition of poetic art, but even inaccuracy, indefiniteness, and lack of eloquence, are held in esteem.' That artistic tradition to which Tolstoy wished to attach himself, and which he wished to revive, was the narratively and morally simple tradition of the people. '. . . the epic of Genesis, the Gospel parables, folk-legends, fairy-tales, and folk-songs, are understood by all.'

The function of art, said Tolstoy, is to aid human progress by spreading better feelings, just as the function of knowledge is to spread better ideas. 'And as the evolution of knowledge proceeds by truer and more necessary knowledge dislodging and replacing what was mistaken and unnecessary, so the evolution of feeling proceeds by means of art—feelings less kind and less necessary for the well-being of mankind being replaced by others kinder and more needful for that end. That is the purpose of art.' Art essentially unites people. It unites the reader with the writer, and with all the other readers, in sharing a more or less powerful impression, and complex of feelings. The art of the future will be of two kinds, according to the two kinds of feeling it unites us in. '. . . first, feelings flowing from a perception of our sonship to God and of the brotherhood of man; and next, the simple feelings of common life accessible to every one without exception—such as feelings of merriment, of pity, of cheerfulness, of tranquillity, and so forth.' This is, phrased in simplistic, pamphleteering terms, part of the cultural theory of art in which many of us who admire *Lolita* were trained up and still believe. But morally powerful as that programme may still seem, it needs no proof that Nabokov's art devotes great energy to doing something quite the opposite. If we needed proof, we would find it in the examples Tolstoy gives from nineteenth-century literature of the first kind of art: Schiller's *The Robbers*, Hugo's *Les Misérables* and *Les Pauvres Gens,* Dickens and Dostoevsky complete, *Uncle Tom's Cabin* and *Adam Bede*. The art of the second kind of feelings he could find no satisfactory examples of. While among those he condemns we find at least one whose example runs through *Lolita* as a kind of sponsor and precursor—Baudelaire—and Nabokov's other sponsors of theme and expression, like Proust and T. S. Eliot, would have seemed hardly any better to Tolstoy.

Chapter XI of *What is Art?* is devoted to the methods of counterfeit art, which replaces true art when sincerity has failed. Those methods it calls borrowing, imitating, striking, and interesting. Borrowing means using previously established poetic subjects, setting, characters, or plot. Imitating means detailed descriptive realism. (*Lolita*'s narrative manner can be described

as an ingenious combination of those two.) Striking means
directly affecting the senses. Interesting means with a subject of
independent interest—like nympholepsy, for instance. Tolstoy
did not say that these methods are incompatible with true art, but
that they are irrelevant to it, and often a substitute for it.

Nabokov borrows, imitates, etc., a great deal, and, more
importantly, that borrowing is far from irrelevant to his essential
meaning—his meaning comes through his borrowing—through
what is borrowed and also through the fact that it is borrowed.
Lolita is a fundamentally counterfeit book, fundamentally not
sincere as Tolstoy used that term, fundamentally tricky. The voice
of the narrator, for instance, though ultimately quite moving and
moved, quite committed on the book's basic issues, and therein
simple, solid, direct, is all these things only after, and through, a
great deal that is the opposite. We have a hundred reasons to
distrust that voice. He is a murderer and a pervert. He
is a dissenter from even the highest norms of thought and feeling.
He is fundamentally ironic and cynical—not only in his thoughts
(about Charlotte) but in his actions (to Valeria). And all this is
true of his character alone, as established by the events he narrates; something more fundamental is to be doubted and distrusted—his existence. Whoever writes the Foreword, signed
John Ray, Jr, Ph.D., is obviously the same person as signs
himself Humbert Humbert. We recognize the same flow of over-
elegant language, always shifting (swelling absurdly, halting
abruptly, changing its brand of elegance) in response to an acute
sense of (taste in) its own glossy falsity. 'If, however, for this
paradoxical prude's comfort, an editor attempted to dilute or omit
scenes that a certain type of mind might call "aphrodisiac" . . .'—
this is the main voice of the novel, whatever it may sign itself,
and to realize that this trick is being played on him rouses all a
reader's distrust—all his gamesmanship.

But John Ray we can forget. Clare Quilty is rooted in the
action of the novel, and it is much more deeply disturbing to
recognize the hints that he too is unreal; that he and Humbert
are two parts of the same personality. The similarity of their
mental habits and sexual tastes, the differentiation between their
moral guilts, the hallucinatory atmosphere of their encounters,
the cousinly and indeed brotherly relationship foisted on them;
by all these hints we are invited to believe that Humbert first
invents Quilty, to take on the worst of his own guilt, and then

kills him, symbolically to purge himself. But if this is true, then a great many of the novel's events must be untrue, and the whole persona of the narrator is one we cannot take at face value.

Indeed, his very physique changes as the novel proceeds. At the beginning he is beetle-browed, pseudo-Celtic, intensely virile, 'lanky, big-boned, woolly-chested', 'a hunk of movieland man-hood', with 'clean-cut jaw, muscular hand, deep sonorous voice, broad shoulder'. By the time he visits Lolita married, he is 'the distant, elegant, slender, forty-year-old valetudinarian in a velvet coat sitting beside her', and, 'The men looked at her fragile, *frileux*, diminutive, old-world, youngish but sickly, father in velvet coat and beige vest, maybe a viscount.' The more virile characteristics have been transferred to Lolita's husband—the blue eyes and black hair, the white teeth, the brawny shoulders and muscular arms. Richard Schiller is the final inheritor of a series of normal men (for instance, big Frank in Elphinstone) who have been contrasted with Humbert to his disadvantage through the second half of the book. Clearly, Humbert's original entity has again been split up, and the parts distributed among different actors, to dramatize an internal movement of self-hatred and self-punishment. The reader has to ask himself whether it is Humbert or Nabokov who does this—whether we can distinguish between what is invented by this narrator and what is reported—and the answer is complicated. The reader has to deal with a highly sophisticated reading experience, which challenges his assumption that he 'knows what is going on', in matters of moral fundamentals as well as of narrative techniques.

And the voice itself, its handling of the language, amplifies all these effects. The tone is always at least double.

'My very photogenic mother died in a freak accident (picnic, lightning) when I was three, and, save for a pocket of warmth in the darkest part, nothing of her subsists within the hollows and dells of memory, over which, if you can still stand my style (I am writing under observation), the sun of my infancy had set; surely, you all know those redolent remnants of day suspended, with the midges, about some hedge in bloom or suddenly entered and traversed by the rambler, at the bottom of a hill, in the summer dusk; a furry warmth, golden midges.'

Here let us note the abrupt change of rhythm in the first parenthesis; the mocking acknowledgement of his own over-elegance

—we have already been told to count on a murderer for a fancy prose-style; and above all the sudden flowering of the image, at the end of the sentence, into something full-blown and beautiful, the reference of which is by no means clear, and the force of which alters the emotional balance and direction of the whole statement. We have to follow such syntax very carefully.

We have to follow the *narrative* very carefully, because so much is conveyed by allusion and by ellipsis. The book is in part a game the narrator is playing against us ('*touché*, reader', he says at one point) and he is not above cheating. He will tell us Lolita had gone for ever, when in fact he merely felt then as if she had, and five lines later she is back. He will put Humbert and Valeria into an anonymous taxi, to discuss Valeria's infidelity, and then spotlight the taxi-driver as her beloved. He will even ascribe speeches and actions to people out of the exuberance of his own fancy. Sometimes he admits this afterwards, as in the case of Charlotte's letter. Sometimes he does not, as in Humbert's absurdly pompous warning about reformatories to Lolita, or in Lolita's letter home, beginning 'Dear Mummy and Hummy'. This narrator is clearly someone both master and servant of his own taste for brilliant language. Anything vivid enough to demand to be said he will say, and retrieve his sincerity later—will temporarily throw away his identity and his serious purposes for an effect. And our instinct that this characteristic must run very deep in the sensibility of which Humbert is the spokesman is corroborated in 'Vladimir Nabokov on a book entitled *Lolita*'.

'After doing my impersonation of suave John Ray, the character in *Lolita* who pens the Foreword, any comments coming straight from me may strike one—may strike me, in fact—as an impersonation of Vladimir Nabokov talking about his own book. A few points, however, have to be discussed; and the autobiographic device may induce mimic and model to blend.'

Autobiography is a device, and to speak in his own voice is a matter of having a model and being a mimic. With Nabokov there is always a mask, and of a self-proclaiming kind. Sincerity is something he achieves not by laying all masks aside, but by the way he manipulates them.

His private tragedy, he tells us there, is that he had to give up his native language for 'a second-rate brand of English, devoid of any of those apparatuses—the baffling mirror, the black velvet backdrop, the implied associations and traditions—which the native illusionist, fractails flying, can use to transcend the heritage in his own way'. This is in itself a tricky statement, for none of our native illusionists has in fact used more of those apparatuses, and few readers would say *Lolita* could be improved by *more* baffling mirrors and black velvet backdrops. But the important point is what is implied in the word illusionist, which is essential to what Nabokov means by an artist, and essentially not what Tolstoy meant—a man of tricks.

Tolstoy's examples of true art may seem at first remote from modern practice; the stories of Isaac, Jacob, and Joseph, the psalms and parables, the Vedas, Homer, and the story of Sakya Muni. But the artistic virtues such a selection is built round are obvious. Cardinal among them, perhaps, are the artist's dignity and simplicity, the loftiness of his message and the plainness of his manner. And if we look for more modern equivalents within our own traditions, and for artist-figures to associate with such art, we find them easily enough, in Emerson and Wordsworth, and in the later Tolstoy himself. Indeed, the ideal he there sketches out is only an extreme version of something we are all familiar with in British literature; George Eliot, Carlyle, Ruskin, Morris, are all figures modelled after the same ideal to some degree. All of them employed their gift of eloquence to proclaim noble truths with noble gestures. It is Nabokov's version of the artist-figure which is the real alien, the enigma and paradox, given our tradition.

'You have to be an artist and a madman, a creature of infinite melancholy, with a bubble of hot poison in your loins and a super-voluptuous flame permanently aglow in your subtle spine (oh, how you have to cringe and hide!), in order to discern at once, by ineffable signs—the slightly feline outline of a cheekbone, the slenderness of a downy limb, and other indices which despair and shame and tears of tenderness forbid me to tabulate—the little deadly demon among the wholesome children; *she* stands unrecognized by them and unconscious herself of her fantastic power.'

The image of the illusionist is blended with the image of the madman and the immoralist. Quilty, not Humbert, is a professional artist. Art is the realm of both the theatrical and the delirious illusion; of the exaggerated, the pretended, the masked, the suggested, the shameful, the feverish, the insane. It deals in truths that are banished from the open air and the daylight and the world of self-respect, truths that have the status only of half-truths or lies, because they cannot be fully faced or frankly stated. And the methods of this art, the gestures of this artist-figure, are appropriate to its subject-matter. There can be no question of noble simplicity or plain directness.

Hence the artifice; the diary entries, the addresses to the jury, the staged scenes, the painted pictures, and all the thousand devices of fantasy and memory, to change the truth away from literalness. 'The arabesques of lighted windows, which, touched up by the coloured inks of sensitive memory, appear to me now like playing cards—presumably because a bridge game was keeping the enemy busy.' Hence too, there are those messages in the text of *Lolita* for people other than the reader—for the printer, for the editor, for Lolita, for his lawyer, for his car, for Gaston Godin— which are yet for the reader too, involving him in an artificial complicity. There is that wealth of literary and linguistic reference, indulged in partly for its own sake, and as a game. There is the French and the German and the mock-Latin, and the constant refrain of references to Carmen and to Catullus and to Poe and to Dante. Related, there is the game with names and titles—Lolita's class-list, and the entries from *Who's Who in the Limelight*. The climax of all this is the system of clues Quilty scatters over the motels' visitors' books. Nabokov is playing with words all through the book, and though his games are organic parts of the action (partly because of Humbert's trickiness of character and characterization) they are so only through being games in and for themselves. They *are* personal displays of cleverness on the writer's part; they *are* what Tolstoy called the marks of bad art.

The poem, 'Wanted, wanted, Dolores Haze', is an example of another kind of trickiness in the novel. Humbert calls it a maniac's masterpiece, but though the rhymes are, as he says, 'stark, stiff, lurid', the spirit of their stiffness is not at all insane. Their spirit is comic-pathetic, and its tactics are most sane and sophisticated, the 'unintentional' effects amplifying the intentional ones both in the wit and in the pathos.

Where are you riding, Dolores Haze?
What make is the magic carpet?
Is a Cream Cougar the present craze?
And where are you parked, my car pet?

If we call the second line an intentional effect of wit, then the clumsiness of the third is 'unintentional' (a guarantee of sincerity), and the fourth is of course both.

My car is limping, Dolores Haze,
And the last long lap is the hardest,
And I shall be dumped where the weed decays,
And the rest is rust and stardust.

Here those two kinds of effect are less easily separated, and what we are more aware of is two kinds of parody; the first which deflates emotion, the second which inflates it, by making the mockery self-mocking—a mockery of expression, that is, and a Romantic inflation of the inexpressible experience. Thus the last phrase expands and asserts the poet's emotion—emotionally. This is typical of much of the writing in the novel, which appeals to our pity, our understanding, our delight, our liking for the hero, after seeming denials and devaluations of those feelings.

In all these ways, *Lolita* is a tricky novel, involving the reader in very risky games, many of the moves of which, and the counters of which, carry a high moral voltage. Neither narratively nor morally is it simple. And at the root of all these differences between the prescriptions of *What is Art?* and the texture and structure of *Lolita*, there is a sharp opposition between their aesthetic theories. Tolstoy saw art as a matter of communication. 'Art is a human activity consisting in this, that one man consciously by means of certain external signs, hands on to others feelings he has lived through, and that others are infected by these feelings and also experience them.' And therefore good art is that kind which communicates good feelings. He completely rejected the ideal of beauty itself, and the giving of pleasure, as the ends of art. He thought such theories merely rationalized the aesthetic interests of an idle and irreligious upper class.

'So these people remained without any religious view of life; and having none, they could have no standard whereby to estimate what was good and what was bad art, except that of personal enjoyment. And having acknowledged their criterion of what was good to be pleasure, that is beauty, these people of the upper classes of European society went back in their comprehension of art to the gross conception of the primitive Greeks, which Plato had already condemned. And conformably to this understanding of life a theory of art was formulated.'

K

Nabokov's position is the opposite. Beauty and pleasure, fused into 'aesthetic bliss', is art's only end and justification.

'I am neither a reader nor a writer of didactic fiction, and despite John Ray's assertion, *Lolita* has no moral in tow. For me a work of fiction exists only in so far as it affords me what I shall bluntly call aesthetic bliss, that is a sense of being somehow, somewhere, connected with other states of being where art (curiosity, tenderness, kindness, ecstasy) is the norm.'

That is by no means an easy sentence to read, but for the moment let us only note the diametrical opposition to Tolstoy. Humbert is even clearer in his rejection of every religious and moral scheme, every ideological synthesis within which art might have some function of cultural service.

'Alas, I was unable to transcend the simple human fact that whatever spiritual solace I might find, whatever lithophanic eternities might be provided for me, nothing could make my Lolita forget the foul lust I had inflicted upon her. Unless it can be proven to me—to me as I am now, today, with my heart and my beard, and my putrefaction—that in the infinite run it does not matter a jot that a North American girl-child named Dolores Haze had been deprived of her childhood by a maniac, unless this can be proven (and if it can, then life is a joke) I see nothing for the treatment of my misery but the melancholy and very local palliative of articulate art. To quote an old poet:

The moral sense in mortals is the duty
We have to pay on mortal sense of beauty.'

Religion, and *any* explanatory scheme, does not take human experience seriously enough. Only an attitude of protest and rage, refusing explanations, does. So art is superior to religion just because it is a melancholy and local palliative. *Lolita* is written as a melancholy and futile reparation to its heroine—'[to] make you live in the minds of later generations. I am thinking of aurochs and angels, the secret of durable pigments, prophetic sonnets, the refuge of art. And this is the only immortality you and I may share, my Lolita.' The consolations of religion and the rigours of morality are both derived from the aesthetic sense. What is beautiful is so because it satisfies our moral sense among other things, but the idea of beauty is the larger. The moral sense is an obligation entailed upon us, which we pay resignedly as a part of the price of beauty.

The interest of putting Nabokov and Tolstoy together at this length is not that they are different, for that would be conceded after a sentence, but that they are so very different. They represent opposite standards, and though Tolstoy's standard is too extreme for us to take seriously any ordinary divergence from it, still to stand, as Nabokov does, so defiantly opposed to all Tolstoy proclaims, that surely is a fact about Lotita which we do take seriously. Putting them together, that is, brings out something in the morality of *Lolita* which does trouble us. Nabokov so flies in the face of all ordinary usable morality, and so defiantly offers us pieces of beauty as his justification for doing so, that some of us are bound to be uneasy. The readers I am assuming are people not prepared to take up either Tolstoy's position or its opposite— some equally stringent exposition of Nabokov's aesthetic bliss. We stand somewhere between the two. There is, for people in that position, surely some force to Tolstoy's account of the duties and accomplishments of art, or at least to the contrast between them and what Nabokov makes art do.

'All that now, independently of the fear of violence and punishment, makes the social life of man possible (and already this is an enormous part of the order of our lives)—all this has been brought about by art. If by art it has been inculcated upon people how they should treat religious objects, their parents, their children, their wives, their relations, strangers, foreigners; how to conduct themselves towards their elders, their superiors, towards those who suffer, towards their enemies, and towards animals; and if this has been obeyed through generations by millions of people, not only unenforced by any violence but so that the force of such customs can be shaken in no way but by means of art: then by art also other customs more in accord with the religious perceptions of our time may be evoked.'

This is the task Tolstoy assigned to the art of the future, and though his phrasing there is too moralistic to serve as a direct imperative to imaginative writers, still even Western literature since Tolstoy's time has contributed to that task in its own way and to some degree. A case like Lawrence's needs no arguing, but even Joyce's *Ulysses* offers us, in the figure of Bloom, a representation of 'our fellow man' and 'our common humanity' brought before us with a most loving intelligence and a most intelligent love. Nabokov stands, in the group of significant Western writers, fairly far out in the direction of freedom from all cultural-moral imperatives, in the direction of rejecting that task.

At the same time, when we compare that group as a whole with the equivalent group of Soviet writers, or with nineteenth-century writers, we see that that direction is what has characterized modern Western literature. So that Nabokov, from this point of view, may be said to represent all our writers, and his case has a representative significance. The Soviet writers have on the whole obeyed Tolstoy's prescriptions, and followed his view of the social function of art, and of aesthetics as a whole. Soviet literature is Tolstoy's 'art of the future'. Our literature is definitely not—is closer to being that development of upper-class exclusive art which he deplored—and though we may on the whole congratulate ourselves on the difference, still some kinds of uneasiness persist, and are likely to be most acute when we are reading *Lolita. Is* this not after all an immoral book—for the way it flouts all cultural responsibility, not merely sexual decency? *Is* it not in fact the product of a corrupt culture—unbelieving, pleasure-seeking, beauty-worshipping? Is not Tolstoy ultimately right, at least about *Lolita* and everything like it?

Before attempting a moral defence of the book we should perhaps try to formulate the charge against it more in terms of its own imaginative life. The sexually perverse enterprises of the main character are made funny, beautiful, pathetic, romantic, tragic; in five or six ways we are made to sympathize with him in them. Above all they are made impressive. When the poem begins, 'Wanted, wanted, Dolores Haze', the pun in the first word has a great deal of power in it, for to want someone, in that sense, is a major fact, even an achievement, in modern literature, in modern culture. Sexual love is a major mythical form of human relationship, and all its pains and pleasures are taken seriously. Moreover, our novels are full of figures who are not able to want each other, or not able to want her or him fully—wanting is an achievement not to be taken for granted. Humbert, we are convinced, does want Lolita fully; he does love her. It is a perverse love, but it is love, and so is to be sympathized with. The novel thus breaks down one of our most intimate and powerful taboos. And the perversity involves Humbert necessarily in other kinds of immoral behaviour —his manipulative marriages, for instance, and his cruel abduction of the child—with which again we are made to sympathize, to participate imaginatively, against our whole moral heritage.

But the sexual perversity gets its full flavour in the book from being type and symbol of a more general perversity; a rebellion against all morality. This rebellion is not harsh or loud; it is humorous, ironic, nonchalant, like most of Humbert's general attitudes; but it is profound. His habitual scepticism about all ordinary moral affirmations is ingrained in the prose. Such prose cannot be made to express affirmations. What it does express, and more naturally, more vividly, more consummately than anyone else's prose, is immoralism.

'I remember once handling an automatic belonging to a fellow student, in the days (I have not spoken of them, I think, but never mind) when I toyed with the idea of enjoying his little sister, a most diaphanous nymphet with a black hair bow, and then shooting myself. I now wondered if Valechka (as the colonel called her) was really worth shooting, or strangling, or drowning. She had very vulnerable legs, and I decided I would limit myself to hurting her very horribly as soon as we were alone.'

It is the gaiety and the nonchalance as much as the substance of the statement which affront our moral sensibility. And the fact that this was a *friend's* sister he thought of 'enjoying', and the friend's gun with which he would then shoot himself, shows the ingenuity with which Humbert's mind works out such affronts.

Then his actual treatment of Valeria, and later of Charlotte, is both cruel in itself and callously indifferent to our response. His sensibility as a whole is inspired by feelings of exasperation and offence taken at life and revenge desired. Take for instance the very funny description of the night noises in the Enchanted Hunters hotel, Chapter 29, Part 1. The humour of this derives from an experience of acute exasperation, and one which fits into a habit of exasperation, one which gives the keynote to a whole range of feelings. Much of the motel-name humour is quite serenely and freely playful, but most of Humbert's wit derives from an impatience so sharp it has cut itself off from all sympathy with its object. This is the essence of the cruelty we feel in him towards Valeria and Charlotte. This expresses itself again in his feud with psychiatrists, in his gratuitous insults to Dr Quilty and Mrs Chatfield at the end of the book, and in his final driving down the wrong side of the road. Of the impulse to do this, he tells us, 'In a way, it was a very spiritual itch.' And indeed behind this impatience, this self-insulation, this radical alienation, does lie something spiritual; a whole sense of himself as a changeling, in disguise, not fully human. He speaks often of his adult male disguise, but it is also a matter of his foreignness, of his other languages, of his hidden history. Nobody knows him as he really is. Of course, we must not make too much of this. Nabokov has made practically nothing. But Humbert clearly is an outsider in the fullest sense, and his sexual perversity is not an unfortunate accident. It is both the root and the emblem of his whole personality. We are being asked to make a hero out of someone in full-scale rebellion against whole systems of our moral inheritance.

And finally, the tone and form of the novel, while they win our sympathy for Humbert, prevent that sympathy from following any conventional outlines of pity and understanding. The wit is insolent, the mockery is triumphant, and Humbert's irony is everywhere in the book. There is no vantage point from which to see beyond and around him. He has been beforehand with us in every tone to take about him. We are forced to succumb to his way of seeing himself and talking about himself.

We do all this at considerable cost to our self-respect, considerable moral mortification if not debilitation, and if all we get in return is a series of very funny incidents and passages of very beautiful writing, then we are likely to react with an unconscious resistance which will cramp the roots of that initial response. We should then be left, as many readers are who are not conscious of having made a moral judgment, with an experience of a clever and amusing novel which we can relegate without trouble to an unimportant literary category. If that is not to happen, we must find a powerful, and (since so well hidden) a quite elaborate moral strategy within the novel.

That strategy can I think be described as a series of concessions, a self-criticism, a self-defence, and a moral theory of art. The major concession is making Lolita sexually experienced before she meets Humbert, and having her seduce him. This is of course right for the novel in several ways, but one most important way is as a concession to the reader's outraged sensibility, an easing of his act of sympathy with Humbert. Let Lolita be entirely innocent, and our feelings about the story would be very different. There are other concessions of the same kind, but let us pass immediately to another kind. In that disturbing episode of

Valeria's confession, and particularly the callous cruelty of Humbert's response, the narration enacts a comic criticism of him. It comments on his vanity; it exaggerates his complacency; it mocks his sense of superiority and security. In effect, we *are* here given a point of vantage from which to see beyond and around Humbert, we are allowed some relief from the effort of identifying ourselves with him. And there are other examples of this kind of concession, too.

But the problem, the challenge, is merely shaped by these concessions. Its resolution is a matter of the self-criticism, the self-defence, and the theory of art. Humbert criticizes himself, indeed hates himself, with an intensity which may perhaps escape our attention at first reading. Its expression is most often unobtrusively placed in the narrative; as for instance in the phrase 'and my putrefaction' in the quoted sentence beginning, 'Unless it can be proven to me,'; or as in this, 'But instead I am lanky, big-boned, woolly-chested Humbert Humbert, with thick black eyebrows and a queer accent, and a cesspoolful of rotting monsters behind his slow boyish smile.' This unobtrusiveness becomes all the more telling as a mode of expression when such remarks are put together with that self-alienation discussed before—note '*his* slow boyish smile'—that poisoning of Humbert's sense of himself. And the counterpart to this is the overwhelming emotionalism, the desire to drown all consciousness in tears, which wells up from time to time. 'Oh let me be mawkish for the nonce! I am so tired of being cynical.' This is most overt at key moments, like the end of Part I, 'At the hotel we had separate rooms, but in the middle of the night she came sobbing into mine, and we made it up very gently. You see, she had absolutely nowhere else to go.' But this note too recurs unobtrusively and obliquely throughout. In the middle of the gay description of the motels, we find, 'And sometimes trains would cry in the monstrously hot and humid night with heartrending and ominous plangency, mingling power and hysteria in one desperate scream.' *Lolita* remains a comic novel, but within the conventions of comedy Humbert is placed for us quite unequivocally, and with a strong sense of horror as well as pity. This horror is what is worked out in terms of plot and characterization by that splitting off of Quilty from Humbert discussed before, and by the killing of Quilty.

But that self-criticism, however unequivocal, is still not satisfyingly prominent in the novel. It is not in any sense the point of the characterization. More important than that is what I have called the self-defence, which is really an involvement of the reader with the hero, a binding together of the two. Humbert Humbert is our protagonist, and we are unable to dissociate ourselves from him self-righteously, because he represents a part of ourselves we are normally proud of. What he represents is amongst other things our intelligence. Humbert is one of the cleverest of novel heroes. His wit is brilliant, his observation ranges over everything, his taste is marvellously alive. When he does so callously make fun of Charlotte and Valeria, he carries us with him intellectually. We feel that they are funny, not just that he is being funny about them, even though we protest that we don't want to laugh. He is ourselves, without our inhibitions, acting out our tendencies. But if so, then we cannot take the moral problems raised lightly; we are bound to undergo them painfully; to the extent that we are identified with Humbert, *Lolita* is a serious novel.

And he is even more importantly our protagonist in the matter of love. As we said before, Humbert does manage to love Lolita, and this is a powerful claim on our respect. He knows her completely, and he loves her completely, sensually and sentimentally and for herself, all at the same time. And he does so in that tradition of romantic love which is so important in our culture. Humbert loves Lolita, he says, in the way that Dante loved Beatrice, the way Petrarch loved Laura, the way Poe loved Virginia, the way Don Jose loved Carmen. The references to these great tragic idealistic love affairs run through the novel and challenge us to deny that Humbert's feelings belong to the same family and deserve the same respect.

Here he remembers his excitement at seeing (he mistakenly thought) a nymphet undressing at an opposite window:

'There was in the fiery phantasm a perfection which made my wild delight also perfect, just because the vision was out of reach, with no possibility of attainment to spoil it by the awareness of an appended taboo; indeed, it may well be that the very attraction immaturity has for me lies not so much in the limpidity of pure young forbidden fairy child beauty as in the security of a situation where infinite perfections fill the gap between the little given and the great promised—the great rosegray never-to-be-had.'

This is, despite the irony of the occasion, one of the great minor chords in the symphony of romantic love; and the great major chord is this.

'She was only the faint violet whiff and dead leaf echo of the nymphet I had rolled myself upon with such cries in the past; an echo on the brink of a russet ravine, with a far wood under a white sky, and brown leaves choking the brook, and one last cricket in the crisp weeds . . . but thank God it was not that echo alone that I worshipped. What I used to pamper among the twisted vines of my heart, *mon grand péché radieux*, had dwindled to its essence: sterile and selfish vice, all *that* I canceled and cursed. You may jeer at me, and threaten to clear the court, but until I am gagged and half-throttled, I will shout my poor truth. I insist the world know how much I loved my Lolita, *this* Lolita, pale and polluted, and big with another's child, but still gray-eyed, still sooty-lashed, still auburn and almond, still Carmencita, still mine; *Changeons de vie, ma Carmen, allons vivre quelque part où nous ne serons jamais séparés*; Ohio? The wilds of Massachusetts? No matter, even if those eyes of hers would fade to myopic fish, and her nipples swell and crack, and her lovely young velvety delicate delta be tainted and torn—even then I would go mad with tenderness at the mere sight of your dear wan face, at the mere sound of your raucous young voice, my Lolita.'

In Humbert's most Mannerist manner—hectic, writhing, self-falsifying, self-caricaturing—this is still sincerity, and faced with this, the reader dare not dissociate himself from Humbert in simple condemnation. With all we now believe and feel about sexuality and self-responsibility, no one can call Humbert's perversity a more significant moral fact than his ability to love. And neither can the reader dissociate himself from the experience in simple titillation or appreciation of the comedy and the fine writing. Nabokov has taken the tradition of romantic fiction, and carried it forward into its next stage; if Carmen, why not Lolita? Whatever answer we make, that is a serious question, and Nabokov has put it to us seriously.

The moral theory I mean is an application of the doctrine of the immortality of art, discussed before. Art can confer immortality, of a consciously limited and conditional kind, by 'singing' its subject, 'celebrating' the experience it describes, however painful or ignoble that may be. This is, however little, the most that man can do to assert his values in the face of life's indifference, and therefore art is glorious, in all its artificiality and trickery. The artist is a kind of hero. Humbert killed Quilty because, 'One had to choose between him and H.H., and one wanted H.H. to exist at least a couple of months longer, so as to have him make you live in the minds of later generations.' And what Humbert wrote *is* the local and melancholy palliative of art, a palliative to his misery, and a reparation to her memory, because it is an immortalizing tribute to their experience. This describes and accounts for the novel as a whole, texture and structure. It could be read by Lolita as his tribute to her and to the events of their relationship. Its tone is true to their tone to each other in the reported conversations and encounters. It does confer upon her the immortality of art, and it is the kind of art—as distinct from the kind of *Madame Bovary* or even *Anna Karenina*—which could be felt as a tribute. And the melancholy and the inadequacy of the reparation are fully acknowledged by—are a part of—the novel.

But *Lolita* was written by Nabokov, not by Humbert, and it is a tribute to more than its heroine. The palliative Nabokov offers us is on a larger scale, though of exactly the same kind, as what Humbert intended. It is a tribute—in the same sense, of a garland of mingled pain and delight, intricately woven—to America. This is not only a matter of the overt hymning of the American landscape, or the affectionate satire of the motels, the cars, the highways, the curiosities, etc. It is also a matter of characterization, and thematic characterization. Lolita herself is a part of America. She and her mother, and their relations with each other, and with their friends, and the house and the town they live in, are vividly American figures, in a vivid sketch of American life, the interest of which is quite independent of Humbert's personal drama. They are also thematically related to previous characterizations, those of Annabel and Valeria, in the way that America as a whole is related to Europe.

This relationship is a development towards realism, a mixed, part painful, part ignominious understanding of life, away from the romantic, the pastoral, the idyllic understanding associated with Europe. The idea of this development is made explicit in several places comparing Lolita with Annabel. It is *implicit* in the tawdry, comic, fake seaside scene in which Humbert first sees Lolita, compared with the real (but so much more simple and 'romantic') seaside in which he had known Annabel. It is implicit again here:

'What drives me insane is the twofold nature of the nymphet—of every nymphet, perhaps; this mixture in my Lolita of tender dreamy childishness and a kind of eerie vulgarity, stemming from the snub-nosed cuteness of ads and magazine pictures, from the blurry pinkness of adolescent maidservants in the Old Country (smelling of crushed daisies and sweat); and from very young harlots disguised as children in provincial brothels; and then again, all this gets mixed up with the exquisite stainless tenderness seeping through the musk and the mud, through the dirt and the death, oh God, oh God.'

He could not have said that about Annabel, and yet he needed to say it, for the full development of his complicated moral and aesthetic harmonies. Not only Lolita herself, but the Lolita experience, is 'American', part beauty, part absurdity, part horror. That mixture of the dreamily childish with the eerily vulgar is what Humbert finds everywhere in America, and the substitution of that mixture for the idyllic simplicities of Europe is the major process of development for the novel. It is the condition of fulfilment of all Nabokov's potentialities as an artist.

The development from Valeria to Charlotte is primarily in substantiality:

'Had Charlotte been Valeria, I would have known how to handle the situation; and "handle" is the word I want. In the good old days, by merely twisting fat Valeria's brittle wrist (the one she had fallen upon from a bicycle) I could make her change her mind instantly; but anything of the sort in regard to Charlotte was unthinkable. Bland American Charlotte frightened me.'

Charlotte is altogether a larger figure in the book, and Humbert is constantly brought up against reality in her. And in her case as in Lolita's her substantiality is a matter of her Americanness. Annabel and Valeria are creatures of pastoral fantasy, in comparison; they fit completely into Humbert's dreams. Lolita and Charlotte continually upset, offend, elude, resist him and his dreams. They, and all America, are reality; though finding reality does not mean, for Nabokov, renouncing romance, but combining that with its opposite, in a stable counterpoint of the idyllic with the grotesque.

Indeed, Humbert himself stands in the same relation to his father as Lolita to Annabel, as Charlotte to Valeria, as America to Europe. His father's debonair and selfish sensuality was able to gratify itself all his life long in an atmosphere of universal admiration and fondness, general gaiety and wit, discriminating elegance and luxury. His father and two grandfathers had sold wine, jewels, and silk; Humbert's uncle sold perfumes; his English grandfathers had amusing scholarly hobbies. Humbert obviously destined himself to a similar career—to be a more intellectual version of his father—but life played the hideous trick of perversity upon him. The grotesque had to be interwoven with the idyllic. The beautiful Hotel Mirana was changed for a series of American motels. The point of the book is that the motels are more interesting, more vivid, more fully alive, than the Mirana; that they, Lolita, America, are embraced in full recognition of their differentness from Europe, their differentness from everything idyllic or even respectable, but in full enthusiastic appreciation. And since they represent more of life, as Nabokov sees life, it is life as a whole that is embraced. Thus the book is a tribute to America, and to human experience, in a way that expands without altering its function as a tribute to Lolita. And the immortality art can confer is thus a larger thing than the formula suggests, a thing closer to Lawrence's and Tolstoy's aims in art, since it is life itself that is immortalized.

We have already discussed the way in which the novel is 'about' romantic love. Let us just say now that this theme—related obviously enough to those just discussed—is developed and resolved according to the pattern of the novel. That is, the major instance of love taken (the American instance, the Lolita instance) is very painful, ugly, unassimilable to romance, it is explicitly contrasted with the minor perfect instance, and then described in insolent and brutal detail; but the total picture created is of a necessary interaction of very beautiful moments with very ugly ones. It is a development from idyllic romanticism to realistic romanticism, by means of interweaving the grotesque with the idealized in a convincing pattern.

It is only in this sense that I can understand Nabokov's sentence about aesthetic bliss. The novel gives us the sensation of being connected with other states of being where art is the norm; and art he either identifies with or groups with curiosity, tenderness, kindness, ecstasy. *Lolita* obviously creates moments for us—we need not specify them now—in which curiosity, tenderness, ecstasy, beauty, art itself, are radiantly realized, and it creates a world within which we can rely on such moments recurring. But to justify a man in entering such a mental world, he needs to be sure that it is 'realistic'—that it has taken adequate account of the ugliness of actual experience, and of the human impulse merely to make up such pretty dreams, merely to make itself see roses and hear violins. So *Lolita* must contain also moments of ugliness and pain as bitter and burning as any Nabokov could devise. And it must be infinitely sceptical about its own search for beauty, infinitely ironic about every mode of romanticism and idyll. Moreover these anti-romantic modes of the imagination must be allowed to interpenetrate the romantic. Hence all the pornographic-seeming detail of the orgasm on the couch, so ugly and shocking as well as so brilliant and gay. Hence too all the trickery, all the warning against believing the narrator, against any unguarded response, throughout the novel. Only by giving full free play to both these anti-romantic tendencies, and by building a world that will contain them too, can the author justify those moments of perfect beauty and win for himself 'aesthetic bliss'.

This is the moral structure of *Lolita*, and it surely is strong enough to support and contain the anti-moral material the novel allows itself. A novel is not pornographic (except in the sense that it can be used as pornography) when its interest in sexual excitement is a necessary part of such large and serious interests. It is not anti-cultural when its cynicism (Humbert's cynicism) dramatizes an alienation which is so movingly, though unobtrusively, placed and judged.

But none of this contradicts Tolstoy's assumed condemnation of the novel. All we have been saying is true only from a point of view completely sympathetic with the author, a view taken from a point, so to speak, inside the novel. This is the perfect reading of the novel, and novels do not exist only in that form. Culturally speaking, they exist much more in the form of imperfect readings—as understood from outside the novel, in very imperfect sympathy with the author's intentions. *Lolita can* be used as pornography; in fact it will be, and almost must be, and by highly trained readers as well as by the untrained. It will also have, in its measure, an anti-cultural effect of weakening taboos and fostering cynicism, etc. There is something powerfully disintegrative in Nabokov's sensibility, and though the novel's form contains and transmutes that something, the total effect of reading it—even on highly trained readers—is not likely to be controlled by the form. *Lolita is* in fact the product and the agent of a corrupt culture.

If then we, like Tolstoy, were ready to judge art primarily by cultural criteria, we could, and would have to, condemn *Lolita.* Tolstoy followed Plato, and said better no art than bad art, which means better aesthetically bad art than morally bad. But we, presumably, are committed to using primarily aesthetic criteria, and to preferring aesthetically good art. We are committed to judging a novel primarily on its perfect reading, seeing it in perfect sympathy with the author's intentions, understanding it from inside; however rare, in cultural fact, such a reading may be; however little that reading may coincide with the book's effective meaning; however 'exclusive', to use Tolstoy's term, the audience for that version of the book.

This obligation on the critic is a necessary correlative of the freedom of the artist, and we of the liberal tradition are pre-sumably committed to that freedom. Nabokov is a fine example of the free artist, and a fine symbol of what we are committed to. He is free first in the sense of refusing all allegiance to non-aesthetic schemes of value, and aggressively, positively refusing, as well as negatively; he affronts and injures those schemes of value; he is not only non-ideological, he is anti-ideological. And this freedom he so fully takes necessitates the other freedom we were discussing—his claim, his right, to be judged only from inside the special world he has created. His justification of those freedoms, and what they cost us, in affronts and injuries to our personal and collective sensibilities, is the novel itself. Given its perfect reading, *Lolita* is a brilliant and beautiful experience, satisfying our most purely moral sense as well as all the others. What is there in Tolstoy's 'art of the future', Soviet literature, that can compare with it? But that comparison is not the point. It is the contrast, within our own case, between what we gain and what we lose, by our effective philosophy of art, which seems to me so interesting.

More exactly, what interested me so much in *Lolita* was—for the purposes of this book—the way it stretches and punishes as well as rewards the sympathies of a reader like me. While on the one hand he must allow such a brilliant writer his reckless assaults on decency, he must on the other feel uneasy, resentful, even ashamed by his own readiness to co-operate with him, his own readiness to play that destructive and degrading game with him. Being a literary man today means being ready to betray—and of course to enjoy betraying—some of one's most serious loyalties.

There is a sense in which being a *writer* today (one who aims high) means being ready to become a monster—to identify oneself with one's unhealth and not with one's health. One must be ready to write about —and that means to live in—one's perversities, one's hatreds, one's disgusts, one's neuroses, one's psychoses. The self-respecting man acknowledges those facts about himself, but he does not identify himself with them; his self is his healthiness, however unexciting, doughy, basely alloyed, that may be, and his unhealthiness is merely the alloy, a private and accidental defect, which debases and diminishes that self. But the modern writer has to explore some area of his self which involves pungent and reckless truth-telling, and unless, like Tolstoy and Lawrence, he is gifted with extraordinary powers of health, he must, like most of the other interesting writers, explore his disease—there is nothing equally risky to be said about his health. (I need not say that neither Tolstoy nor Lawrence were simply or perfectly healthy; far from it; but their diseases are ignorable, as nobody else's are, because they could manifest their genius in the other way.) Whether the writer becomes a monster in his everyday life also is something that depends on other factors in his personality, and therefore varies according to cases. What is constant is that in his self as writer—however that may manifest itself—he must be ready to ignore those rules of moderation and decency, of measure and shapeliness, of modesty and due limit, which normal people impose on themselves.

As a humanist, I feel strongly attracted to the idea that a man ought never to make himself a monster, even if the reward of writing a brilliant novel awaits him. This is not an idea one finds expressed often among literary people—naturally enough—but Gorky gives voice to it in a letter to Andreyev. It is no accident that Gorky belonged to that movement in Russian literature most opposed to the one from which Nabokov derived. This is a classic confrontation.

Gorky wrote, 'It is nobody's business what is hurting me, if anything hurts. To display one's scratches to the world, to rub them in public and let the pus run over oneself, to squirt one's bile into other people's eyes, as many do, and most disgustingly of all, our cruel genius Feodor Dostoevsky used to do—that is an odious business and harmful, of course.' The choice for the writers of a given culture, to agree with

Gorky here, or to disagree, is a crucial one for the literature of that culture. Upon it depends the character of what gets written—perhaps even the selection of who writes. How much would Tennessee Williams have written, if he had felt that it was nobody's business what was hurting him?

Gorky continues, 'All of us will die, the world will go on living; it has shown me and fastened on to me much dirt and meanness, but I do not want and will not adopt its abominations. I take, and have taken, what is good in the world, I have no reason to revenge myself on it, no reason to poison men with the shameful spectacle of my wounds and ulcers, to deafen them with my squealing.

' "Brotherhood" most certainly does not consist in showing one's brother one's inward nastiness and filth—but if one can't destroy it, at least in keeping tactfully quiet about it.'

The idea that a writer should ever have a duty to keep quiet about anything, especially anything ugly or shameful, is something so fresh in our literary climate that I feel again—as so often—that all the people with whom one wants to argue about literature are in Russia. Surely there is a great deal of truth in what Gorky says, of health in what he feels? Certainly I disagree with the Western scholar who, after quoting that letter, comments that art revenged itself on Gorky for 'scorning that self-knowledge through which alone one man may gain understanding of others'. The point at issue is not self-knowledge but self-display, or at best a literary *presentation* of the act of self-knowledge—one can very easily have one without the other. Besides, 'understanding of others' is of many kinds, not all of which are arrived at through a self-knowing which amounts to knowing one's diseases (even when that self-knowledge is dissociated from literary presentation).

And yet I must admit that Gorky's work *does* often fail through artistic insincerity, and this *is* related to his insufficient concern with personal and private truth as opposed to public and responsible truth. I still face, that is, a conflict in loyalties. Nabokov is a much greater artist than Gorky, and a humanist must therefore respond to him more, let him into the secret places of his mind, however much that goes against his grain. Tolstoy's theory of literature is as extremist in the opposite direction, as Ellman's is, and ultimately just as unacceptable. It would destroy the freedom the best literature needs. We have to allow literature to produce—that is, we have to learn to respond to—the most lurid of images, the most destructive of meanings.

The solution for a humanist—or at least the solution I have so far arrived at—is to keep open access to other sources of imaginative life besides art. Not to admit the pretensions of modern art to be an ultimate authority in all fields of the imaginative life, and to foster the quite different stimulations of modern science, and of religion as that is mediated to us by von Hügel. By so doing, one draws on a supply of other images of life and value, far different from those images of purely 'bodily' life in which modern art is pre-eminent. One keeps a greater imaginative respect for even Karenin, that embodiment of abstract system. One can respond to *Mansfield Park,* so challengingly on the side of system, and not on the side of (bodily) life. One can see the work of Descartes, St Thomas, all the great system-builders, as something more than mere dry insect cumulativeness, mere scuttling scarab dung-rolling, a mere by-product of any healthy human life monstrously magnified into an overweening rival to that life itself, a toppling structure threatening the future of mankind. Perhaps no one thinks quite that, of Descartes or of atomic physics. Perhaps everyone, except the obviously sick, draws on other sources of imaginative life beside the arts, consciously or unconsciously. The humanist differs from other people in that he *acknowledges* science, etc., as imaginative, as similar in function to the arts themselves. And within the field of the arts, he looks for other things besides the 'life' created. He turns with special receptivity to authors who serve other interests, even though with less brilliant success than Nabokov achieves in the service of art. He turns with that receptivity to Gorky and his successors in Russia today.

Throughout Soviet literature, including the most recent, one finds evidence of a similar scrupulousness and niceness of mind about the writer's calling, a humanist moderateness and normality. Paustovsky, one of the most immediately engaging of modern writers, tells us in his autobiography how his youthful aestheticism was modified into something broader, how his narrow faith in his own generation of aesthetes and intellectuals—whom he thought 'would reshape the world'—was replaced by a growing awareness of 'the people'. 'It was a sense of truth which could not be charmed away by music and poetry, however beautiful, nor obscured by the fog of Bergsonian philosophy, fashionable at the time. I felt it everywhere, as inescapable as a fixed, expectant regard.' The generation he refers to—a generation of 'restless dreamers and idealists'—is of course the Symbolist generation from which both Nabokov and Pasternak derive; a Symbolism essentially like that from which, through Yeats and others, our own literary climate of ideas derives. And it is just because Russian writers on the whole reacted away from 'my generation' to 'the people', and Western writers on the whole did not, that the two literatures are in such opposite predicaments today. I dare say it is arguable that Paustovsky would have become a more exciting writer if he had kept his faith in music and poetry, and dodged the fixed inescapable regard of the people. But in that case he would almost certainly have become something of a monster—quite certainly a less engaging personality.

Even Evtushenko expresses a strangely modest idea to our eyes of his own rôle as poet. The poet, he says, is the mouthpiece of others. 'I know that there are people who enrich society by their original ideas, which society uses as weapons in its struggle. Theirs is perhaps the highest form of creativity, but I am not of their number.

'The new thoughts I express in my poetry were there in Soviet society before I began to write, they had only not been expressed in verse. Someone else would have put them into poetry if I hadn't.'

At the same time, this modesty about the poet's function goes with a claim for it prouder in another way than our poets would make. 'To a Russian the word "poet" has the resonance of the word "fighter". Russia's poets were always fighters for the future of their country and for justice.' He refers to Nekrassov, Mayakovsky, and even Blok, in support of this argument, and obviously his society supplies him with a full tradition of ideas about literature's social place.

Of course one cannot rear much of an argument on the base of such remarks as those of Evtushenko, and perhaps those of Paustovsky just as much; which are all too obviously the pietisms of their society, not particularly reminted or regenerated by their utterers. And of course the ugly side of the Soviet handling of literature is important too, though I can't imagine many readers of a book like this who are likely to forget that. Even the dreary side—the party polemics against Joyce and Proust —is surely self-condemnatory. The humanism I have been describing has no sympathy with the political proscription of great writers, how-ever much it demands the right—for political reasons among others— to argue with them, quarrel with them, even condemn them, while appreciating, admiring, responding. Even Tolstoy's position in *What is Art?* is not acceptable to a humanist. It is an extreme case of that moral-cultural approach which (in its extreme cases) is just as far from humanism as aestheticism is, though in the opposite direction. While one is surrounded by Symbolists and semi-Symbolists, one turns to *What is Art?* with respect as well as relief. If one were ever surrounded by Tolstoyans, one would perhaps turn to *Studies in the Renaissance* with those feelings.

But in fact the atmosphere in which we live is dominated by plati-tudes opposite to but as dead as those of Paustovsky and Evtushenko, and it is an atmosphere in which we choke. The attitude of Western literary men to, for instance, the question of censorship, and all control of literature, is so often hysterically defensive. Even among scholars of Russian literature and society one must expect to find this kind of thing. 'Utility as a criterion of artistic value is not unknown, of course, in other societies, including our own. . . . When Flaubert is dragged into court by the French police, when books are banned in Jersey City or Boston, when Pushkin's work is put under the surveillance of the Tsar, when Dickens reports the enormous pressure on him of Victorian expectations, we are in the presence of the police sergeant's fear of literature as a profound disturber of the peace.'

Thus Rufus W. Mathewson, Jr, in *The Positive Hero in Russian*

Literature. Obviously this statement will not stand up to even the gentlest scrutiny. The Dickens example has very little to do with the police sergeant's fear of literature. And the items so loosely jumbled together and so loudly cursed are too disparate to prove anything except muddle in the writer's mind. If Evtushenko's remarks are the pietisms of a Communist, cultural, literary theory, Mathewson's are those of our, Symbolist, theory, and of the two I prefer the first. Those sentences are typical examples of the moral and social childishness one is likely to stumble across anywhere in our literary world, masquerading as devotion to literature. Without making the Soviet theory into a cultural model—and there is surely no danger of that—we have a great deal to learn from it. Without making Sholokhov our example of what the great novelist should be—he is not even in the first rank of novel-writers—we must learn to give him some parity of esteem and attention with, say, Pasternak.

Sholokhov and the Russian cultural tradition

Many Russians said that Sholokhov should have got the Nobel Prize in 1958, when it was given to Pasternak. Some of them probably said this to cover their indignation at Pasternak's getting it, an indignation which had an uglier emotional character than they wished to let appear, but others were equally probably sincere. A man sensitive to literature certainly *could* think Sholokhov just as remarkable a talent. And he obviously *was* the novelist Russia herself had judged to be her greatest, and obviously had written the same kind of novel as *Doctor Zhivago*—a long chronicle tragedy of the Revolution and the Civil War. To give the international award to Pasternak immediately his novel appeared, and to continue to ignore *The Quiet Don*, the first volume of which was published thirty years before, could have seemed a calculated insult. It must have seemed to many a political manœuvre, or at the least a political distortion of aesthetic judgment—the West was finding *Doctor Zhivago* aesthetically impressive because it was politically 'liberal'.

In fact, of course, the enthusiasm in the West was perfectly sincere, even though politically opportune. This was one of the rare occasions on which aesthetic judgment spontaneously coincided with diplomatic expediency, and literary men could co-operate with politicals in good conscience. And the lack of enthusiasm over Sholokhov's novel and prize is equally sincere. Most Western readers nowadays don't find *The Quiet Don* anything to get excited over; just as most Russian readers are less enthusiastic than we are about *Doctor Zhivago*. (For obvious reasons, this last judgment is based on very little evidence. Almost the only extended Russian discussion of the novel occurs in the letter from *Novy Mir* refusing to publish it. But, however political the disapproval of *Novy Mir*'s editors may have been, one cannot feel, reading their letter to Pasternak, that they were suppressing any aesthetic enthusiasm for the novel.) In both cases, it is admitted that the writer has great talent, and that the book is a major undertaking, in size and depth, a major slice of its author's life. But the novel is found to be not really satisfying, not really exciting or impressive. This is an aesthetic, not a political response, but aesthetics are of course a cultural matter. Sholokhov's novel derives from and expresses a whole set of ideas about the relations between literature and society, a whole tradition of cultural thought. And because Western literature today is dominated by the rival tradition, the Symbolist tradition, we find even our scholars of Russian studies unsympathetic to his work. We find one of them, for instance, saying that *The Quiet Don* is the best Soviet novel about the Civil War, but,

'To be sure, as an exemplar of the best in this respect one may prefer *Doctor Zhivago*, which is also concerned with the struggle between old and new in war and civil war and is likewise written in the tradition of nineteenth-century Russian realism, although Pasternak has brought to it his own increment of originality. Pasternak's masterpiece, however, though steeped in the tragedy of Soviet life, is really devoid of the typicalness of Soviet literature, for it rises above the battle into the clear air of universal art.'[1]

This is surely an illusion. *Doctor Zhivago* does not rise above the political-historical battle—it takes its stand clearly enough. And in the cultural-literary battle it crosses over to the other side, *our* side, which naturally seems to *us* like 'universal art' and 'clear air', but is in fact Symbolist or semi-Symbolist art.

Moreover, *The Quiet Don* is a very considerable achievement, by no means incommensurable with *Doctor Zhivago*. Judging by the consensus of praise for Pasternak's poetry, he was the more gifted man of the two, but neither the tradition of subject and treatment in which he wrote his novel, nor the final product, seem to me so clearly superior. In any case, since that tradition is our tradition, it behooves us to become critical of it—to make some effort of sympathy with the other.

Sholokhov set out to give an accurate, 'historically correct', account of the Cossack rising of 1920–21 and what led up to it; and to instruct as well as to move his readers, by *explaining* this piece of history, naming the rights and wrongs, the heroes and villains, as well as the whys and wherefores, the victims and

[1] Ernest J. Simmons, *Introduction to Russian Realism*, Indiana, 1965.

sufferings. The first part of this programme is not as evident to the readers of the English translation as it is in the original, because a great deal of detail is omitted from the English version. Professor Simmons calculates that about a hundred pages have been omitted; that is, *And Quiet Flows the Don* would have been 850 pages, instead of 750, if the translation had been complete.[1] Some of these omissions are not a matter of detail but of complete episodes—the most important being Timofei's diary—but a good many of those missing pages are accounted for by generalized summaries in the English of what in the Russian is painstakingly particular; names of cities and provinces, generals and colonels, numbers of guns and troops and transport, measurements of distances and provisions, descriptions of the front as a whole, the texts of historical speeches, telegrams, pamphlets, inventories. There are historical figures in *The Quiet Don*, some of whom play sizeable parts, like Podtielkov and Krivoshlikov, but even when they are not on the page, the book presents itself as a true account—in every sense of the word true.

It is that, Sholokhov's intention to encompass also the literal kinds of truth, which is most unfamiliar to our minds, and which places him most firmly in the other tradition—he acknowledges social, economic, and political truths. But his explicative and interpretative, his *literary*, truths, are also in the Soviet tradition. Not so much because of his choice of heroes and villains as because of his manner of presenting them to us, his tone in addressing us. Sholokhov makes it plain that he is addressing not connoisseurs of literature but 'the people', and his figures excite our laughter, our tears, our admiration, our disgust, by broadly obvious gestures and postures. He is attempting to educate his whole nation in much more simple ways than any major Western writer has for a long time thought artistically possible—the ways Tolstoy described in *What Is Art?*

But he is not therefore as crude in his tactics as he is sometimes supposed to be. There is, for instance, and here we must contradict Sholokhov's Marxist as well as Western critics, no 'positive hero' in *The Quiet Don*. This is the phrase Russians use about the exemplary figures (for instance, Rakhmetov in Chernyshevsky's novel, *What Is To Be Done?*) which writers in the revolutionary

---

[1] Throughout this essay I shall be using the paginations and the transliterations of *And Quiet Flows the Don*, London, 1934, translated by Stephen Garry: and *The Don Flows Home to the Sea*, London, 1940.

and Soviet tradition incorporated into their novels. Sholokhov is no submissive conformer to the tradition he has chosen. He has not even a fully representative hero, like Tolstoy's Levin or Lermontov's Pechorin. His Gregor Melekhov is, ideologically, quite strikingly unheroic for a Soviet novel, and even a Russian novel. He is obviously no model of behaviour or thought—he is categorically wrong; and Mishka Koshevoi, who is categoric-ally right, is never put forward as a hero. This is no aesthetic or intellectual muddle in Sholokhov. He distinguishes perfectly clearly between right-and-wrong, historical right-and-wrong, and fictional splendour-and-vitality. Mishka is right, but Gregor is splendid. Nor does this division imply the sort of anguished struggle and defeat in the author's mind which Western readers expect, and which they look for so industriously in Sholokhov. Western writers, having each invented his own scale of right and wrong, as an expression of his deepest feelings, must be seriously troubled when their responses to some particular incident or person violate that scale. But Sholokhov's right and wrong are rooted outside himself, in politics and economics, and a conflict between that and his 'feelings' is not a conflict within himself.

Thus Helen Muchnic seems to me on the wrong track when she tries to show that Mishka is made to triumph in every way in the novel. If we take the two key passages describing the division of Mishka from Gregor, we see that Sholokhov clearly awards the human dignity more to Gregor, and stresses the human cost to Mishka and Ivan—without impugning their rightness. The first of these passages occurs in Chapters 14 and 15 of Part I of *The Don Flows Home to the Sea*, between pages 125 and 135. After Gregor has complained against the Red régime to Mishka and Ivan, and they have argued with him, the section ends like this:

'Mishka and Ivan went off together. Ivan began to tell of his meeting with the district chairman, but when he spoke the colour and significance of it all had faded. He tried to recover his previous buoyant mood, but could not: something stood athwart the road, preventing him from living joyously and breathing in the fresh, frosty air. Gregor and his talk were the obstacle. As he recalled the discussion he said with hatred in his voice:

"Such men as Gregor only get between your legs. The scum! He never reaches the shore and floats along like cow-dung. If he comes again I'll give him one. And if he starts agitating we'll find a quiet little seat for him. What do you think? How are things going, Mishka?"

Mishka turned to him, a smile flickering over his girlish lips:

"What a rotten thing politics is, by the devil! You can talk about whatever else you like, but you won't ever cause so much bad blood. Here's Gregor: we've been friends ever since we went to school together, we ran after the girls together, he was like my own brother to me, and now we begin to talk and I get so wild that my heart comes near to bursting, as though it was a water-melon. It was like he was taking something from me, robbing me! And I could have killed him as we talked. There are no brothers or cousins in this war. You just draw a line, and follow it." Mishka's voice trembled with his unbearable sense of injury. "Not over any girl he'd won from me did I ever get so angry as over his words. That shows you how far we've got!" '

And a few pages later, after several old men of the village have been arrested and—to Ivan's horror—shot, Stockman, the ortho-dox Communist, delivers an angry sermon.

'You "can't make a revolution with the gloves on", as Lenin said. Was it necessary to shoot these men in this case? I think it was. Maybe not all, but certainly Korshunov. That's clear. And there's Gregor Melekhov: he's got away for the time being. We should have caught him in the act. He is more dangerous than all the others taken together. That talk he had with you was the talk of a man who will be an enemy tomorrow. And what we're going through here is nothing. On the fronts the finest sons of the work-ing class are perishing, and in their thousands. We must be sorry for them, and not for those who are killing them or waiting for the opportunity to strike us in the back. And now you see daylight, don't you, Ivan?'

These are the crucial passages for this parting of the ways, divid-ing Gregor from his former friends, and Sholokhov clearly does not make Gregor seem wrong, in human terms. In human terms, it is politics that is to blame. Stockman's argument is a rationalization, and emotionally inadequate, in two or three ways. It justifies the action taken without redeeming it.

And when Mishka and Gregor have their climactic and retrospective long conversation at the end of the action, six hundred pages later, it is Gregor who has all the human dignity and poignancy. He, explicitly, will forget the past (that Mishka killed his brother). Mishka, explicitly, refuses to forget. Mishka declares he would have killed Gregor, too, if he could have caught him. Gregor, truthfully, declares that when *he* heard *Mishka* was in danger, from Gregor's friends, he hurried to save him. Mishka, it is made clear, has had to sacrifice some of his humanity to his cause. This does not mean, as it would do in a Western novelist's character, as it does in Pasternak's Pasha, that Mishka is wrong. On the other hand, he is not wholly right. Sholokhov is more complex than Western critics are willing to to give him credit for. Gregor is wrong, but this is not due to a tragic flaw in his personality which the novel gradually reveals, as Professor Muchnic says. It makes more sense to attribute his weakness, as the Marxist critics do, to his being a 'middle' Cossack, whose class loyalties are fatally confused. But in fact Sholokhov does not need to explain, in any ambitious sense, why Gregor goes wrong politically. He only needs to make us see and feel that he does. Sholokhov does not penetrate that far inside people or events. This is no accusation of his art, but a definition of it.

Sholokhov has combined with his socialist realism other literary elements, which he did not derive from the same aesthetic, but which are part of the folk heritage, elements of legend and epic. His enormous novel is essentially a panorama, in which event follows event partly because factually this is the way it was —the narration of this sequence of events is the purpose and justification of the rest of the novel, not *vice versa*—and partly because each piece of action has the vivid colours of savagery or tenderness or excitement or fun which Sholokhov wants for this part of his panorama. Events do not derive from the people concerned so much as happen to them. Even such an internal force as Gregor and Aksinia's love seems to act on them from outside. Psychologically everyone is simplified down; we may say that everything is soaked in blood, sweat and tears, not to mention the other bodily secretions. (Sweat is Sholokhov's speciality, and it is remarkable how many different kinds he can distinguish.) Nothing is to be understood with dry intelligence. Everything is to be felt. And the narrative voice is epically immediate and yet impersonal, moving easily into lyric apostrophes to the soil, and presenting Pantaleimon's dances of rage, or Chikamasov's insistence that Lenin must be a Cossack, with a confident expectation that all the readers will share the family joke, that the whole circle of listeners is equidistant from the storyteller.

Sholokhov achieves many kinds of epic and legendary beauty, especially in the second half of his novel, where he is much more the master of his method. The death of Aksinia at the end, for instance, has often and rightly been contrasted with the earlier death of Anna Pogoodko, for tact and nobility and power. The death of Ilinichna is also very moving and impressive, and the whole of the end of the novel is beautifully modulated. The passages of natural description, often at the beginning of chapters, express a wealth of exact observation and passionate response, and are often astonishingly beautiful. In the humorous scenes, and the passages of savage brutality, the reader feels the price the writer pays for his disregard of sophisticated response, but there is rarely anything false or bad.

I would call attention to just one of these epic effects, one that is pervasive, and far from simple in the pleasure it gives. I mean the interfusion of a natural setting into the consciousness of someone not primarily attending to it, or into events indifferent to that setting. Let us take the beginning of *The Don Flows Home to the Sea*. In Chapter I, Section 3, Gregor, worried by something his brother has said, is also oppressed by the weather.

'Next day Piotra led half the squadron back towards Vieshenska. The remaining youngsters set out under Gregor's command for Arzemovsk. From early morning the sun baked mercilessly. The steppe seethed in a brown haze. Behind them loomed the blue lines of hills, and sand stretched in a saffron flood. The sweating horses swung along at a walking pace. The cossacks' faces browned and flushed beneath the sun. The saddle-peaks, stirrups and snaffles were so hot that they could not be touched with the bare hand. There was no cool even in the forest: there also hung a steaming vapour and the strong scent of rain.

Gregor was troubled by a dull yearning. All day as he swayed in the saddle he thought disconnectedly of the future. Like the beads of a glass necklace Piotra's words tinkled in his ears. The bitter taste of wormwood burned his lips, the road smoked with the heat. Under the sun the golden-brown steppe extended full length, while arid breezes wandered over it and sent the dust flying.

Towards evening a translucent mist veiled the sun. The sky faded and greyed. In the west clouds gathered mournfully, hanging almost motionless on the fine-spun thread of the horizon. Then, driven before the wind, they floated on menacingly dragging their brown tails irritatingly low, their edges turning a sugary whiteness.'

This dull yearning finds relief in a sexual encounter, as the night coolness relieves the day's sultriness.

'This unknown, childishly naïve soul opened simply to Gregor's eyes, as simply as a little dew-fed flower opens. Gregor was intoxicated, and his pity was aroused. He caressingly stroked the rumpled hair of his new-found friend, and closed his weary eyes.

The fading light of the moon soaked through the reed roof of the shed. A falling star sped violently towards the horizon, leaving a dying phosphorescent trail in the ashen sky. A duck quacked on the pond, and the drake called with an amorous hoarseness.

Gregor went off to the hut, lightly carrying his chilly body, flooded with a delicious ringing weariness. He fell asleep with the salty taste of her lips on his lips, carefully preserving in his memory the cossack woman's yearning body and its scent: a complex scent of herb honey, sweat and warmth.'

We must always remember that Sholokhov may have been much better served by his translators than Pasternak, but a passage like that is attempting something so like passages in *Doctor Zhivago*, that it is difficult not to draw an implicit comparison, and to prefer Sholokhov.

A more conventional example, but extremely beautiful, is the description of Mishka with the horses on the steppe during a thunderstorm; Part I, Chapter 3, Section 2. That is too long to quote effectively, but perhaps this passage from *And Quiet Flows the Don*, page 97, will show how magnificently Sholokhov could command the epic manner even at the beginning of the book, though less consistently and subtly.

'The green, spiked-leaf wheat breaks through the ground and grows; within a few weeks a rook can fly into its midst and not be seen. The corn sucks the juices from the earth and comes to ear, the grain swells with the sweet and scented milk; then it flowers and a golden dust covers the ear. The farmer goes out into the steppe and stands gazing, but cannot rejoice. Wherever he looks a herd of cattle has strayed into the corn; they have trodden the laden grain into the glebe. Wherever they have thronged is a circle of crushed wheat: the farmer grows bitter and savage at the sight.

So with Aksinia. Over her feelings, ripened to golden flower, Gregor had trodden with his heavy, raw-hide boots. He had sullied them, burnt them to ash—and that was all.

As she came back from the Melekhovs' sunflower garden Aksinia's spirit grew empty and wild, like a forgotten farmyard overgrown with goose-grass and scrub. She walked along chewing the ends of her kerchief, and a cry swelled her throat. She entered the hut and fell to the floor, choking with tears, with torment, with the dreary emptiness that lashed through her head. But then it passed. The piercing pain was drawn down and exhausted at the bottom of her heart.

The grain trampled by the cattle stands again. With the dew and the sun the trodden stalks rise; at first bowed like a man under a too heavy burden, then erect, lifting their heads; and the days shine on them and the winds set them swinging.'

Certainly there is a great deal that Sholokhov (no doubt wisely) does not attempt. Moreover, though he seems to understand his limitations well, even *The Quiet Don* occasionally addresses itself to subjects which it cannot encompass. People who cannot be epically distanced and made picturesque, people like Stockman, Mishka and Bunchuk, are not really satisfying characters. If our gaze is allowed to dwell on them long, and especially in their off-duty moments, we become aware of something second-rate— Sholokhov does not have anything first-rate to tell us about them. Bunchuk and Anna Pogoodko, for instance, are embarrassing in their love-speeches to each other, and in their visions of the Communist future. Timofei's diary, which has to present us with an educated consciousness, has nothing of Sholokhov in it. The Listnitskys do not develop, and though Olga seems, on her first appearance, at least visually vivid, even that effect is explained away when her husband commends her to Eugene as 'a woman from Turgenev's pages'. Even within the village of Tatarsky, the Mokhovs seem too rich, too educated, too contemporary and self-conscious, for Sholokhov to handle them freely and vividly.

And if our sense of inclusiveness, of scope, is poorly satisfied in *The Quiet Don*, so is our sense of structure and pattern; and these are surely two of the senses an epic most arouses in us, the appetites it most promises to satisfy. We do not expect to get deeper inside Gregor and Aksinia, with their every reappearance and conjunction, but we do expect some sense of chiming recurrence, or significant variation, some satisfying connection between the various vivid scenes in which they meet. This sense is, it seems to me, but meagrely provided for by Sholokhov. We recognize, of course, general forms like 'a quarrel', 'a parting', 'a reunion', but we don't find, I think, that each parting differs from the preceding one in a formally interesting way.

What holds the novel together is much more the feeling for fact than the feeling for epic form; the feeling for history, the feeling that all this really happened. But this feeling, though one we in the West are not used to see function as a formal principle, does seem to me adequate to the task assigned to it. It does hold the novel together satisfyingly. There is a sense of 'fate', though we really need another word for something so different from what we usually mean by it, engendered by this recital of 'what happened'. Just as there is a moral 'complexity', though it is something calmer than what we usually call complexity, in the distinction between the right and the splendid.

Perhaps the most impressive thing about the novel, from the craft point of view, is the skill with which Sholokhov has united the factual-historical principles of socialist realism, with these epic and legendary principles which roughly coincide with revolutionary romanticism. The first book is almost entirely devoted to describing the Cossack way of life, in picturesque terms. The feeling is not historical but legendary. There is little sense of a particular year, but of recurrent seasons, customs, festivals, seedtime and harvest. The characters are distanced from the reader by their folk ways, their costumes, and games, and songs, and by the primitive simplicity and force of their instinctual life. With the outbreak of the war, the novel becomes in some scenes historical and realistic, but the legendary simplicity of the Cossack characters serves in these scenes to make them represent the historical process. And as the civil war develops, Gregor Melekhov rises to the point of historical significance—as a commander of a division—without losing his legendary anonymity—as just another brave Cossack. His high rank, like his foreign blood, gives him a differentness from those he represents which only makes more vivid his power to represent them.

The Quiet Don is of course the Soviet Government's prime exhibit in the case for socialist realism, and for state socialism in the arts. How much it proves in either argument is not the point here. We should not become so much involved in these arguments that we cannot see for instance the difference between this novel and Sholokhov's other large scale work, translated over here as *Virgin Soil Upturned* and *Harvest on the Don*. The second half of the latter is very inferior, and the first half is only respectable literature-as-propaganda. *The Quiet Don* is perhaps propaganda in some sense, but not in that sense which marks a betrayal of literary values.

We should remind ourselves that although Sholokhov has accepted Communism, and party control of literature, with a completeness that disconcerts us, his career has not been one of submissiveness, nor of artistic consciencelessness. His career in fact shows how much integrity is compatible with great success by a literary man under the Soviet system. His political orthodoxy has not made his literary path easy. Volume I of *The Quiet Don* would have been rejected from publication but for the lucky chance that Serafimovich, a Cossack writer himself, read the manuscript. When it was published, Serafimovich alone among the critics praised it. The second volume was even more severely criticized in Russia. The hero was said to be reactionary and embittered, and the rumour went round literary Moscow that the novel was not written by Sholokhov but by a White Guard officer. When volume 3 was submitted, RAPP (the Russian Association of Proletarian Writers) demanded so many changes before they would publish it that Sholokhov appealed to Gorky to intervene, saying that if he made all the changes required he would have to rewrite three-quarters. Volume 4 did not appear till twelve years after Volume I, and it is commonly supposed that this delay was because of Sholokhov's refusal to make Gregor finally become a Communist. Stalin himself is said to have held up the publication of the last volume two years for this reason.

Even *Virgin Soil Upturned*, so completely a propaganda work for the first Five Year Plan, was rejected by *Novy Mir* as unpublishable without important changes, because of the ugly picture it painted of the dispossession of the kulaks. Again Sholokhov had to appeal, this time to the Central Committee of the Communist Party, before he could get it accepted. And the long delay in the publication of the second volume—nearly thirty years—is believed to have been due to Stalin's ruthlessness against the peasants, and to the misery in which they consequently lived, which made truthful propaganda like the first volume impossible. Thus all six volumes of his two major works had trouble in getting published, or in getting read.

Sholokhov's struggles have been mostly with the literary world, and its bureaucracy, from which he has kept himself at a distance —often attacking the Union of Soviet Writers, for instance. He has been able to appeal to the party and its leaders over the head of the Union. But he is known to have written to Stalin in 1933 in protest against the peasants, just as in 1937 he is known to have protested against the purges, and to have refused to join in official press statements condemning the victims.

He has himself had to yield to party pressure in aesthetic matters. The 1953 edition of *The Quiet Don* included a good many changes; the characters of White generals were further smeared, and Communist leaders were shown more favourably, Lenin and Stalin appeared on the horizon of the novel, the Party and the Red Army were shown winning more applause, the love affair of Anna and Bunchuk was much subdued. But there were also a great many changes in style and narrative order, in the direction of refinement and purification of effect. These changes are said to be at the expense, on the whole, of vitality and picturesqueness. Nevertheless, they are clearly evidence of artistic conscientiousness, and they have been a feature of other new editions of Sholokhov's work.

I am not arguing that Sholokhov is the novelist we have all been waiting for, or even that he deserves more from us than Pasternak does, but that our aesthetic response to him has as clearly been distorted—diminished—for cultural reasons as the Russian response to Pasternak. More exactly, my argument is that in both Russia and the West the cultural bias has become exaggerated and distorted, and the aesthetic sense correspondingly unhealthy and untrustworthy. I don't want to reduce the problem to safe and academic proportions by implying an equality and balance of blame. The social servitude of art in Russia is a grosser and grimmer fact than the aesthetic autarchy and cultural anarchy in the West. But our own failures naturally loom larger in our own eyes, because they are what we are responsible for; I mean the

emotional and moral squalor connected with the arts in the West
—the intellectual decadence and even depravity; and within
literary sensibility itself the worse than average distortions of
taste and limitations of response. Above all, we have been
insidiously persuaded to think of our own aesthetic position
(even when we admit its disadvantages) as profoundly humanist,
and the Communist position as the reverse, whereas the truth is
far from that simple. We have therefore every reason to try to
stand back from ourselves, to understand how we came to be as
we are, to find a point of leverage from which to move ourselves.
The position most obviously outside our own is the Russian, and
the cases of Sholokhov and Pasternak provide a good opportunity for examining that position.

But in order to understand the very striking differences
between the two authors and between the Russian and the
Western responses to them—the quite instinctive and spontaneous attractions and repulsions of the aesthetic sensibility,
which yet turn out to be so predictable and meaningfully opposite
in the two cases—we need to rehearse some of the cultural history
of Russia in the nineteenth and twentieth centuries. This history
is interesting also for its direct relevance to our larger concern. It
presents us with a particularly clear picture of the two alternatives
we always face in devising an aesthetic policy. It offers a paradigm
of our own dilemma; the choice between, to label them crudely,
a 'cultural' and an 'aesthetic' idea of the arts.

To define our terms, by humanism, or by culture,[1] I mean the
practice and study of the arts (and other things) when these are
understood as the expression of serious thought and feeling about
the life of the individual in society. It therefore describes both
an approach to the arts and one kind of artistic product, and the
adjective 'cultural' or 'humanist' has the same scope. Cultural
literary criticism, for instance, is that kind which acknowledges
a responsibility to the life of society—a responsibility on the part
of both the writer and the critic. From certain points of view (as

---

[1] I need two words because I use cultural in both a good and a bad sense. In the good
sense, it means much the same as humanist, and that sense I define above. In the bad
sense, it means a theory of culture which stresses the social origins and ends of art
too much—allows insufficient independence to the artist and to art. The feature that
differentiates humanism from culture (and from its opposite, aestheticism) is its
insistence on allowing full value to all the interests engaged in the cultural enterprise:
its weakness, correspondingly, is that the links it makes between those interests are
often loose and lax.

a rallying slogan, and because culture now means so many other things too) humanism and humanist seem to me preferable terms, and I shall talk most often of a humanist rather than of a cultural idea of literature when I contrast that with the aesthetic idea; the latter allowing the arts much more autonomy, attributing to the artist his own kind of religious and philosophic power, absolving him from all cultural duties that might involve subordination—subordination to the scientist or the moralist or the philosopher. The humanist idea, and the kind of literature it produces, occur where creative artists and critics and thinkers and responsible citizens share a common vocation—to save society— and therefore build a common vocabulary, in order to debate with each other on shared premises of passionate commitment; and the debate may of course be within the individual as well as within a group. This produces an especially substantial kind of literature, and it is this that we in the West have turned away from in recent years.

The ideas covered in the nineteenth century by the English word culture (the equivalent Russian word was perhaps *narodnost*, nationality) had a development and an effectiveness in Russia quite comparable with what they had in England. (In America, on the other hand, they were very much less effective.) This seems to have been most importantly because of the very vigorous interaction of a line of critics with a line of novelists; or at least that interaction was a major manifestation of the ultimate cause, which was a specially energetic coming together of literary and moral ideas. The most important of those critics were Belinsky, Chernyshevsky, and Dobrolyubov, and they demanded from their novelists, Gogol, Turgenev, Tolstoy and Dostoevsky, a more than aesthetic conscientiousness. They demanded that a novelist tell the truth, the saving truth, about and to Russia. At least in the case of Belinsky, it seems clear that this imposition of a social duty did not derive from any meagreness of purely literary response, and in all these critics it was an expression of a high enthusiasm for literature and for life. This idea of nationalist culture, now heavily institutionalized in Russia, is the one to which Sholokhov has affiliated himself.

The great Russian novelists did not simply comply with the critics' demands on them. In one way or another, indeed, they all positively refused to acknowledge the authority behind those demands. But their refusals were not firm or final; after *Fathers*

M

and Sons, Turgenev acknowledged, 'I had no right to give our reactionary riff-raff the opportunity to seize upon a sobriquet [nihilist] . . . the writer in me should have made this sacrifice to the citizen.' After *War and Peace* and *Anna Karenina*, Tolstoy acknowledged that his social and moral responsibilities demanded more than purely aesthetic expression.

In Tolstoy's case it is particularly clear that such a decision did not amount merely to submitting to, say, Chernyshevsky; but it did amount to acknowledging the force of ideas, moral ideas, ideas of the social responsibility of the literary man, which acted in the Russian climate of opinion more fiercely than anywhere else. All these novelists wrote about Russia, about what was wrong with her, and about her would-be saviours in the intelligentsia, with an intensity that English novelists did not achieve for the English equivalent. And they could do so just because those ideas were forced on them, were in the air, kept alive by the critics' indignation and enthusiasm, given shape by the critics' definitions and distinctions. This happened in England to the 'condition of England question'—Carlyle, Mill, Ruskin, etc. making ideas vivid for Dickens, George Eliot, Mrs Gaskell—but there was a passionate centrality in the Russian equivalent, mirrored in the Russian tradition of the novel hero, which English fiction never achieved. English novel heroes of the nineteenth century were never as interesting as Raskolnikov, Levin, Bazarov, or a dozen others.

The Russian tradition of the novel hero goes back before this line of novelists and critics, and continues long after. It is important to our understanding of Pasternak's Zhivago and Sholokhov's Melekhov, and it can be said to have begun with Pushkin and Griboyedov. (Belinsky traced it back as far as Karamzin.) The heroes of *Woe from Wit* and *Evgeny Onegin* are recognizably Romantic figures, recognizably transplanted from the pages of Byron, Goethe, Chateaubriand, Constant; but they are also Russian figures. What these Romantic types mean when they appear in Russian society, and how they relate to older Russian types, are important questions within the books.

But Pushkin, Griboyedov, and Lermontov were perhaps precursors of (rather than participators in) the cultural tradition I am describing, just because they were not confronted by those literary critics who were to form such an important part of it. Their social consciences as artists were freer than those of later writers, and their work is more obliquely related to 'the problems of our day'. They offer no clue to what is to be done about such problems, no simply endorsed solutions or positive heroes. It is the force of quite contradictory emotions expressed in the complex called 'the Romantic hero' which makes Evgeny Onegin a hero of his times. We are drawn both to condemn and to admire him, to sympathize with him and to withdraw from all contact; but all the time we feel that this is 'true'—that a figure like this represents a human potentiality peculiarly significant in this time and place. And in that effect, this Russian Romanticism was already a kind of cultural art, and a very central kind. English novelists did not draw such heroes, and the heroes they did draw—Rochester, Pendennis, Adam Bede—are a pale substitute.

After Lermontov's novel, of 1840, the next we are told belongs to the tradition is Herzen's *Who is to Blame?*, of 1846. And with Herzen we come to that fuller interaction between critic and writer mentioned before, both in his relation with Belinsky and within his own mind, between himself as imaginative artist and himself as thinker. For not only was he a significant critic himself, he was a man of ideas in that crucial sense which Pushkin and Lermontov were not—that is, a serious political radical. He was indeed a personal friend of Belinsky. Those two, with Bakunin and Turgenev, were the core of the group Annenkov described in his essay 'The Marvellous Decade', the men of the forties. The rich intercourse of talents, ideas, tastes, and above all energies, which those names represent, are another sign of what Russian culture achieved then.

But there had been some partial interaction between critic and author before. Though Pushkin and Lermontov were not personal friends of Belinsky, nor influenced by his criticism, *they* were very important to *him*. And his critical writings became the forum in which these artists' images encountered the ideas of contemporary philosophy and politics, and thus became fully a part of culture. Belinsky declared that *A Hero of our Time* was indeed the portrait of its generation; he explained and endorsed Lermontov's meaning for the intellectual public. And his eleven essays on Pushkin gave the latter his peculiar place in Russian letters, as the origin as well as the standard of everything later—a place like Shakespeare's in English literature. But more important than his shaping of the literary past was his shaping of the future. Belinsky more than anybody else spoke for Russian literature to Gogol, Turgenev, Goncharov, and Dostoevsky. He praised them, he blamed them, he told them what they had achieved, and what they must go on to achieve; and all with a passion both personal and national.

The extraordinary tone he could take with them is best represented by his famous open letter to Gogol, of 1847, after the latter's *Selected Passages from Correspondence with Friends.* 'Yes, you must indeed be sick, preacher of the whip, apostle of ignorance, champion of obscurantism and dark ignorance, defender of a Tartar way of life. Look at the ground beneath your feet. You are standing on the edge of an abyss. . . . Why, if you had made an attempt on my life I could not have hated you more than for these disgraceful lines.'[1] The denunciation was in part on political grounds. (This was the letter Dostoevsky was accused of reading out to a circle when he was arrested and condemned to death.) By recommending personal piety and the Orthodox religion, Belinsky declared, Gogol had betrayed his calling as a writer and as a member of the intelligentsia.

'. . . Russia sees her salvation not in mysticism, nor asceticism, nor pietism, but in the successes of civilization, enlightenment and humanity. What she needs is not sermons (she has heard enough of them!) or prayers (she has repeated them too often!), but the awakening in the people of a sense of their human dignity lost for so many centuries among the dirt and refuse; she needs rights and laws conforming not with the preaching of the church but with common sense and justice, and their strictest possible observance.'

But this power of political disapproval was complemented by, fused with, his power of cultural enthusiasm for writers as such— for Gogol himself. 'Yes, I loved you with all the passion with which a man, bound by ties of blood to his native country, can love its hope, its honours, its glory, one of the great leaders on its path of consciousness, development, and progress.' He honoured writers primarily for their place in culture. 'Only literature, despite the Tartar censorship, shows signs of life and progressive movement. That is why the title of writers is held in such esteem among us, that is why literary success is easy among us even for a writer of small talent. The title of poet and writer has long since

[1] I am using the translation in *Selected Philosophical Works,* Moscow, 1948.

eclipsed the tinsel of epaulettes and gaudy uniforms.' But he loved them as writers, as artists, not as propagandists. As he said in another place: 'Poetry has no purpose beyond itself. . . . Do not worry about the incarnation of ideas. If you are a poet, your works will contain them without your knowledge—they will be both moral and national if you follow your inspiration freely.' He believed that a return to the great classical works of art would give readers the answers to life's problems, would regenerate and ennoble them. But those works of art must have their own self-generated form and self-justifying structure.

In his last years Belinsky was a revolutionary democrat, and when he died moves were being made to have him arrested. His whole life, as well as what he wrote, was important for the cultural tradition we are discussing. 'His life and personality became a myth,' Isaiah Berlin tells us, 'He lived as an idealized, severe, and morally immaculate figure in the hearts of so many of his contemporaries that, after mention of his name was once again tolerated by the authorities, they vied with each other in composing glowing epitaphs to his memory.' This was true of Turgenev, for instance; Belinsky was, we are told, the great ideal figure who divided with Flaubert Turgenev's moral and imaginative loyalties. And Belinsky's is the name Soviet literary criticism always invokes, when it claims its heritage and justifies its values. But his importance for us is not so much his strictly personal heroism, as the communal debate in which he involved others— the tradition of cultural criticism he created.

To return to Herzen, *Who is to Blame?* has a romantic hero, Beltov, who is like Onegin and Pechorin, but the people whose lives he ruins are in a new style and more interesting. As Belinsky pointed out, the book is most interesting when it deals with the social structure, and the personal enigma, so authoritative in Lermontov's novel, is derivative here. It is important in this tradition as an assimilative work, bringing together Gogol's provincial backgrounds with Pushkin's hero, but subduing both imaginative modes to a general sobriety of tone which expresses all-round normality and responsibility. Herzen was not a great novelist, but he gave this cultural tradition what it needed, the keynote of moral-emotional health and sanity. Pushkin and Gogol by themselves could be called the direct ancestors of Pasternak (even Nabokov) and thus of a quite non-cultural idea of art. But a tradition that includes Herzen also begins to turn away decisively from aestheticism, begins to make demands Pasternak and Nabokov will not meet.

Turgenev is the artist of stature who most fully exemplifies the power of this tradition. In his first novel, *Rudin* (1856), the hero-figure reflects his times as much as Onegin did, and indeed inherits something from him, but modifies it. Rudin is much more fully committed to the values of political liberalism; he dies on the barricades of Paris in 1848. And in *On the Eve* (1860) Turgenev gave his readers the perfect revolutionary, Insarov, and in *Fathers and Sons*, the more equivocal portrait of Bazarov. But by then the 'men of the sixties' dominated the world of ideas, and the novelists of the forties, like Turgenev, were being condemned as ineffectual individualists. The tradition we are discussing was changing again.

The relationship between critic and writer became still closer and more demanding, which was probably a change for the worse. A writer's freedom is always in some sense diminished by his acceptance of cultural duties. But up to a point (which varies from case to case) that loss in freedom is more than balanced by a gain in substantiality. Surely it is clear, for instance, that the interest of most of Turgenev's fiction depends on, derives from, his concern for ideas. Ignore that, and what you have left is surely something very thinly graceful. When Western criticism, with its current bias, denies that, it seems to me to diminish itself. A recent translation of *On the Eve* has a preface which calls it 'an unconscious tribute to Turgenev's powers of characterization' that the readers of the time discussed Elena's radicalism and Insarov's patriotism so eagerly. The modern reader in the West, it goes on, knows that this is really 'a tale of two lovers'; though behind the Iron Curtain it may be that the political and sociological aspects of *On the Eve* are still discussed. (The same bias is evident in Western pronouncements on *Doctor Zhivago*, into discussion of which, it is implied, only Communist prejudice insists on introducing the subject of Pasternak's treatment of history.) Surely such discussion will always be relevant, and its discussability in those terms will always be the best measure that *On the Eve* remains alive. Without that, the charming sketches of manners and character, though full of wit and sentiment, are not very engrossing, and the famous lyricism by itself would scarcely make the author major. Turgenev has often been compared with Tennyson, and what gives him the greater dignity in the comparison is surely just that his understanding of the ideas of his time was so much livelier—which is to say that he benefited from the Russian cultural tradition.

To return to the change in that tradition, it was in 1859 with the publication of Goncharov's *Oblomov*, that the critics had made their most famous demand on the novelists. Dobrolyubov wrote an article called 'What is Oblomovism?', declaring that all the Russian novel heroes up till then had been Oblomovs, in that they found the real world less interesting than their own imaginations, that they refused to act, that they were psychic invalids. This included Onegin, Pechorin, Rudin, etc., who were all only romanticized portrayals of Oblomov. Dobrolyubov called for novels with positive heroes; in whom Russian readers could invest, by sympathy, all the active and healthy faculties of their imaginations, by identification with whom their natures would be energized. The critics were no longer satisfied with heroes who were relevant to the age; they demanded that they be also useful. This is the form of the tradition we associate most often with Soviet criticism and with Sholokhov, though, as we have seen, he cannot be said to have complied with all its demands.

Dobrolyubov, who died in 1861 from consumption, at the age of 24, himself became a semi-mythical figure in Russian literary culture. Like Belinsky, he stood for an angry severity of manners and standards, an uncompromising and uncouth commitment, though it seems to be agreed that he did not have the breadth and disinterestedness of response which his master had. This, we gather, was true of all the critics in this line after Belinsky, and it was the great weakness of this cultural tradition in the second half of the century. The leading men on the critical side were not very good critics, and the novelists could afford to neglect them. Chernyshevsky, Antonovich, Pisarev, were loud consciences rather than subtle sensibilities; they represented the conscience of the country, but it was possible to imagine another representation more relevant to literary questions and just as authentic morally. (I rely here on E. Lampert's *Sons Against Fathers*, London, 1965.)

These literary critics were, however, also cultural heroes— Chernyshevsky passed nearly half his life in prison and exile— and as such they challenged even the greatest of the novelists. *What Is To Be Done?* was written while Chernyshevsky was a prisoner in the Peter and Paul Fortress. It was a kind of answer to *Fathers and Sons*—in which Turgenev was thought to have slandered the radicals—and it provoked Dostoevsky to write *Notes from Underground*, which appeared the following year, 1864. Moreover, when *Crime and Punishment* came out two years later, Raskolnikov was taken as a 'comment on' Rakhmetov, and *The Possessed* clearly depicts circles like those Chernyshevsky idealizes, seen by Dostoevsky from an opposite point of view. Dostoevsky was the most virulent of all the novelists in rejecting the critics' ideology, but Tolstoy too made fun of the marriage ideal of *What Is To Be Done?*, and in his own novels the ultimate answers to life's problems are invested in, not liberal intellectuals like Sergei Ivanovitch, but very opposite figures like Platon Karatayev. Nevertheless, it is in *War and Peace*, and in Dostoevsky's novels, that one best sees the intensity of thought and feeling for which this cultural tradition was responsible. They are all novels of passionate argument, born out of debate, personal and more than personal. And though Tolstoy and Dostoevsky rejected the critics' demand for positive heroes, they both present their fully representative heroes, Bezukhov and Levin, Prince Myshkin and Alyosha Karamazov; clearly defining and rejecting the other hero-types culturally available—Prince Andrey, for instance, who is clearly related to the Onegin-Pechorin line, and the unregenerate Raskolnikov, who is another Rakhmetov.

Chekhov treated some of these same figures and issues (in *Ivanov*, for instance), but on the whole this phase of the Russian cultural tradition ended with the Golden Age of the novel. At its most self-conscious, this series of declarations and counter-declarations, essays 'answering' novels, and novels 'answering' essays, was no doubt a mixed blessing. But as the background to a novelist's profession, as the less immediate context of his work, it was wonderfully stimulating and sustaining. As indeed it was to the whole profession of letters. A remark of Belinsky's, 'I am a littérateur. I say this with a painful and yet proud and happy feeling. Russian literature is my life and my blood', shows how the whole profession of letters was put into relation with the rest of life. And this tradition remained in force to the end of the century.

Vladimir Korolenko declared, 'My country is not Russia, my country is Russian literature.' In any other country, this would have been a declaration of aestheticism. In Russia, with its cultural tradition of literature, it was a declaration of political commitment—in this case, of revolutionary radicalism.

Surely we must agree that, with all reservations made, this

tradition of cultural thinking was, in important measure, responsible for a great period of great literature. At any rate it will stand as our example of what we mean by a cultural idea of literature, as well as our explanatory background to Sholokhov.

But by 1890 the energies of both this line of novelists and this line of critics were exhausted, and the cultural theory, or complex of attitudes, which was expressed in their action, no longer had the power to inspire significant new writers. (Gorky is the only major exception—a very significant one for Sholokhov, since Gorky kept that tradition alive for him.) A very different theory of literature was being formed. Writers were called on for personal exaltation more than for social responsibility, for splendour of beauty more than for accuracy of analysis. This was more than a gradual or partial change. It was a revolution in sensibility. Mirsky says, 'In 1890 the sole function of art in Russian was to "express ideas"; in 1915 Russian society was aesthetically one of the most cultivated and experienced in Europe.' This was the result of the movement sometimes split up between Decadence and Symbolism, sometimes called simply Symbolism. Mirsky says, 'It was at once an aesthetic and a mystical movement: it raised the level of poetical craftsmanship, and it was united by a mystical attitude towards the world, which is expressed in the very name of Symbolism.' Poetry and craftsmanship were much more central to its literary concerns than the novel and ideas; and in nearly every other way it was the opposite of the theory it replaced. This movement had of course no direct effect on Sholokhov, but it is impossible to understand Pasternak without knowing about it. Moreover, it is related importantly to our own dominant aesthetic theory; it is a vivid case of the alternative to 'culture'.

The mystical side of the movement is most importantly represented by the names of Solovyev, Shestov and Rozanov, though Merezhkovsky, now ignored, was the most immediately influential. There was an important series of books on Dostoevsky, developing his ideas, and using them in an attack on the prophets of progress, the priests of rationalism and moralism, the Westernizers, the ideologues, the social critics. Solovyev's *Three Addresses in Commemoration of Dostoevsky*, 1881–3, seems to have been the first. Solovyev was said to be the original of Alyosha in *The Brothers Karamazov*; and Rozanov had an even more personal connection, since he married Dostoevsky's ex-mistress.

In this series of books, Dostoevsky was habitually put into opposition to Tolstoy, and often into alliance with Nietzsche. Shestov brought out *The Good in the Teachings of Tolstoy and Nietzsche* in 1900, and *Dostoevsky and Nietzsche*; *The Philosophy of Tragedy* in 1901. He said that the thousand year reign of conscience and reason was over, and the era of psychology, of which Dostoevsky was the prophet, was about to begin. Then there was Merezhkovsky's *Tolstoy and Dostoevsky*, 1901, Rozanov's *Legend of the Grand Inquisitor*, 1890, Bely's book in 1911, and Vyacheslav Ivanov's in 1932. All this writing was explicitly anti-rationalist and anti-moralist, and implicitly, much of it, anti-rational and anti-moral. The spiritual exaltation was blended with both aestheticism and sensualism—in Rozanov and Shestov most vividly, we gather. This was also true of the purely literary works they themselves produced and of those whose authors they influenced, like Sologub and Bryusov, Blok and Bely. For Blok, as for Solovyev, Sophia was three things: an abstraction, Wisdom or Russia; a supernatural being, with its own vitality; and a fleshly reality, the woman he loved. (Lara Guishar, who is explicitly identified with Russia, and with life itself, appears to Yurii Zhivago in the forest, in the form of a vision.)

But this was an aesthetic as well as a mystical movement. Although Russian symbolism was closer to the German than to the French equivalent, and so more metaphysical than we would expect from our Anglo-American symbolists, there was a powerful concentration on form and beauty, and an energetic dismissal of all social and moral restrictions and demands. And since so many of the other principles of knowledge and judgment were depreciated, taste, the aesthetic sense, whether or not in co-operation with the mystical sense, became in effect a powerful arbiter of destiny. It dominated the imagination. Appropriately, that taste's preferences were highly 'aesthetic'—were for the bold, the bizarre, the colourful, the exotic. There was much interest in music and painting among literary men, and in effects transferred from one art to another. Scryabin, who was very important to Pasternak as a young man, is a vivid example. Mirsky says that the movement was purest in the visual arts, and it is perhaps worth remembering that the editor of *Mir Iskusstva,* when it was founded, in 1898, was Diaghilev, and that Benois, who worked with him there, also wrote the scenario and painted the scenery for the ballet *Petrushka,* for which Stravinsky wrote the music. The Russian ballet is, therefore, a convenient emblem of that taste, and, in part, of the whole symbolist movement in Russia. (It is striking how often in *Doctor Zhivago* representations of life are suffused with a brilliant colouring, or music, which subdues their factuality to a boldly aesthetic effect.)

It is clear how completely this goes against the cultural tradition I described before, which set such limits to the literary artist's autonomy. That tradition too awarded the writer great dignity, asking him to prophesy, to save the community, but it did not allow him to do so entirely on his own terms. It insisted on the critical relevance of social, economic, and political criteria. It imposed the community's demands (as interpreted by intelligent critics) on the writer as well as welcoming the writer's pronouncements on the community. The fallacy that lies in wait for such critics is of course that they will feel they know in advance what the writer ought to be saying and how he ought to be saying it. The cultural theory behind Symbolism had quite opposite strengths and weaknesses. It admitted no limits to the writer's autonomy. The artist listened to the music of the universe direct, and recreated that music in what he wrote. Music can perhaps best be defined as the symbolists' name for the Dionysian forces of the world, accessible to man's apprehension only in non-rational and non-moral ways. No one else was in such direct contact with the truth (because 'truth' was only a part of that music) and so no one could tell the artist what he ought to be saying, or do anything but listen humbly and gratefully to what he *was* saying.

But it is perhaps worth noticing that the Symbolist theory did have one feature in common with that of the social critics. In their own way the Symbolists left the line dividing life from art just as vague, though in their case this did not result in any usurpation by life of art's autonomy, but rather the opposite. As Khodasevich said,

'Symbolism did not wish to be only a school of art, a literary trend. It was always striving to become a mode of creativity and living, and in this lay its deepest, perhaps unrealizable, reality; but in truth, its entire history was passed in the constant pursuit of this reality. It was a series of attempts, sometimes truly heroic, to fuse life and creation, to find a kind of philosopher's stone of art.'

This was particularly true of the personal life of the artist. Victor Erlich says, 'Many a poem of Blok seems to have served as a literary scenario to be acted out in real life . . . life and art alike were shaped here by a third force, the myth of the artist as a tragic hero, as a dedicated custodian of "music".' And what Eichenbaum said in 1921, shows us how completely the contemporary 'audience' responded to this myth. 'For us Blok became a tragic actor who played himself . . . his youthful figure has fused with his poetry in the same way in which the make-up of a tragic actor is inseparable from his monologue. Each time Blok appeared before us, we felt a shiver down our spines. So much did he resemble himself.' This idea of the poet (which we must keep in mind to understand Pasternak) is familiar to us from our knowledge of Rilke, and, in modified form, Yeats. Russian Symbolism was importantly related to Symbolism in the rest of Europe and therefore to the whole modern movement in Western literature. For all that movement, the figure of the poet, the artist, is an extraordinarily glamorous and powerful one, who effectively knows no limits or duties, save to his own talent. He knows, in his own way, all the theologian knows, all the mystic knows, all the scientist and the social scientist know. His overwhelming duty is to not let them impose their ways of knowing on him, but to deliver to us, pure, *his* truths, known in *his* way. He does not merely write them down, he lives them, he embodies them. And because this is so hard a task, in our day, he is a tragic hero, struggling against insuperable odds, redeeming us with his blood. These are the ideas that lie behind the figure of Yurii Zhivago, and indeed behind Pasternak's life, and which Sholokhov's life and work flatly contradict.

To return now to Sholokhov and Pasternak, one could say that the first has written in the 'cultural' tradition we can identify with the name of Belinsky, and the second has rebelled against that, in favour of the Symbolist tradition. (In fact, *Doctor Zhivago* is not in substance and structure a Symbolist novel, as we shall see, but it contains many Symbolist features.) More exactly, Sholokhov has written in the much cruder version of Belinsky's tradition enforced by the Soviet government. This is cruder in several ways. One hears of no significant literary critics involved; there had been no debate comparable with that of the nineteenth century; much of the freedom necessary to a writer if he is to be a creative critic of his society has been denied him. All that remains is the fire-gutted framework of that tradition—the idea of the artist's responsibility to his culture.

And even though these modern ideas are so much cruder, and so much more crudely enforced, Sholokhov has not rebelled against them in his personal life as Tolstoy and Dostoevsky rebelled against the nineteenth-century equivalents. That is what is so hard for us to understand, or to accept. At the same time, it will not do, as we have seen, to condemn him as corrupt or to ignore him as insignificant. Given Russian cultural conditions, Sholokhov's career, like his work, is an achievement, something to be proud of. We have to keep reminding ourselves how different those conditions are, that culture is, from what we are used to. That perhaps becomes easier when we remind ourselves of certain other aspects of that difference.

There can be small doubt that Sholokhov's independence and integrity has been easier for him because he is not at all an intellectual or even, like Pasternak, a literary man. He lives where he was born, and among the people he describes in his novels. His leisure time is spent in hunting, fishing and cattle-breeding. He has never spent much time in the capitals or in literary centres. He has made himself a man of the people, with something of the same earthiness of style of Khrushchev, and it is easy to see why the latter took him as a companion on his visit to America.

In all these ways, the Western writer he is most like is perhaps Faulkner, and I would suggest that a comparison of the two is interesting. Both are very unintellectual men, who turned their backs on the literary and intellectual worlds of their time, rooting themselves in the provinces, in an agricultural life, and amongst a people 'left behind' by the century. Both assumed a heartily masculine and philistine persona, as hunters and farmers. In their work both turned to legend and local myth, making intensive use of their region, its speech, its types, its social problems. Their humour is very broad and folklorish. Their action is brutal, shocking, savage. Their characters are usually emotionally obsessed, and unavailable for subtle intellectual or psychological analysis. Their men are insistently and wholly virile, their women insistently and wholly female. Their work is full of passages of lyrical natural description. Their view of life is 'tragic'; that is, dominated by the awareness of suffering, injustice and horror.

Someone may perhaps object that Sholokhov is optimistic, Faulkner pessimistic. That seems to me a meaningful distinction, but it is surely the result of the two literary cultures within which the writers operate, and is a superficial difference compared with the 'tragic' quality they both more personally exemplify. One might perhaps say that they are alike in the superficiality and yet thoroughness of that optimism or pessimism. For although each writer turned his back on his literary culture, he remained in some ways unusually responsive to the directives it issued—no doubt just because he did not confront them directly. Thus the equivalent of Sholokhov's Communist 'message' is Faulkner's symbolist 'messagelessness', his enigmatic ambiguities. Veshenskaya is Sholokhov's Yoknapatawpha, Moscow is his Memphis, the Cossacks and peasants are his Southern whites and negroes, and their humour—for instance, their stories of horse-trading—is of strikingly the same kind.

If one accepts all these likenesses between the two minds and talents, then what strikes one most in the differences between the finished products is the price Faulkner paid for belonging to a liberal democracy with a symbolist aesthetic. He was dissuaded from that use of fact and history that lends Sholokhov's work such solidity and simplicity, such dignity and innocence. He was persuaded into an obscurity of style and loftiness of symbol which was most often inappropriate to his very simple understanding of problems and issues. He was dissuaded from any clear evaluation or explanation of characters or actions. He was encouraged to scatter hints, ambiguities, ironies, from behind the god-like mask of the artist persona. Above all, he was given no sense of the function of his calling, the limits and scope of literary knowledge and intuition, the ways they co-operate with other kinds of knowledge. It is this sense Sholokhov has, as a result of the humanist cultural tradition he works within, even in the distorted form given that tradition by the Soviet government. Even in that form, that tradition is more humanist, though so much less humane, than our own symbolist-dominated literary culture.

It is a monitory exemplum, a symbolist critic like Helen Muchnic assessing a Communist novel like *The Quiet Don*. She tells us that Sholokhov's understanding of men is thoroughly materialistic; that there is no free play of emotion in his characters; because every

emotion in them is created by an object, and has in it nothing
interesting except in so far as it eventuates in action. She is invoking
in effect a standard of literary refinement, of imaginative gentility,
which in principle she would surely repudiate. After comparing
Sholokhov with Homer, Dante, Tolstoy, she says, 'Only in our day
and age does physical agony seem to have become important in itself.
This is in keeping with a materialistic, pragmatic view of life.' She
points out that when Sholokhov's battle scenes are compared with
Tolstoy's, the former are seen to be much more crudely shocking in
their effects. And that in his work in general, 'The senses are not
subordinate to the imagination. Meaning and value reside in the
physical world, and little exists beyond the evidence of sight, hearing,
taste, smell, touch.' All this is true in so far as it describes the kind of
novel Sholokhov wrote—and proves that that kind has a narrower
range than Tolstoy's. In so far as it implies that his mind is too crude to
be capable of interesting art, it is surely untrue. Brilliant writers of all
kinds have worked with cruder effects and narrower ranges than
Sholokkov, and the primitive epics he demands to be compared with,
from the Odyssey and the Iliad to the Chanson de Roland and the
Icelandic Sagas, work within very similar limits.

I need not say that in a case like Sholokhov's, as much as in Powers's,
one could easily show the tax exacted from the artist for his cultural
security—the tax on his artistic freedom. Equally, it is Powers's sense
of cultural responsibility which helps save him from the wild extravagancies of form and content that Faulkner was betrayed into, just as
Sholokhov's saves him. Now clearly, after my fourth essay, *I* of all
people cannot argue that just being a Catholic novelist saves Powers
from all extravagancies of form and feeling; but then neither does just
being a Communist writer save Sholokhov. Individual talent and
personal taste matter too. The Communist novels with really positive
heroes in them, like Furmanov's *Chapayev* (1923), Gladkov's *Cement*
(1925), and Ostrovsky's *The Tempering of Steel* (1932), are examples of
how being a Communist writer can betray a novelist, which one could
parallel with the Catholic novels discussed before. Sholokhov, like
Powers, has had to find an artistically right way to be a Communist
(Catholic) novelist. The credit is personal to them; but it is not entirely
unrelated to their creeds, since they chose to become the media by
which those creeds found artistic expression, and since that choice
has clearly helped make their novels different from, again, Faulkner's.
It seems to me that in all these cases one can see the same pattern, of
the same advantages and the same disadvantages going with the choice
of ideological commitment and cultural responsibility. Just as when
one turns to cases of the opposite choice (Yeats, Rilke, Nabokov,
Pasternak) one sees a pattern of opposite disadvantages going with the
refusal of commitment and responsibility. It must be somewhere

between these two extremes that the humanist can find a position which does not bring such disabling disqualifications.

These disqualifications disable the reader as much as the writer. Much Western criticism seems really baffled by *The Quiet Don,* circling round it, tentatively ascribing to it qualities and features that go against all probability. 'And one wonders,' says Professor Muchnic, 'is Sholokhov's voice quite so self-assured as it has seemed? The quaver one detects in it argues something discordant and unbalanced, as if its cadences and timbre were inappropriate to his theme.' Sholokhov's voice is one of the least quavering in all literature. It is Western criticism that insists there must be some hidden protest in this author, some dissent from the values he proclaims, because the Western idea of an artist demands it.

As soon as one turns to the Western criticism of Pasternak from that of Sholokhov, one finds oneself in the land of superlatives and hyperboles. Because that 'Western idea of an artist' is *embodied* in Pasternak. He provides the happy ending to Professor Muchnic's book on twentieth-century Russian literature, *From Gorky to Pasternak.* The other writers all went wrong from time to time. Even Blok sometimes forced himself out from the privacy an artist needs into the public forum. Only, 'Pasternak, the freest, wisest spirit of them all, is always at home wherever he may be.' And thus, 'His life and work, like those of Marcel Proust, were a dissertation on art.' All the devices of Pasternak's art are described as if they were magical, or religious. The coincidences in *Doctor Zhivago,* says Professor Muchnic, are symbols of Pasternak's awe before the play of fate; they are exempla, necessary demonstrations of a world of mystery; not the mystery of terror but a sense of the inscrutable, and of a reasoned conviction that to be honest man must stop short of ultimate conclusions; and that a poet can only deal with the particular, however spellbound he may be by generalities. These ideas remind us of Yeats, Blok, and Rilke; and the last two were obviously of prime importance in the formation of Pasternak's ideas and personality. His autobiography, *Safe Conduct,* is dedicated to Rilke, from whom he says that he 'received' his reminiscences. And the way Pasternak handles abstractions and things in his poetry is very Rilkean; for instance, the title *My Sister, Life.*

This is interesting, because Rilke is perhaps the most vivid of all examples of the problem the great Symbolist poet sets his self-respecting reader. For Rilke, to be a poet was more than to write verses, or to build a career centred on that; it was a divine calling and a total fate, which absorbed all of his strength and all of his interests, and incidentally absolved him from the duties and responsibilities of ordinary men—his version of family life may serve as our example of that. Moreover, Rilke insisted that his life, his version of his life, was our concern if we are literary men at all. He insisted that his manner of living was the poet's manner. The reader must either believe that, or dissent in a way that carries some far-reaching implications for his reading of the poems. Thus we find one scholar-critic, Heerikhuizen, who says that Rilke's life 'has not the appearance of a twentieth-century life; it was lived in Biblical and Dantesque proportions'. While another, E. M. Butler, finds Rilke's life and personality so un-attractive, as we shall see, that she can hardly respond to any of the statements in the poems.

As for myself, I can see a truth in Heerikhuizen's remark, but it is a half-truth. The proportions, the massiveness, suggested by the Bible and the *Divine Comedy*, are after all the product of more than an indi-vidual sensibility working in a vacuum—which is what, comparatively speaking, Rilke's did. Dante was the poet of the Middle Ages; that is, he accepted, absorbed, identified himself with the established culture of his times, including its philosophy and its religion, as Rilke never began to do. The proportions, the pretensions, of Rilke's life, were supported largely by his private sensibility and his private will.

Heerikhuizen's phrase represents the response Rilke called for; which, by the present decorum of literary criticism, is the only correct one for a critic. But if one goes on giving Rilke those responses, one finds oneself in country as strange as the ideology of Yeats scholarship. The humanist will find himself asked to betray his beliefs, his very balance of mind, in order to respond to the poet and his poetry. Thus Edmond Jaloux, drawing a distinction between Rilke, who was a poet, and other men who just wrote poetry: '. . . but when Rilke began to talk he introduced me to a world that was his own and into which I could enter only by some sort of miracle. The marvellous, the fantastic grew with his words and through him I escaped at last from the hell of logic.' It is true that in Rilke's poetry everything is transformed, and that this gives his poetry its force; but those of us who don't find logic a hell are not so happy to escape from it completely.

In Rilke's case the challenge, how am I to respond, how completely am I to yield my mind to this writer who denies my deepest beliefs, is particularly sharp, and finds particularly interesting answers. In his introduction to *Rainer Maria Rilke; Selected Works*, Vol. I, J. B. Leish-man talks about the translator, Gertrude Craig Houston, a woman who devoted much of her life to reading and translating Rilke.

'She attached, as I have said, much importance to the cultivation of insight and perception, which were her special gifts, and Rilke's innumerable insights and perceptions and his most subtle, delicate and original expression of them enabled her to extend the depth and range of her own. For this she was grateful, and expected other readers to be grateful. But for the right use of these acquisitions, as of all other gifts, natural or acquired, for their relation to the whole duty of man, for

N

their place and importance *sub specie aeternitatis*—she knew that neither Rilke nor any other poet could teach her that, and she often became impatient with those who expected to learn from poets what they should have learned at their mother's knee, or to find in poets a substitute for what each must work out, with fear and trembling, for himself.'

This is an admirably sensible answer, on Miss Craig Houston's part, but I think Mr Leishman's account of the original problem makes rather too light of it. First of all, Rilke would not have been satisfied with this attitude—he would have found Miss Craig Houston very philistine—and consequently her answer to the problem involves disagreeing with his idea of poetry quite importantly. Secondly, her answer amounts to making all poetry subordinate to religion, assigning it the secondary role of cultivating the sensibility, and is thus the answer of a religious humanist. Obviously I have no reason to object to that, but I must insist that it cannot be taken for granted—that only a religious humanist can make that answer, that not many readers today are even secular humanists, and that those who are still face problems in reading Rilke's poetry. Miss Craig Houston must have felt pretty divided in her response to many of the poems.

It seems to me that Guardini is unanswerable when he says:

'Rilke thus demands more from his reader than appreciation of the beauty of his verses or comprehension of great thoughts. His work does not require "enlightenment", but—Rilke emphasizes the distinction—"submission", in other words, "faith". His own relation to his work is that of a prophet—an inspired vessel filled with a divine voice which speaks through him. He himself had to listen to his own words and "penetrate" them gradually.

This claim which Rilke makes is so far-reaching that the reader is entitled to ask whether or not it is authentic. Usually a claim of this kind is given an aesthetic interpretation as evidence of the poet's inspiration and faith in his own work. We respect his claim and acknowledge the significance of his writings. But this would not have satisfied Rilke at all, for his own meaning was utterly different. . . .

In view of the far-reaching claims which the poet makes for his work we are not merely justified—we are *obliged* to examine how far they can be substantiated.'

Guardini goes on to examine the Elegies in detail, accepting and rejecting what he finds there, as true or not true.

'Our interpretation—as was stressed in the Introduction—does not aim simply at exposition of the "thought-content of the *Elegy*" or of "Rilke's idea". Over and above the definition of his idea we must try to examine the truth of the idea as well, and here it must be affirmed that Rilke's construction is false and disastrous—just as false and disastrous as that dualism

which, in its gnostic form, pervades the whole of Western thought.'
E. M. Butler, in her book on Rilke, is even sharper in her tone about
him. The question is, she says, 'Has the work of the greatest German
poet since Hölderlin real religious validity; or is it merely the
mysterious expression of a one-man dream?' Her book endorses the
second of those answers. 'His gentle manners, his sensitive mind, the
skill and fluency with which he used religious terms seemed to prove
that he loved humanity and worshipped God. Whereas in reality he
recognized the god of art and Rainer Maria Rilke his prophet. and was
stirred to deepest and purest enthusiasm for those kindred spirits who
felt and did the same.' She goes through all the different aspects of his
career and work with the same combination of enthusiasm and indignation. For instance, she quotes his letter of 1915, in which he exclaimed,
why is there not even one person to protest publicly against the war.

'Had Rilke been a saint or a martyr he would undoubtedly, feeling as
he did, have testified against the war in the market-place and suffered
the penalty at the incalculable price of *Duino Elegies* and *Sonnets to
Orpheus*. Had he been even a normal compassionate human being, he
would have volunteered for light hospital duty twelve months before
and have found some measure of relief. But the author of those
excruciating pages on Paris hospitals never learned how to roll a
bandage or to pad a splint. He was a pure poet, whose mysterious gifts
were allied to a child-like irresponsibility.'

Obviously, Professor Butler is badly torn in her feelings. Her
vocabulary expresses violently shifting sympathies. There is much to
make us uncomfortable in her book, and indeed in Guardini's. We are
not used to such an alternation of reverent exegesis and scornful scepticism, and perhaps there is something essentially indigestible in it.
But if so, surely Rilke is the person most to blame, for imposing such
an unmanageable strain on the conventions of criticism. It is clear that
both Guardini and Butler enthusiastically appreciate the poetry,
completely acknowledge the poet's powers, but find full consenting
response impossible. And if the reader is to read with his full self,
bringing all his experience and all his knowledge to bear on the poetry,
I don't see how he can escape the same bafflement. This is surely a
classic case of the conflict between poetry and belief which only a too
abstract theory can completely resolve.

Today, as we have seen, that conflict is usually decided in poetry's
favour. Guardini acknowledges in advance the resistance his readers will
feel to what he is doing. 'An undertaking of this kind may be difficult
to understand today. The author has already provoked a certain amount
of criticism whenever he left the path of historical or aesthetic appreciation in order to make a philosophical assessment of poetic works—in
other words whenever he was concerned with the question of their

objective truth.' His answer, to which he returns several times through the book, is that in the past serious poetry was always examined this way. 'In ancient times and in the Middle Ages men were convinced—just as the more sensitive minds of today are convinced—that the words of a poet convey greater depths of truth than could be seen through our own observation. It follows as a matter of course that we must not only ask the poet what he wants to say about life, but also whether what he says is true.'

Guardini's concern is more limited than Professor Butler's. He discusses only the Elegies, and the large ideas expressed in them. The points that he raises are all extremely interesting from our point of view, and I will include one reference to perhaps the most important of them, Rilke's 'weak sense of human personality', because this relates so directly to the question of extreme individualism so important in Yeats and Pasternak and all our representatives of modern art. Rilke, one of the most thorough-going of all individualists, who could never bring himself to accept any ties or bonds as final, ended by objectifying even his own personality and regarding it as a disturbing factor, to be eliminated as far as possible. 'There is one feature running through all the *Elegies* which should be emphasized here in conclusion. This is the dangerous tendency to deny the value of the human person. In this matter Rilke does not speak for himself alone. He is the spokesman of our time.' We think immediately of Nazism; Guardini is saying that the humanism which should be our instinctive defence against all totalitarian temptations is betrayed where it should be strongest by Rilke's kind of individualism.

Guardini's book is of particular interest to me because it is a Catholic humanist's approach to a representative modern poet. It repeats the confrontation of Yeats and von Hügel with which I began. It may be said to be von Hügel's reply to Yeats; and no unworthy one, no ideological broadside. Guardini can concentrate his fire on the aesthetic problem proper, and above all he can give that problem its deepest range of meaning. 'His style opened up new possibilities of expression but it also has had a destructive effect. The new frequencies which he sets in motion and the light which he throws on hidden places are to a large extent the product of sacrificial fires which devoured something intrinsic in the structure—one is tempted to say the *dignity* of language.' This is what I mean by humanist literary criticism.

And side by side with Yeats and Rilke, perhaps the last of the modern poets to attract general attention in the West, is Pasternak. His work exemplifies ideas very much like Rilke's, but I am interested above all in the reception it received, which illustrates how powerful still is the tendency in our literary world to accept all the Symbolist artist's claims, at whatever cost to the reader's self-respect and independence of mind.

Doctor Zhivago and the critics[1]

1. The Western Critics. (This in effect means British and American.)

The circumstances of publication, together with the quality of the novel itself, provoked an enthusiastic response from Western intellectuals, as to something more than a mere book. Thus J. M. Cohen wrote, in terms quite unlike the common currency of literary discussion, 'The presentation of *Doctor Zhivago* to the State Publishing House was as conscious and symbolic an action as that of the Christ of his poem awaiting the "thieves and nondescripts" with Judas at their head.' This was written in 1962, in a discussion of Pasternak's later poetry, and the more immediate response to the novel was even more emotional. Edmund Wilson called it, 'one of the great events in man's literary and moral history'. Edward Crankshaw said, 'He was not alone in this battle for the truth; but he is alone among living Soviet writers in having fought it unremittingly and without compromise to the wonderful, the miraculous end, when his Truth suddenly and shatteringly broke through every barrier to flood the world'. This was an honourable response, perhaps the most honourable response to make at the time. As Irving Howe said, reproaching Isaac Deutscher for the latter's ungenerous disparagement of the novel and its author, any intellectual surely ought to feel at least a deep comradeship with Pasternak, both for what he had done and for what he had suffered.

But this tone and this attitude have also been—at the level of discussion we are concerned with—equally a response to the novel itself, as a novel. It has been generally agreed that *Doctor Zhivago* is great by purely artistic standards, that its greatness is a function of its economy as a work of art, and independent of all political and biographical reference.

---

[1] I have read only a few passages in Russian, the poems and places where the translation seemed suspicious, so my remarks must be taken to apply to the English version of the novel.

There has not yet been any full-scale analysis of that economy —Donald Davie's book on the poems perhaps answers most nearly to that description—but there have been several essays which sketch out its main principles, and explicate this or that feature. These various readings have all this much in common, that they treat the action as having a symbolic meaning which is more important than the literal one, and therefore value the novel for things hidden from the common reader, and different from the things most novels offer. One of the most recent compares *Doctor Zhivago* with *The Leopard*, and the main point is the transcendent superiority of the former. Lampedusa's novel is a fine piece of work, but *Doctor Zhivago* exists in a different dimension. Pasternak's coincidences, for example, are quite different from what they first seem, and his use of them is quite different from other writers'. Seen structurally they are 'a prime organizing factor'; seen thematically they are 'examples of what Jung has called synchronicity'. This is a concept to be found in *I Ching*, an ancient book of Chinese wisdom, for which the material and the spiritual are simply 'aspects of one coherent reality', and 'the conjunctions of time and place have a significance that cannot be accounted for causally'. *Doctor Zhivago* as a whole is a 'seamless web of coincidences', and 'a pattern of timeless moments', which have 'the smell of Providence about them'. The novel's value, on this theory, derives from no exterior considerations.

Anyone familiar with modern symbolist criticism will recognize such phrasing as the mark of its highest approval. *Doctor Zhivago* has stimulated that criticism into efforts in its characteristic mode of appreciation which must often be called excesses. Nicola Chiaramonte, in one of the more moderately phrased, says *Doctor Zhivago*

'is, in substance, a meditation on history, that is, on the infinite distance which separates the human conscience from the violence of history and permits a man to remain a man, to rediscover the track of truth that the whirlwind of events continually cancels and confuses. One might say that all of *Doctor Zhivago* is dedicated to a description of this distance, and to the insistent representation of the truth manifested in it.'

Does it mean anything to say that a novel is a meditation on a distance, or that it is dedicated to a description of that distance, or of the truth manifested in that distance? Well, yes, each phrase means something, but not anything one can be too clear about, too firm in the grasp of, too able to proceed from in any rigorous sequence of thought. This is a congenital weakness of all literary comment, but symbolist comment, and the discourse built up out of it, is particularly weak in this way.

Edmund Wilson's two essays show us the symbolist analytic system at work on Pasternak's text, and their strengths and weaknesses let us measure how appropriate it is. That the word '*zhivago*' means 'living' in Old Church Russian, and is used in the Russian Gospel and twice in the Russian liturgy, is obviously relevant to any account of the novel's meaning. But that Yurii means George, and that Pasternak himself is like St George, in having been attracted to Christianity by the experience of the Thirties purges (St George was first attracted to the religion by the behaviour of Christians during martyrdom) and in having finally signed political denunciations (St George was finally forced to sacrifice to idols) is obviously much less relevant; to me it seems that it is simply irrelevant. And that St George died and was resurrected three times, as Zhivago was three times 'recalled to life' by his brother Evgraf; that Evgraf in the Russian calendar means writer, and that he is said to 'descend upon' his brother, just like the latter's force of inspiration or creative genius; these are surely inadequate bits of evidence, put in the context of the whole novel, for saying we must associate Yurii with St George or Evgraf with literature.

Then we are told that Larisa means seagull; that Lara is often described in terms of water and wind; that in one legend of Poseidon, he has a wife called Larisa; that in Lebanon the cult of St George sometimes confuses him with Poseidon; and that somewhere else the story of St George and the dragon derives something from that of Perseus and the sea-monster. Such connections as these are surely too frail taken individually, too disconnected to be taken together, and above all too tangential to most of Lara's nature and behaviour, for us to take them as meaningful. They can neither act as directives to the reader's imagination, nor stand as the outward and visible signs of a deep and total identification. By such a system of signs, after all, Yurii's second wife is much more clearly identified with water and the sea than ever Lara is; by her name, Marina, and by her most vivid action, helping him with the water-carrying. It is clear that Pasternak intends no such identification—though the water-carrying *has* a broad non-esoteric significance in our understanding of Marina, just as the sea-imagery has in our understanding of Lara—and that in general Pasternak is not using any such system of signs, because his characterization quite plainly exemplifies other principles.

Lara is also, Mr Wilson says, identified with the revolution, or rather with the possibility of freedom which the revolution announced. The direction to us to make this identification is largely a matter of dates. Lara arrives in Moscow at the time of the earliest revolutionary unrest. In July 1905 came the first signs of her seduction by Komarovsky. In August 1905 the Tsar dismissed his reactionary ministers and promised to convoke the Duma. That winter she was seduced. In December there was an insurrection in Moscow. Six months of the relationship with Komarovsky led her to desperate action. Six months after his manifesto of 30 October, the Tsar withdrew the liberties granted in it. In 1911 Lara shot at Komarovsky but hit Moscow's assistant attorney-general; in the same year revolutionaries assassinated Stolypin, a minister who was in fact improving the economic situation. After that Lara disappeared from Moscow till 1917; so did the revolution.

It is true that in the section titled 'A Girl from a Different World' Pasternak narrates the events of Lara's life alternately with events that embody the revolution; and that the violence and energy, the youthful hope and the youthful despair, of the one story, are reflected in the other. But to make that reflection into a symbolism, to make that association into an identification, is surely to pervert and ruin what Pasternak has done. When the dates are juxtaposed in isolation, as Mr Wilson juxtaposes them, what becomes clear is how independent of the revolution Lara's career is. When the stories are loosely and picturesquely inter-woven, as Pasternak interweaves them, what is suggested is an emotional similarity (as much a matter of the novelist's emotion as of anything intrinsic to the events), a similarity as ordinary as, perhaps more ordinary than, the emotional similarity between the different stories of *A Tale of Two Cities*, and quite undeserving the description 'symbolism'. The symbolic reference of characters in *Doctor Zhivago* to events in history is of quite a humble kind; that kind—and obviously this use of 'symbolism' has nothing to do with the grander meanings of the word—by which Kologrivov represents those liberal industrialist millionaires like Morozov, who contributed generously to the funds of the revolutionaries who were in the act of destroying capitalism.

Let us say immediately that the novel does invite a symbolic reading. Parallels between Zhivago and Christ and Hamlet are certainly drawn, from time to time, and between Lara and Mary Magdalene, and there is a gradual apotheosis of Zhivago the person into Zhivago the poet. Our disagreement is with the theory that these are major principles of structure, and that this is therefore a symbolist novel. We have the alternative of saying that they are 'put into the novel' as Pasternak said they were, 'to warm it up like a stove'. He also said that Edmund Wilson's 'theological' interpretation 'could not be further removed from my understanding of the world', and clearly implied that the novel was not organized round any comparable idea or point of view. 'The great heroic devotion to one point of view is very alien to me—it's a lack of humility.' This rings true to my understanding of Pasternak and his novel, but I can see how little reason there is to take such remarks as by themselves a conclusive refutation of a reading by Edmund Wilson.

Especially when one sets *Doctor Zhivago* in the context of Pasternak's symbolist past, one expects to interpret it as, in Mr Wilson's phrase, 'an enormous metaphor for the author's vision of life'; which means that its non-metaphorical aspects, its George Eliot-like representations of general experience, will be comparatively unimportant. But the novels that phrase fits best are perhaps novels like Kafka's, and novels like Joyce's last work. And when Mr Wilson goes on to say that *Doctor Zhivago* was obviously much influenced by *Finnegans Wake*, that Yurii and Evgraf are like Shem and Shaun, Lara like Anna Livia, and that Zhivago is Hamlet, Jesus, and St George in the same way as H. C. Earwicker is Adam, Tristram and Finnegan, then surely what becomes clear is the much more important way in which the books are unlike. What becomes clear is that *Doctor Zhivago* is not a metaphor about life but a representation of it. The meanings Mr Wilson works out for the Moreau and Vetchinkin bill-board, involving puns in three languages, show both how far he pushes the parallel with Joyce, and how implausible the parallel is.

The last examples I shall take are of two attempts to interpret the poems as guides to the novel. As one would expect, most symbolist readings of *Doctor Zhivago* assign great importance to the poems, which have so much more fully the character which symbolist criticism would like to attribute to all literature; the formal perfection, the use of a special language, the independence of external reference, and so on. F. D. Reeve says that Pasternak may be said to have invented the character Zhivago to go along with the poems. Donald Davie says that until we read the poems in the right way we have failed to read all the rest of the novel— because they undermine its apparent meaning and give it a new one. Both these critics take the novel to be about the processes of art, which is perhaps the classic theme of all symbolist literature. 'In an almost literal and fantastic sense, Zhivago becomes his poems,' says Mr Reeve; the destruction of his 'normal' personality, due to the tragic circumstances of his life, leads to the apotheosis of the 'idea' of his personality—the person is destroyed, the artist is created. The justification and purpose of Zhivago's life come more and more to be his art. At the end, he does not lose Lara, but sends her away, because he cannot endure the continued immediacy of so much life. He turns her into poetry, because he has become a poet rather than a lover.

On any such reading of the novel, the poems are of course its key. Donald Davie (who largely agrees with this reading) sets out to show that the poems all derive from Zhivago's experience, *not* Pasternak's, and that some of that experience is described in prose *only* for the purpose of later illuminating one or other of the poems. I underline these words because only with these emphases can the proposition, when proved, help make *Doctor Zhivago* the special kind of novel it is said to be; and Dr Davie accepts that responsibility honestly. He sets out to show that for every poem there is a prose passage as 'source', and that the relation *between* the two is significant.

In some places his enterprise does throw light on both the prose and the verse, but in more it does not, and in just as many it leads him into strained extravagances of interpretation which seem to me self-condemnatory. This happens, for instance, in the discussion of 'In Holy Week' (of which a better translation would surely be 'In Passiontide'). Here the prose passage which relates to the poem (Chapter 10, section 2) is a meditation in the mind of Galuzina, a person Zhivago never met, about Krestovozdvizhensk, a town he never visited. How then can we be asked to believe that he, not Pasternak, wrote this poem? Dr Davie is forced to conclude that Galuzina's sister, Tyagunova, gave

Zhivago all the details mentioned in the poem during a brief conversation in Pazhinsk. This very strained explanation might seem like a major disaster for Dr Davie's system of interpretation, but he continues, snatching victory from the jaws of defeat,

'What is interesting is that Pasternak should pose the problem and make us work out the solution. (I cannot see that the second section of Chapter 11 has any other function than just to supply it.) Evidently it was important to him to establish in this way how much a poet like Zhivago can make out of only a couple of bare hints.'

This is not evident at all. Surely a novelist so recklessly ready to invent a piece of human life—merely to supply a clue in a literary acrostic like this—could also invent a way to *show* us a poet proceeding from his initial hints to his final product. More important, surely literature does not work this way. When a pattern of interpretation is incomplete, surely we do not take the exceptional instance as being just as significant as those that fit the pattern; we do not take its exceptionality as proving the existence of *another* pattern, or as a signpost to some major message. When we find apples growing on what we had thought was an orange tree, we do not say, 'Despite the smooth green skin this must be a kind of orange. And this is meant to show us that oranges are not to be thought of as just fruit with thick yellow rinds.' No; that would be a crazy way to reason about nature, and it is equally crazy about art; we say, 'Evidently this is not an orange tree, after all.' For a literary example, take the pattern of parallels between Ursula and Gudrun in *Women in Love*. What happens to the one sister happens, with significant differences, to the other. This is a much more clearly established pattern than that relating the prose of *Doctor Zhivago* to the poems. But when that pattern does not complete itself, when there is no clear equivalent, for Ursula, of the chapter 'Gudrun in the Pompadour', it is not that exceptionality that is significant. Lawrence is not posing us a problem, and forcing us to work out why there is no such chapter for Ursula, the answer to which is what he wants to 'establish'.

The poem 'White Night' Dr Davie connects with the Gordon-Dudorov conversation at the end of the novel, and he identifies the young lady from Kursk (mentioned in the poem) with the city of Moscow (called, in the conversation, the heroine of

Zhivago's life-story). Even after that, he is faced with the difficulty that this poem is emphatically about Leningrad, not Moscow. He solves this problem the way he solved the last one.

'By this insistence, right at the end of the story, on how completely Zhivago is a Muscovite, Pasternak goes out of his way to make us notice how the second city of Russia, Petersburg or Leningrad, plays no part at all and is the locale of not a single incident in the whole book. There could hardly be a clearer directive to the reader; when he turns a few pages and comes to a poem which insists on how it is a poem of Petersburg, what is he to think? Surely he is meant to realize that this is a poem not to be read literally. It is to be read allegorically or symbolically.'

Obviously the reader is much more likely to think—to 'realize'—that Zhivago did not write the poem. What is this talk of clear directives? What *is* clear is that the connection between the poems and the prose, strong in some cases, is feeble in others, and not there at all in some; and that consequently there is no pattern of interpretation of the novel to be derived from the poems. Though even if there were, it would not support the gymnastics of negative inference from it which Dr Davie attempts. Negative inference is one of the fallacies of symbolist reading, and I have dwelt on these two cases because their interest is partly independent of the case of *Doctor Zhivago*. Dr Davie is a very shrewd critic, more on his guard than most against these fallacies.

Only rarely do the poems clearly derive from Zhivago's experience rather than Pasternak's. We have Pasternak's authority (*via* George Katkov) for saying that 'The Breach' is a description of his own feelings when he learned of the first arrest of Ivinskaya in 1948, and that 'Daybreak' is addressed directly to Christ (which goes against the interpretation demanded by its relation to the prose). And as against the whole symbolist interpretation, we know of course that Pasternak declared that he had become a realist when he published *Doctor Zhivago*, and that he repudiated his earlier, symbolist, work. More important, the efforts of the Western critics to show how the symbolist elements in the book can organize and dominate the rest, have proved, by their repeated failure, the reverse. On the whole, the Soviet critics' comments are much more useful and illuminating.

2. *The Soviet critics*

I am referring here only to the letter written by the editorial board of *Novy Mir*, published in 1958, but allegedly sent to Pasternak in 1956, when he submitted his manuscript to the magazine for serialization. The political-moral attitude to a writer's duties expressed in this letter is one we all agree to condemn, and many of the purely critical remarks are mistaken, stupid, unjust, and even unforgivable. But on the other hand, the basic account of the book given is more faithful to its page-by-page personality than that of most Western writers. These critics are concerned with only part of the truth, but that is a part which most of our critics seem to have dismissed much too quickly.

For instance, Edward Crankshaw confidently condemned the letter for describing Zhivago as the 'hero' of the novel, and took it for granted that such terms betrayed a way of thinking about literature far too crude to be useful.

'In this attack the English reader familiar with the novel will find a fair amount of distortion and false emphasis. But this seems to me inevitable and unimportant. What is truly interesting and revealing is the attitude of Pasternak's colleagues to novel-writing as such. In brief, the editorial board of *Novy Mir* is clearly unable to think of a novel without a hero in the most elementary sense of the word. Zhivago is the leading character, therefore, by definition, he is intended as the hero. Therefore Pasternak must approve whole-heartedly of everything Zhivago says and does. . . . So the whole criticism, while reasonable and subtle up to a point, and moderately presented, misses the target absolutely. And the writers of the letter, some of whom are themselves distinguished novelists, clearly think they have scored a bull. If this is shown by nothing else, it is shown conclusively by the fact that they have chosen in full a key passage from the novel (Part 4 and Chapter 11: "The Forest Brotherhood") to prove their point—namely that Zhivago is no hero; as if Pasternak thought otherwise.'

But in this matter surely the Russian critics are right. Zhivago is the hero of the novel, in all the relevant senses of the word. He is overwhelmingly the centre of interest; he represents the author; he is proved right by events; he is liked by the good people and disliked by the bad; all his behaviour is so explained to us as to seem inevitable; his ideas are expounded to us directly—and by others as well as himself—with the slightest possible dramatic or ironic distancing. This is what being the hero of a novel means, not performing picturesque exploits which are conventionally considered 'heroic'. Zhivago's experiences are what Pasternak wants us to undergo; Zhivago's actions and judgments are to be, as far as Pasternak can contrive, while we are reading the novel, ours.

Few Western novels have a hero-character in such a full sense, on such a large scale, and in all that do that character is of central importance. He is, more than anything else, the meaning of the novel, and to define him is to understand it. Russian novels have made much more use of such characters, throughout the nineteenth and twentieth centuries, and *Doctor Zhivago* belongs to that tradition. This is what the Russian critics saw, and what the Western critics have in effect proved blind to. They have looked for the meaning of the book in its metaphors, in the coincidences of its plot, in the poems attached to it. Of course they have believed that these interpretations would prove to be indirectly—and amongst other things—ways towards defining Zhivago; but a novel hero of this kind reveals himself most of all directly, in his major actions and reactions, his behaviour and his thoughts.

Crankshaw continues:

'If the main attack had been along the lines that Zhivago was "anti-hero" and that this was a bad thing to be condemned it would be understandable, if, one might think, wrong-headed. But what I myself find most disturbing in this letter is not the attack as such, but the total failure to see what Pasternak was trying to do on the part of men trying their level best to be reasonable and moderate. Far more than to the orthodox viciousness of the hatchet men of Soviet literature this letter testifies to the existence of a gulf between the human and the Soviet way of looking at things that will be far more difficult to bridge than the political differences, which obsess us all today.'

The Soviet way of reading *Doctor Zhivago* was certainly not non-human, as we shall see, nor was there any total failure to see what Pasternak was trying to do. What the letter rather suggests is critics who understood quite well most of what the novel was trying to do, but some of whom were not trying to be reasonable and moderate.

They begin by dividing the novel into two parts, the first third and the rest, and considering how each part represents the history it deals with.

'The first third of your novel, covering a period of 20 years before the revolution, does not itself contain a clearly expressed non-acceptance of the coming revolution, but, to our mind, the roots of this non-acceptance are already there. Later, when you begin to describe the accomplished revolution, your views develop into a system that is more orderly, more forthright in its non-acceptance of the revolution. In the first third of the novel they are still as contradictory. On the one hand, you admit—in a general, abstract way—that the world of bourgeois property and bourgeois inequality is unjust, and you not only reject it as an ideal, but actually regard it as unacceptable to the mankind of the future. But once you turn from general declarations to a description of life, to actual people, these people—both the masters of unjust, bourgeois life and their intellectual lackeys, helping to preserve the iniquity you admit in general—turn out to be, with extremely rare exceptions, such as, for instance, the black-guard Komarovsky, the nicest, the kindest, the subtlest of spirits, who do good, who seek, who suffer, and who are actually incapable of hurting a fly.'

This, so far as it goes, is surely true; and it goes no negligible distance—not towards condemning the book, of course, but towards defining it, in its treatment of its major subject-matter.

The next paragraph continues with the same point, providing more specific analysis. '. . . capitalists donate to the revolution and live honestly; intellectuals enjoy a complete freedom of thought and are intellectually independent of the bureaucratic machine of the Tsarist régime; poor girls find rich and disinterested protectors; while sons of workmen and concierges find no difficulty in getting an education.' This again is rather strikingly to the point. It is only when we come to the next paragraph that we must disagree. 'The novel gives no real picture of the country or the people. Nor, consequently, does it explain why revolution became inevitable in Russia, or reveal a measure of the intolerable depravity, suffering and social injustice that had led the people to it.' We cannot admit either that Pasternak's picture of the country

bears the character of distortion, or that there can be any single
'reality' with which all artists must be concerned.

However, the substance of this account of the book, ignoring
for the moment the evaluation it 'supports', is perfectly solid.

'Most of the characters whom the author has lovingly invested
with a part of his spirit are people who have grown accustomed
to living in an atmosphere of talk about the revolution, which,
however, has not become a necessity for any one of them. They
like to talk about it in one way or another, but they can also do
very well without it, and there was nothing in their life before
the revolution that was either intolerable or merely poisoned
their life, if no more than spiritually. And there are no other
people in the novel (if we are to confine ourselves to characters
who enjoy the author's sympathy and who are drawn up with
anything like a similar measure of penetration and detail).'

All we can say to this is 'yes, true—though it doesn't prove all
you think it does'. We cannot say 'no, untrue', unless we go on
to claim that the novel needs to be read from a radically different
point of view, without major reference to its character as a
description of history, as a cultural document. If *Doctor Zhivago*
has *any* cultural character, it surely is the one the Soviet critics
describe; and they assumed, very naturally about a novel describing living history in such detail and with so much 'judgment',
that this cultural character is the substance of the book. The
Western critics have assumed that the substance of the book is
something much more purely aesthetic—is the symbolist economy
of the novel's art—and that its judgments on history and politics
are merely an inevitable by-product.

This theory of how great literature works is a very agreeable
one for a literary intellectual to hold, attributing to him as it does
a minimum of social obligation with a maximum of social
effectiveness. According to this theory, the great writer delivers
major truths about society and life, but can never be held to
account for them, because he is really only concerned with art.
He triumphs over history and politics doubly, since he can deliver
major truths about them as mere by-products of work as his real,
difficult, *artistic* concerns. And, in a case like that of *Doctor
Zhivago*, the liberal democratic man of letters finds himself for
once the valued ally of his political rulers. There are therefore

powerful vested interests at work in this theory, and especially
in the effort to include *Doctor Zhivago* within its scope. But that
effort, as we have seen, has so far proved unsuccessful, and we
have to return to the simpler Russian account of the novel.

Of course that account is incomplete and unsympathetic—
sometimes crudely and outrageously so. Its main attack, on the
chapter in which Zhivago fires on the Whites with whom he
sympathizes, is an example. It is absurd to talk of his 'picking off
three men one after another', and monstrous to talk of his 'triple
if not quadruple betrayal'. This episode is in fact one of the most
moving and memorable in the whole novel, because of the way
it dramatizes the dilemma of the man of moderate convictions
and minor abilities but powerful imagination, the hero of sensibility in a heroic situation for which he is temperamentally
disqualified.

But it is only rarely that the Soviet critics can be said to have
misread the novel in that sense. Most of the time they have followed the author's account of his characters closely enough,
though they have refused to respond as he intended. His heroes are
admitted to be not

'property-grabbers, gourmets, or sybarites. They need all this
not for its own sake but merely as a means of continuing, in
safety, their spiritual life.

What lives? Why, the ones they led in the past, for nothing
new enters their spiritual lives and nothing changes them. They
regard the possibility of continuing them, without outside inter-
ference, as the greatest blessing not only for themselves, but for
all mankind, and since the revolution steadfastly requires them to
act, to say "for" or "against", they turn, in self-defence, from a
feeling of alienation from the revolution to a feeling of active
hostility to it.'

The same character is to be found in their remarks about Zhivago
himself.

When he finds himself surrounded by terrible nation-wide
suffering, Doctor Zhivago forgets everything but his own "I"
and, as an appendix to it, people related to this "I", directly or
indirectly. This "I", as embodied in himself and his dear ones, is
not only the sole thing worth bothering about but, indeed, the
only thing of value in the whole universe. It embraces the past

and the future, and if it were to die, everything would die with it.'

The tone of this language is of course hostile, but it is otherwise very little different from the language in which Western critics have, most enthusiastically, interpreted to us Western writers' social thought. It is very little different from the way those writers described their own and their heroes' disengagement from the social tragedy. Consider the first World War and the self-disengagement of writers as different as D. H. Lawrence, Ezra Pound, and Hemingway.

'The personality of Zhivago is the supreme value in your eyes. Doctor Zhivago's spiritual wealth is the highest stage of spiritual perfection, and for the sake of preserving this highest spiritual attainment and his life as a vessel containing this value—for the sake of this, everything may be trespassed.'

This is surely a fair enough account, from an unsympathetic point of view, of the moral position Pasternak takes up—following the example of most Western writers. To dismiss this account indignantly is surely to claim a special immunity from challenge for him and them—their moral position can only be described in a friendly and respectful way, and all the flights of controversial rhetoric are to be reserved to them; an immunity which amounts to declining, on their behalf, all full engagement in the debate. If their moral position is worthy of our respect, it must be able to accept and answer a description so clearly similar to their own.

Pasternak in *Doctor Zhivago* describes and judges the Revolution in one of the most direct and expressive ways open to a man. This is probably the major fact about the novel from any point of view; and therefore it makes small sense to say that Pasternak's enemy was not the Revolution but Pharisaism, or that his criticism was all a function of his love of Russia. Pasternak was describing and judging a piece of contemporary history. He was not taking from that history the materials for a work of art which would transform these materials into something different from what they had been, something self-sustaining and independent of all non-artistic reference. This may fairly be said to happen in some of Yeats's poems about the Irish rebellion, and in Blok's poems about the Russian Revolution, and even in Bely's novel about the 1905 revolt, *St Petersburg*. But *Doctor Zhivago* is an example of the novel as cultural document, and the method to follow in reading it is the Soviet critics' method.

3. The novel

What account of the novel can we then give, that will expand the Russian account in both scope and sympathy, and that will help us towards some ultimate response and judgment? First of all, let us try to place the novel's 'ideas' in the tradition to which they belong, for the English reader who knows nothing of that tradition will miss some of their significance.

The philosophical ideas in *Doctor Zhivago* are unusually consistent with each other, and unusually clear in their relation to the novel's intention in the largest sense. We are flatly told that Yurii and his uncle are superior to all their rivals and critics, as thinkers and as artists. Their views are reported at length, sometimes in the form of discourses, commented on only by enthusiastic endorsement from their interlocutors. These views are the novel's message, and though they are fictionalized, the author still bears responsibility for them—they reach to the core of what he has to say—as he does in any novel of this kind. Like *Women in Love, Doctor Zhivago* deals with not only its author's experience, but his attempt to think about that, his 'struggle towards verbal consciousness'. 'This struggle for verbal consciousness should not be left out in art,' Lawrence says. 'It is a very great part of life. It is not superimposition of a theory. It is the passionate struggle into conscious being.'

Doctor Zhivago's ideas belong to the intellectual world of Pasternak's youth, and in particular to the Vekhovtsy, the writers who contributed essays to *Vekhi, Landmarks*. This collection, edited by M. O. Gershensohn, came out in 1909, and was inspired by the failure of the 1905 revolution. The writers agreed, in a common revulsion of feeling, that the whole idea of the revolution as salvation had been wrong, as a major investment of thought and feeling by the intelligentsia, who had been busying themselves with public affairs instead of with their proper intellectual and spiritual duties. The Russian intellectual had been living 'outside himself', 'in the streets', 'in the market-place'. These writers, however much they differed in their interests, the preface said, held in common the principle that 'the inner life of the individual was the only creative force of human existence . . .

the only sound basis for any social structure'. This was a denial of the whole intellectual and literary tradition since Belinsky. Lenin understandably called *Vekhi* 'an encyclopaedia of perfidy', and for him and Gorky 'Vekhovtsy' became a term of abuse. (I take these details from Helen Muchnic's account of the book in her *From Gorky to Pasternak*.)

Nikolai Vedeniapin belongs with these writers (Bulgakov, Berdyaev, Struve, Frank, and others) and with the philosophers of Symbolism, Merezhkovsky, Shestov, Rozanov, and above all Solovyev. These are the thinkers on whom Blok, Bely and Vyacheslav Ivanov drew, as Yurii Zhivago drew on Vedeniapin. In the writings and the lives of Bely and Blok one can find many of the enigmatic features of Pasternak's novel foreshadowed and made plain. The coincidences of Zhivago's life, for instance, are of exactly the same kind as those that marked the friendship and meetings of Blok with Bely, which are discussed at length in Bely's *Reminiscences of Blok*. Vedeniapin was to his nephew Zhivago what Solovyev was to *his* nephew, and to Blok who was also Solovyev's relative.

This parallel is hinted at over and over again. We are told that Vedeniapin 'passionately sought an idea, inspired, graspable, which in its movement would clearly point the way towards change, an idea like a flash of lightning or a roll of thunder, capable of speaking even to a child or an illiterate'. Obviously he must be a special kind of philosopher, one who belongs, like Solovyev, as much to theology and to prophecy as to philosophy. And in his conversation with 'the Tolstoyan', Vedeniapin is shown to belong, like Solovyev, to the alternative and anti-thetical type of literary intellectual, the Dostoevskian, with that type's characteristic interest in the new symbolist writers. For one important way in which the theorists mentioned above defined their position was by rejecting Tolstoy (primarily as a thinker, but as an artistic model too) and preferring Dostoevsky, and often Nietzsche.

Vedeniapin was interested not in the ethical content of Christianity, but in the mystery of its spirit.

'Wait, let me tell you what I think. I think that if the beast in man could be held down by threats—any kind of threat, whether of jail or of retribution after death—then the highest emblem of humanity would be the lion tamer in the circus with his whip, not the prophet who sacrificed himself. But don't you see, this is just the point—what has for centuries raised man above the beast is not the cudgel but an inward music: the irresistible power of unarmed truth, the powerful attraction of its example.'[1]

Perhaps the unobtrusive phrase about music is the most important of all those; for Bely and Blok, among others, the kind of truth and of ideas that matter, ideas that transcend and transform reality, are a kind of music. Music is the supreme example of that power men can feel, in themselves and outside, when irreducible brute fact is reduced, and the mysterious, the irrational, the emotionally meaningful takes over.

Such ideas belong to a kind of philosophical idealism. This kind, in Russia at the turn of the century, was much involved with a mystical eroticism, a mystical aestheticism, and a messianic religiousness. (All three of these are recognizable, and important, in *Doctor Zhivago*.) But this religion, though centred on Christ, does not bear much resemblance to the faith of most church members. Dogma is responded to imaginatively with great fervour, but intellectually it is interpreted away without much respect. Yurii writes in his diary, 'It has always seemed to me that every conception is immaculate and that this dogma, concerning the Mother of God, expresses the idea of all motherhood.' Or he declares, 'Resurrection. In the crude form in which it is preached to console the weak, it is alien to me. I have always understood Christ's words about the living and the dead in a different sense.' But at the same time, both Yurii and his uncle insist that their ideas are derived from the Gospel;

'. . . [that] history as we know it now began with Christ, and that Christ's Gospel is its foundation . . You can't make such discoveries without spiritual equipment. And the basic elements of this equipment are in the Gospels. What are they? To begin with, love of one's neighbour, which is the supreme form of vital energy. Once it fills the heart of man, it has to overflow and spend itself. And then the two basic ideals of modern man—without them he is unthinkable—the idea of free personality and the idea of life as sacrifice.'

Of these two ideas, the first is developed in the novel most

[1] I take this quotation, and all that follows, from the translation by Max Hayward and Manya Harari.

importantly in Yurii's rebellion against the demands of the state, his claim that his private life, his private self, is of an absolute importance. The second is most vividly expressed, in a single action, in his sending Lara away with Komarovsky at the end; and more generally in his renunciation of the heroic stance, his identification of himself as inefficient, feeble, indecisive; he accepts pain, passivity, and death as a large part of his experience, and as part of his vocation as poet.

Neither of these ideas is specifically Christian; neither is even Deist. The significance of Christ is the way he transformed history —'began history'. This is made clear in a paragraph from Vedeniapin's diary.

'And then, into this tasteless heap of gold and marble, He came, light and clothed in an aura, emphatically human, deliberately provincial, Galilean, and at that moment gods and nations ceased to be and man came into being—man the carpenter, man the ploughman, man the shepherd with his flock of sheep at sunset, man who does not sound in the least proud, man thankfully celebrated in all the cradle songs of mothers and in all the picture galleries the world over.'

That is, Christ announces the superiority of the private individual over every social organism, the precedency of the private life over every social corporateness. He abolished nations and gods in the name of man; and man's primary qualities are henceforth those that make for personal happiness, in personal relations, in the creation and appreciation of art, in social manners, in the exchange of ideas in conversation, in all the life of a small and mutually selective group.

With this aspect of Christ, as philosopher, is associated another, as artist. This is not so much an ethical or an eschatological Christ as an aesthetic or symbolist one, though 'aesthetic' and 'symbolist' carry larger connotations than are usual in the West.

'It has always been assumed that the most important things in the Gospels are the ethical maxims and commandments. But for me the most important thing is that Christ speaks in parables taken from life, that He explains the truth in terms of everyday reality. The idea that underlies this is that communion between mortals is immortal, and that the whole of life is symbolic because it is meaningful.'

Christ has redeemed man by redeeming common (and above all private) experience—by showing that such experience can be a means of communication—rather than by having died on the Cross. This is of course what an artist can do, if he uses his art properly. It is in conjunction with this idea that we should read the notes on urban poetry found among Zhivago's papers after his death. There we see the artist finding the material for *his* parables—'following Christ' in the sense this version of Christianity makes central.

Art, on this theory, means more than either craftsmanship or a category of objects and ideas.

'I have always thought that art is not a category, not a realm covering innumerable concepts and derivative phenomena, but that, on the contrary, it is something concentrated, strictly limited. It is a principle that is present in every work of art, a force applied to it and a truth worked out in it. And I have never seen art as form but rather as a hidden, secret part of content. All this is as clear to me as daylight.'

And this principle can also be found outside all works of art, in one's way of understanding life. Thus Vedeniapin is an artist, even though it is philosophy he works in. When he meets Yurii again, '. . . the moment they began to speak of the things that really matter to creative minds, all other ties between them vanished, their kinship and difference of age were forgotten, all that was left was the confrontation of elemental forces, of energies and principles.' A philosophy like Vedeniapin's (and Solovyev's) is a work of the imagination in itself, as well as legislating the triumph of the imaginative way of looking at life over all other ways. And if the philosophical essayist is an artist, the poet is a philosopher. Yurii is called on by others to explain life and death, and history, and ethics.

This enthusiasm for the artist and for art-values is associated with a devotion to life-values; perhaps more closely than we are used to in England and America. Yurii's major declarations of faith are in life.

'Reshaping life! People who can say that have never understood a thing about life—they have never felt its breath, its heartbeat—however much they may have seen or done. They look on it as a lump of raw material that needs to be possessed by them, to be ennobled by their touch. But life is never a material, a substance to be moulded. If you want to know, life is the principle of self-renewal, it is constantly renewing and remaking and changing and transfiguring itself, it is infinitely beyond your or my obtuse theories about it.'

There the enemy is of course the politicians and social engineers, who deal with public life, public and corporate affairs, which are not really life at all.

'. . . those who inspired the revolution aren't at home in anything except change and turmoil, they aren't happy with anything that's on less than a world scale. For them transitional periods, worlds in the making, are an end in themselves. They aren't trained for anything else, they don't know anything except that. And do you know why these never-ending preparations are so futile? It's because these men haven't any real capacities, they are incompetent. Man is born to live, not to prepare for life. Life itself, the phenomenon of life, the gift of life, is so breathtakingly serious! So why substitute this childish harlequinade of immature fantasies, these schoolboy escapades?'

Real capacities, *real* competence, is for life (as understood here, private life) and art. Public life is seen as unreal, as a preparation for, or a scaffolding around, private life.

How then are public events handled, when they constitute so much of the subject-matter of the novel? Surely the answer is, by being kept remote from the major ideas and the other subject-matter—those blocks of private experience, in personal relations and in speculation, which *are* fully related to the novel's philosophy. The public events are treated (by the traditional Symbolist technique) as natural phenomena, sweeping down upon individuals, and altering their lives, their real lives, from outside. The most frequent image is of a storm; rain and wind, ice and snow, avalanche and glacier. And when public affairs demand to be taken on their own terms, as the action of people-in-society, the novel runs into difficulties. Zhivago's voice, and Pasternak's, becomes shrill and cracked. Yurii makes an attempt to describe public events in 'his own language', when he comments on the Bolsheviks' seizing of power, 'It has something of Pushkin's uncompromising clarity and of Tolstoy's unwavering faithfulness to the facts'. There is obviously something very strained in this, something incipiently foolish, and in fact Yurii lives to repent bitterly this one attempt to confront public events directly.

'Only once in his life had this uncompromising language and single-mindedness filled him with enthusiasm. Was it possible that he must pay for that rash enthusiasm all his life by never hearing, year after year, anything but these unchanging shrill, crazy exclamations and demands, which became progressively more impractical, meaningless, and unfulfillable as time went by? Was it possible that because of one moment of overgenerous response he had been enslaved forever?'

The first passage occurs a third of the way through the novel, the second two-thirds of the way through. The second recalling the first announces that this is a major theme, and invites us to scrutinize its treatment. But when we do so, we must surely be disappointed. Yurii deserves our sympathy but his way of handling the experience cannot impress, and the novel gives us no hint of how to criticize him while remaining loyal to Pasternak. The shrill petulance of the second quotation is the natural complement of the shrill eagerness of before, and the exaggerated egotism of the final exclamation is ultimately the hero's, and the author's, responsibility. Yurii cannot, in fact, deal with public affairs as human behaviour. He, and Pasternak, can only deal with them as phenomena of 'nature'.

Understanding the ideas leads us therefore to a critical judgment directly, and almost equally so, to a comment on characterization. For the major representative of the life idea is Lara; and she represents vividly too its relation to art. This is explicit. Yurii says to himself in Yuriatin,

'Oh, how sweet to be alive! How good to be alive and to love life! Oh, the ever-present longing to thank life, thank existence itself, to thank them as one being to another being.

This was exactly what Lara was. You could not communicate with life and existence, but she was their representative, their expression, in her the inarticulate principle of existence became sensitive and capable of speech.'

This had been her rôle from the beginning.

'Lara felt her size and her position in bed with two points of her body—the salient of her left shoulder and the big toe of her right foot. Everything else was more or less herself, her soul or inner being, harmoniously fitted into her contours and impatiently strained towards the future.'

She has a natural style, a self-completion in whatever she does, a perfect adaptation to the earth and life.

'In the reading room I thought she was absorbed in her reading with the ardour she would give to a real, hard physical task. Now I see that the reverse is also true: she carried water from the well as lightly and effortlessly as if she were reading. There is the same gracefulness in everything she does, as if she had taken a flying start early in life, way back in her childhood, and now everything she does follows this momentum, easily, naturally. This quality is in the line of her back when she bends down and in her smile as it parts her lips and rounds her chin, and in her words and thoughts.'

The relation of this quality to art is made clear in the passage describing how she would walk from the station to Duplyanka when she arrived there for the summer.

'Lara walked along the tracks following a path worn by pilgrims and then turned into the fields. Here she stopped and, closing her eyes, took a deep breath of the flower-scented air of the broad expanse around her. It was dearer to her than her kin, better than a lover, wiser than a book. For a moment she rediscovered the purpose of her life. She was here on earth to grasp the meaning of its wild enchantment and to call each thing by its right name, or, if this were not within her power, to give birth out of love for life to successors who would do it in her place.'

This helps us understand her relation to Yurii, psychologically as well as thematically. If poetry were what she cared about most, he would be a very glamorous figure in her eyes, and his inefficiency in the practical world, and in public affairs, could seem the signs of his vocation. This would fit in with her mishandling of her husband—not a poet, not an original sensibility, but a superbly effective man of action—her instinctive recoil from Samdeviatov and other confident 'strong' men, and her own tendency to take charge, to run things, to dominate. She instinctively allots her men the passive and feminine rôle in relationships with her, and only with a man who achieves something brilliant and powerful in that rôle, as a poet does, can she form a stable and satisfying love-relationship.

However, this psychological theory is something the reader has to piece together for himself. Most of what Pasternak tells us about Lara, and Yurii, goes against it, or at best ignores it. Lara we are told *is* life and health. Her beauty is wholly natural and alive.

'Coming home at night, hungry and tired, he found Lara busy at her domestic chores, cooking and washing. In this prosaic, weekday aspect of her being, dishevelled, with her sleeves rolled and her skirts tucked up, she almost frightened him by her regal attractiveness, more breath-taking than if he had found her on the point of going to a ball, taller in high-heeled shoes and in a long low-cut gown with a sweeping, rustling skirt.'

As such she is natural mistress of Varykino, which has been presented from the beginning as the home of life. Their love affair is equally a matter of life.

'They loved each other, not driven by necessity, by the "blaze of passion" often falsely ascribed to love. They loved each other because everything around them willed it, the trees and the clouds and the sky over their heads and the earth under their feet. Perhaps their surrounding world, the strangers they met in the street, the wide expanses they saw on their walks, the rooms in which they lived or met, took more delight in their love than they did themselves.

Ah, that was just what had united them and had made them so akin! Never, never, even in their moments of richest and wildest happiness, were they unaware of a sublime joy in the total design of the universe, a feeling that they themselves were a part of that whole, an element in the beauty of the cosmos.

This unity with the whole was the breath of life to them. And the elevation of man above the rest of nature, the modern coddling and worship of man, never appealed to them. A social system based on such a false premise, as well as its political application, struck them as pathetically amateurish and made no sense to them.'

Yurii embraces all of 'Russia', all of life, when he embraces Lara; and she embraces all of art, and thought, in him. The two concepts are not opposed. They are related in a clear enough way. Art is life raised to a higher pitch of intensity, but losing, by its fineness, some of the toughness, the coarse substantiality, of the humbler medium. All this 'thematic characterization' is interesting enough, and if Pasternak chooses to sacrifice to this the 'psychological characterization' whose possibility we glimpsed before, then we have no right to complain.

But there are important facts about Lara that are thematically discordant. She is identified with Mary Magdalene, she remains all her life in some sense corrupt, and her primary allegiance is always to Komarovsky. Indeed Yurii's love for her is not always healthy and sane. It is expressed often in romantically destructive terms: 'I love you madly, irrationally, infinitely.' The idyll at Varykino is an idyll of death and tragedy, something they know cannot last, and in which they are both very uneasy. And their love is from beginning to end *guilty*. All this surely expresses a very different idea of Lara and of love, as of something doomed and death-directed, against the will of the gods and the laws of nature. This idea is clearly the opposite of the other one, and it plays havoc with any thematic characterization. It makes the reader feel that the author has imposed hasty schematizations on his experience which do not fully express or organize it.

If we turn now to narrative and structural techniques, the first thing to say is that *Doctor Zhivago* is a very loosely constructed book. The simplest example of this looseness is Chapter 10, 'The Highway', in which all the characters and stories we have been following up to then are snatched away, and we find ourselves without warning inside the consciousness of a woman we never heard of before, and one whom we realize, at the end of the novel, could not well have been less important to either plot or theme. This is the most spectacular example, but by no means the only one. That disconnectedness is characteristic of *Doctor Zhivago*. Though our critics have discussed it as if it were as tightly organized as *Women in Love*, it is in fact much looser than even *The Rainbow*. That is, the relation of event to idea, of one event to another, of one idea to another, of the whole order of ideas to that of events, is less immediate, less significant, and less patterned.

The main pattern in *Doctor Zhivago* is the developing love (more destiny than relationship) between Yurii and Lara. Their meetings, so far between and brief and accidental (though always significant) in the first part of the book, become progressively more frequent, more charged with emotion, more fatal in the largest sense, till they end in the catastrophe. This is not a matter of literal meetings only; Lara appears in Zhivago's mind—at first in the form of unnamed echoes and unidentified yearnings—in Varykino, in the middle of the book; later, in the forest, she appears there again, as a literal hallucination, almost overwhelming his consciousness. When he sees her again in the flesh, his life is absorbed in her, and the novel is absorbed in them; they do not part again until the catastrophe, and the tempo of the writing becomes and remains much more excited, emotional and romantic.

This recurrence is the major structural principle, and if we compare *Doctor Zhivago* with *The Rainbow*, with its linked group of thematic concerns and symbols, recurring through three generations, we see how much looser this is. Quite simply, *Doctor Zhivago* is about so many other things besides this love affair that, in the intervals between these recurrences, we can have no very taut expectation of the next one. Of course all the themes are related in the ordinary way themes are related in any half-successful novel; and of course in *Doctor Zhivago* the different stories are connected by the famous coincidences; but there is nothing through which both theme and story, the total meaning of one part of the book, is related to another. When we are not in Lara's presence, or in Yurii's mind when he is thinking of Lara, there is nothing to remind us of her and all that she represents. (Nothing, let me say again, that is a major structural device.)

More than in most novels, the interest of each successful episode in *Doctor Zhivago* is generated by what it contains—as would be expected in a realistic account of contemporary history. There are several narrative patterns which continue through the book, but it is striking that these patterns are desultorily developed, and are separate one from another. Take for instance the story of Yurii's lifelong friends, Gordon and Dudorov. They are introduced importantly, but then disappear, and their recurrences cannot be said to generate any sense of development, or even of pattern. They have no continuity of function, very little of identity. And if they have an obvious and unexciting relation to the theme of the intelligentsia in the revolution, they have no relation to Lara's theme at all. Above all, the novelist's handling of them so baffles our every attempt to find a meaningful pattern in it that we are bound to feel that he is not in control of his material.

The novel's structural *tactics* seem to be a large-scale version of the narrative impressionism we find in a paragraph like this:

'Once more it ended in tears. His uncle woke up, spoke to him of Christ, and tried to comfort him, then yawned and stood thoughtfully by the window. Day was breaking. They began to dress.'

Here the atmosphere of a half hour is captured by noting a number of event-fragments, seen from the outside and described 'unsympathetically', which when put in sequence generate a sense of that inside to the moment which was not directly rendered—only a fleeting sense, and permeated with a feeling of that moment's frailty and uncertainty, but a vivid sense. In the novel as a whole Pasternak sets out to capture the atmosphere of years and decades by the same technique.

This sequence of disconnected fragments can give an air of significance to details which proves deceitful. This air is probably accentuated in translation, and one would suggest that it has provoked some of the wilder guesses of the commentators. The surface of Pasternak's prose in English is very enigmatic and 'meaningful'. At the Gromekos' musical evening:

'The men came in out of the cold in high clumsy snow boots, and every one of them, without exception, did his best to look like a country bumpkin; but their wives, on the contrary, their faces glowing from the frost, coats unbuttoned, shawls pushed back and hair spangled with rime, looked like hardened coquettes, cunning itself. "Cui's nephew", the whisper went round as the new pianist came in.'

The difference between the men and the women here I take to be purely visual and purely momentary. It has no significance beyond itself. Pasternak is being a transparent eyeball at such moments. And just so with larger effects in the novel. Of course they have connections with what goes before and after, but what is much more striking in their aesthetic character is their disconnectedness, their demand to be taken simply and limitedly for what they are. That demand is one which modern reading methods find it hard to meet.

This narrative manner at its most successful, on a small scale, we can perhaps demonstrate with an example from 'The Sventitskys' Christmas Party'.

'Yura stood uneasily in the middle of the ballroom, watching Tonia dancing with a stranger. She swept up to him, flounced her short satin train—like a fish waving its fin—and vanished in the crowd.

She was very excited. During the interval, she had refused tea and had slaked her thirst with innumerable tangerines, peeling them and wiping her fingers and the corners of her mouth on a handkerchief the size of a fruit blossom. Laughing and talking incessantly, she kept taking the handkerchief out and unthinkingly putting it back inside her sash or her sleeve.

Now, as she brushed past the frowning Yura, spinning with her unknown partner, she caught and pressed his hand and smiled eloquently. The handkerchief she had been holding stayed in his hand. He pressed it to his lips and closed his eyes. The handkerchief smelled equally enchantingly of tangerines and of Tonia's hand. This was something new in Yura's life, something he had never felt before, something sharp that pierced him from top to toe. This naïvely childish smell was as intimate and understandable as a word whispered in the dark. He pressed the handkerchief to his eyes and lips, breathing through it. Suddenly a shot rang out inside.'

The style here reflects the excitement described—'innumerable' tangerines, and a handkerchief the size of a fruit blossom, and the comparison to a fish waving its fin. The complex psychology of the relationship, and of each of the two personalities, taken separately, is shattered by this excitement, and all that remain are these irrational, almost hallucinatory, intuitions. And supervening on these agitations comes the incongruity and climax of the shot. This method of short sharp impressions could be called central to Pasternak's way of presenting the private lives and personal stories he is concerned with.

He has a different narrative manner for presenting the Revolution and history. We see this perhaps first in section 5 of Chapter 2, which begins, 'That autumn there was unrest among the railway workers on the Moscow network.' And in section 8 of that chapter we get the description of the demonstration.

'Down the street people came pouring in a torrent—faces, faces, faces, quilted winter coats and sheepskin hats, men and women students, old men, children, railwaymen in uniform, workers from the trolley depot and telephone exchange in knee boots and leather jackets, girls and schoolboys.'

This is in effect the official Soviet style for describing crowd movements which we have seen in many other novels and histories, in films, and in photographs. Naturally, there is much more sense of an impersonal narrator, and of a responsible connected account. Looking for Pasternak's species within this genus, we should say that Pasternak's use of this style emphasizes effects of fragmentation and disconnection.

The primary method Pasternak uses to present the history, however, is not that 'official' style but the telling of anecdotes, about persons and events that emblemize the times. These anecdotes are highly-coloured, semi-legendary, rough-hewn; about people like Ustinia and Mlle Fleury, Pamphil, Kubarkha, Tania, Galuzina, Commissar Gints and Pogorevshikh, Bacchus, Vasia, the people on the train.

One of the striking things about this material and this method is how unrelated it is to Zhivago as a character, and therefore to all that he represents as a character; in distinction, that is, from what he represents as author's mask. In the case of Chapter 10, of course, Zhivago is not present in any sense. But in other cases he is present in the literal sense, but his reactions to what he sees or hears are not reported. They would be artistically irrelevant, even unassimilable. We are upset when it *is* reported to us, about Pamphil, that 'to Yurii Andreievitch this gloomy and unsociable giant, soulless and narrow-minded, seemed sub-normal, almost a degenerate'. Such a judgment makes Yurii momentarily a character within the novel, himself to be judged, instead of being the synonym for Pasternak we had assumed him to be, the name for the novel's central vision. Not that Yurii's judgment is opposed to the narrator's, but it is formulated and determinate, where the latter's is embryonic and indeterminate, not a judgment but an awareness, carefully left to us to crystallize for ourselves.

This anecdotal style is sometimes applied to the doings of the central characters, but the material is then less highly-coloured and rough-hewn. This is true of, for instance, the account of life in Moscow in 1917. Moreover, those central characters then appear as average citizens, not as the persons they are in their private stories. When Tonia ponders which things to take on the journey to Varykino, she does so without revealing her inner self at all—as Anna Karenina does in her household arrangements, for instance. Tonia's ponderings reveal only the barter-lore of Moscow in 1918. (This is another example of what we mean by calling the novel's structure loose and disconnected.)

Whenever he is using the anecdotal style, Pasternak is able to create an atmosphere of the legendary, of the romantic, of the mysterious, which is a prime interest of his. Even in the anecdotes concerning the central characters in Moscow, this effect can be seen; for instance, in the story of the mysterious place between Serebriany and Molchanovka. Even the confusion of rumours at the railway station when Yurii and Tonia leave Moscow is not presented as primarily inefficiency, or even as an annoyance, but as a release into the world of unreason, the world of fantasy, in which anything might be true. There is a sense in which everything in the novel is so described as to produce the impression described here, which refers in context to Yurii's journey from the partisan camp to Yuriatin.

'These scenes and incidents had the strangeness of the transcendental, as if they were snatches torn from lives on other planets that had somehow drifted to the earth. Only nature had remained true to history and appeared in the guise it assumed in modern art.'

When this 'strangeness' is not ascribed to social forces, it is produced by delirium, incipient illness, hunger, exhaustion, emotional stress, in one of the characters, or quite simply and directly by an aesthetic device 'imposed' by the author. For example, events are often described by transposing one kind of sense-impression into terms of another sense—Pasternak is particularly fond of rendering vivid visual effects in terms of drinks and fruits and sweetmeats. In this last example he simply allows a visual effect—the pattern of a cotton print—to take over and dominate a scene involving people and emotions, just as it might in a Matisse.

'Anxious not to seem ungrateful, she [Tonia] kept apologizing, going next door and coming back with presents for the woman—blouses and lengths of cotton and silk prints. And the dark materials, with their white check or polka-dot patterns, were like the dark snow-bound street checkered with bricks and covered with white dots which, that farewell night, looked in through the uncurtained windows.'

Pasternak creates a world in which reason, and prudence, and common-sense, and literal-mindedness, are constantly being outreached and confounded. That is the essential function of his striking interest in mistakes and accidents, as well as in omens and coincidences and mysteries. He goes out of his way to tell us that:

'For many years Tiverzin thought that it was he alone who had stopped work and traffic on the line that night. Only much later, at the trial, when he was charged with complicity in the strike but not with inciting it, did he learn the truth.'

He makes a point of the coincidence and confusion of Yurii's diagnostic success and the birth of his son—the congratulations are several times confused. He makes a point of the mistake over Pasha Antipov's capture, when he was reported dead. There are many mistakes of this kind noted throughout the book, which give a slight blur of doubt (not the full Hawthornian unreality) to figures and events.

Donald Davie describes one of these incidents as 'the best hint on how to read the novel'. This is the matter of the wardrobe which caused Anna Ivanovna's fall, after which she became ill. 'She nicknamed it the tomb of Askold; she meant the horse of Prince Oleg, which had caused its master's death. She had read a great deal, but haphazardly, and she tended to confuse related ideas.' Nothing more is made of this mistake, and this is certainly very characteristic of Pasternak's manner, but Dr Davie says this incident 'represents as it were a poem offered to Zhivago which he never got round to writing'. Surely to introduce the idea of poetry here is only to confuse matters. This is simply an example of the confusion of error and accident and coincidence (after the fall she developed a pulmonary weakness) which Pasternak sees as marking human life. Things that have no explanation or larger significance yet seem to demand one, and Pasternak presents us with both that demand and its unfulfilment. This puts the events into a broad and lofty perspective which resists, indeed renounces, all 'explanation'.

Some of the coincidences have the same function, of creating that broad and detached perspective. One of the most successful is the first one described, in section 5 of Chapter 1, where Yura is in some sense within sight of his father at the moment of the latter's death. The physical distance between observer and observed—already dramatized by the broad plain and shining river—is further enhanced by the coincidence; and all this together enhances the drama of the death. But Yura himself does not see the train, and though he does think of his father, it is unemotionally and in response to no special intimation. This blend of the dramatic and the casual, of the remarkable coincidence and the plausible accident, helps make the incident so satisfying. As is usual in Pasternak, the coincidence is multiple. Misha Gordon, to be Yura's lifelong friend, is in the train, and has met Zhivago senior; and Komarovsky, who is to ruin Lara's life, and so Yura's, has in effect caused the suicide. This concatenation is royal in its abundance, without offending against any of the laws governing this effect. But when we are told that Tiverzina was also present, we are conscious of something else, which we might describe as a nervous tic in the aesthetic sense. Pasternak seems at such times to be obsessed with the aesthete's love of pattern, combined with the irrationalist's love of mystery. This is not a question of ordinary plausibility. I think that if we had been told that Lara was on that same train, or observing it, like Yura, we should not be offended. That could fill out the thematic pattern of the book. What is wrong with Tiverzina's presence is that it has no thematic significance. She might as well not be there. Her presence is an offence against the law of artistic economy, that law which shaped Yura's awareness of his father into something so casual and unemphatic.

When Yurii sees the candle at the window of Pasha's room on the night of the Christmas party, we recognize the same concentrated dramatic suggestiveness of the earlier coincidence: and something of the same tact in the insignificance of the sign, and the disparity of the different excitements people were feeling. And if the perspective is not this time broad and high, but closely brooding over these people, it is just as authentic. But that Yurii should end his life in that same room seems as lacking in tact as the introduction of Tiverzina before. That he should have died in Kamerger Street would have set up the resonances Pasternak wants, but that it should be the same room seems crudely overemphatic and unmodulated. This crudity of taste and clumsiness of touch—if I interpret rightly what Pasternak was intending—is recurrent. It would seem to mark the amateur or at least the apprentice at fiction. Perhaps the grossest example of this sort of failing occurs in the most large-scale of all the coincidences. Here Pasternak is reduced to explaining the identities of the people involved after the event.

'The man who had just died was Private Gimazetdin; the excited officer who had been shouting in the wood was his son, Lt Galiullin; the nurse was Lara. Gordon and Zhivago were the witnesses. All these people were there together, in one place. But some of them had never known each other, while others failed to recognize each other now. And there were things about them which were never to be known for certain, while others were not to be revealed until a future time, a later meeting.'

Here that closely brooding perspective becomes absurd. We are too conscious of who it is who *does* know what all these people don't know. The author is delightedly moving his chessmen together into extraordinary groupings, and calling on us to share his glee.

By the time we come to the description of Zhivago's death, we expect that the old lady in the lilac dress who walks parallel with his trolley will turn out to be someone who had already figured in the action. We also expect, unfortunately, to be kept waiting a long time for the identification, and then to find that it does not add much to the effect. That this should be Mlle Fleury does not seem to enrich the scene significantly. The effect seems to be almost wholly concentrated in the fact that this is *someone* out of the past, or better, *like* someone out of the past; that pattern is suggested, again, a last time, as elusively as ever. But in that case, surely what Pasternak needed to convey was that an old lady passing Zhivago's trolley looked like Mlle Fleury—that it could well literally be her—but not flatly to assert that it was. For such assertions are not merely unsubtle in their immediate effect. They are brutally extravagant in a long-range way. Such reckless manipulations of characters and events remind us of Dickens more than of Shakespeare—it is of course the latter who has been called on to sponsor them, by Pasternak's Western admirers. But Dickens succeeds because he so fully accepts his rôle as manipulator, so energetically conjures up an other-than-objective reality for his events and people. Dickens pays the necessary price of his vivid patterns in the insubstantiality of the things he patterned, the incomplete reality of his world. Pasternak cannot afford any such price, cannot afford to appear a manipulator, both because he is half the time a historian and because the other half he is arguing the inexplicability of events, their mysterious otherness.

Of the omens and portents, one of the most large-scale and the most successful is that in section 9 of Chapter 5; the night storm after Lara has left Meliuzeievo, which awakens Mlle Fleury and Zhivago, and which deceives them into thinking she is knocking on the door. Several critics have tried to connect this with other incidents in the novel, and with other aspects of Lara's personality. But the essence of such an incident is that it should remain inexplicable, unrelated, meaningless. It is again the suggestion of significance Pasternak is working at, not its definition. He is presenting that kind of experience which *seems* pregnant with meaning; and for us to find that it *is* and then to define that meaning, is to miss half the point he is making. This is a case rather like those Robert Frost poems in which the centre of the subject is the *possibility* of an allegorical meaning to the events described.

This effect of suggestion is amplified in ordinary ways, as for instance by making the characters themselves omen-seekers, and thus relieving the author of sole responsibility. Thus as soon as Tonia hears from Yurii that he has met at Meliuzeievo the girl he had met on the night of Anna Ivanovna's death, she replies:

'In sentences broken by sobs and with tear-stains and ink-blots for punctuation, she begged him not to come back to Moscow but to go straight to the Urals with that wonderful nurse whose progress through life was marked by portents and coincidences so miraculous that her own, Tania's modest life could not possibly compete with it.'

And as soon as she has met Samdeviatov, she declares, 'I don't know about you but I feel he's a godsend. I think he'll play some sort of part in our lives.'

Yurii is equally superstitious, about Evgraf and about that mysterious section of street in Moscow. And when he returns to Yuriatin, after being with the Forest Partisans:

'His sudden weakness earlier that afternoon as he approached the town and walked through it an hour or two ago had made Yurii Andreievitch think that he was ill, and had filled him with fears. Now, the sameness of the light in the house and in the street exhilarated him. Bathed in the same chilled air as the passers-by, he felt a kinship with them, an identity with the mood of the town, with life in the world. This dispelled his fears. He no longer thought he would be ill. The transparency of the spring evening, the all-penetrating light were a good omen, a promise of generous fulfilment of distant and far-reaching hopes. All would be well, he would achieve all he wanted in life, he would find and reunite and reconcile them all, he would think everything out and find all the right words. He waited for the joy of seeing Lara as an immediate proof that all the rest would follow.'

Passages of this kind are typical of the whole 'climate of belief' in the book. Pasternak is more interested in, and more pleased with, such states of mind than with more rational, more organized, or more conscientious states. Of course, he does not exclude sceptical states of mind, or rational explanations, but he subordinates them. Take for instance the story of the chiming clock which the Moscow supplier thinks has frightened his wife into a nervous decline. This turns out not to be true—she has typhus —and when the Zhivagos' clock also unexpectedly chimes, Yurii makes a joke of the coincidence and of the portent. But he does in fact catch typhus. The 'explanation' is presumably that he was infected by his patient. But what interests Pasternak, what counts in the novel, is not the explanation, but the portent.

Lara's emotional life is equally influenced by superstitions. Her whole relationship to Komarovsky is superstitious, as well as irrational. When she hears of the part he has already played in Yurii's life, she says, 'It isn't possible! It's extraordinary! Can it really be true? So he was your evil genius, too! It brings us even closer! It must be predestination!' And when she hears that Yurii has met Pasha, she is equally excited, and brings in the idea of predestination again. 'It's as if you were predestined to meet.'

And all these mysteries within the events themselves and in the characters' responses are compounded by purely narrative mysteries created arbitrarily by the author. Two major examples are the story of Lara's child by Yurii, and the identity of Strelnikov. In the first case, we have it hinted to us that Lara is pregnant before she leaves with Komarovsky, we have the wild rhetoric of her speech to Evgraf, we have the mysterious facial likeness between Tania and Yurii, and we have the terrible anecdote of Tania's childhood. These are the standard devices of melodrama-mystery. We find them all in Dickens (Lady Dedlock and Esther Summerson) and in Dostoevsky. As such, they seem quite out of keeping with, quite disconnected from, the fictional world built up in other parts of the novel, especially the open-air, life-worshipping world built round Lara. The second case is even more striking. We are given every conspiratorial hint that Strelnikov is Pasha Antipov from as soon as we meet him—there is no gradual accumulation of suspicion, no natural and probable growth of knowledge—and yet after the fact has been 'established', we are given reason to doubt it (Yurii disbelieves the story, and Lara's belief is over-emotional) though in fact, as we later learn, it was true.

Pasternak was not a skilful narrator. He often gives us a series of events in ineffective order, and sometimes has to halt his story and reverse his direction, in order to explain something the consequences of which we have just seen. The two cases we have just discussed are examples of a kind of narrative which it is particularly difficult to combine with serious thematic concern. Both Dickens's and Dostoevsky's novels sometimes suffer from a conflict of interest between their love of mystery and their seriousness of feeling, and Pasternak could not rival either of them in narrative skill. His fictional successes are in the rôle of the novelist as poet, not as serial thriller.

In such places, he manufactures a narrative interest of a kind which lies inertly alongside the book's other motives, which plainly engage him much more deeply. Perhaps the most effective co-operation of this interest with the others occurs in 'Return to Varykino', in the signs that the house has been occupied, and in the shots from the gully later, all afterwards explained as the work of Strelnikov. This succeeds better surely because the dominant emotional character of this episode is idyllic. These are a few days snatched from Fate, this is an enclave from which the enemy has been—for just a moment—excluded. This hectic and romantic emotional atmosphere is much more compatible with melodramatic narrative devices than those parts of the novel that calmly affirm life and health.

Many prominent features of the book demand to be explained by the theory that the author's control of fictional techniques was fumbling and half-hearted. The attempt to write convincing dialogue, for instance, is clearly abandoned in several places; Sima's lecture to Lara; Lara's explanation to Yurii of the breakdown of her marriage; the Gordon-Dudorov conversation in the 'Epilogue'. The characters are sometimes described to us in an abrupt summation that implies a judging and acting narrator who at other times is conspicuously absent. Thus we are told that, in his adolescence, 'Everything in Yura's mind was still helter-skelter, but his views, his habits, and his inclinations were all distinctly his own. He was unusually impressionable, and the originality of his vision was great.' And later, 'All around, people continued to deceive themselves, to talk endlessly. Everyday life struggled on, by force of habit, limping and shuffling. But the doctor saw life as it was.' Ordinary authorial tact is abandoned; we are suddenly directed how to feel, and at the top of the writer's voice.

'Their love was great. Most people experience love without becoming aware of the extraordinary nature of this emotion. But to them—and this made them exceptional—the moments when passion visited their doomed human existence like a breath of eternity were moments of revelation, of continually new discoveries about themselves and life.'

Passages of description, introduced as the work of a character, are quite transparently the work of the author; when Yurii has to describe to Gordon the Tsar's visit to the Carpathian front, we are told, 'He told his story well', and with that Pasternak takes over. After a description of the flowers around Zhivago's coffin, Pasternak suddenly steps forward and meditates in his own voice, along lines previously attributed to his character.

'The vegetable kingdom can easily be thought of as the nearest neighbour of the kingdom of death. Perhaps the mysteries of evolution and the riddles of life that so puzzle us are contained in the green of the earth, among the trees and the flowers of graveyards. Mary Magdalene did not recognize Jesus risen from the grave, "supposing Him to be the gardener . . ."'

Finally, in characterization too we find this same clumsiness. We have already pointed out how sketchily Pasternak treats matters of psychological interest, in our comments on the relationship between Lara and Yurii. The same could be said of the relationship between Lara and Antipov, and of the whole characterization of Komarovsky. In all these cases, a thematic significance is made to override the psychological intricacies of the figure, and yet characterological features are allowed to obtrude which are incompatible with that significance. Komarovsky, for instance, as he appears at the end of the novel, and in his speech at Lara's wedding, and in his behaviour after the shooting, is far from the 'pure-bred animal' we are told about, the cold-blooded sensualist, the wholly corrupt representative of evil. He is sentimental, self-deceiving, well-meaning, comic.

What Pasternak has attempted, apparently, is the kind of characterization we find in *Women in Love,* but he has not achieved that adjustment of perspective by which a complicated personal psychology—say Gerald Crich's—can focus the eye on one large thematic truth without sacrificing any of its own necessary intricacies.

Our account of the novel must then be that it is very interesting as a cultural document, and interesting, often beautifully successful, as an experiment with fictional techniques; but not very distinguished in its handling of human emotions and behaviour, and rather inept in various simple matters of narrative and characterization. Above all, it is not a tightly organized or highly integrated novel. Paradoxically, it is partly because it is so loosely organized that it has been thought to be so mysteriously complete and impeccable. Partly, of course, this mistake has been made because Pasternak plainly *invites* us to think that his is a symbolic novel in the most ambitious sense (we may point to *Passage to India* as a successful example in English literature of what we mean). But in part the paradox holds. Modern criticism identifies loose organization with artistic failure so exaggeratedly that it is faced with the responsibility of condemning every novel in which it cannot find a stringent artistic economy. Unable thus to condemn *Doctor Zhivago*—because of its obvious artistic vitality as well as for less valid reasons—it has had to invent an economy for it so esoteric that common-sense dared not lay hold of any episode in isolation from 'the whole'. The entire episode is a cautionary tale for modern literary studies.

Pasternak was a typical modern poet even in the way he looked— and perhaps even in the way he made himself look. One surely must suspect that that extraordinary long upper lip and those hollow cheeks were the result of histrionic art. He was pulling his lip down and sucking his cheeks in. At least in some unposed snapshots he appears quite different—a handsome man in a much more ordinary style. And there is evidence enough, from the accounts of people sympathetic to him, of his intense self-consciousness about his looks, and his readiness for a certain amount of posturing. In his youth, Annenkov tells us,

'He had large eyes, full lips, a proud and dreamy bearing, a good figure, a rhythmic way of walking, and a strong, pleasant voice. People in the street turned instinctively to look at him without knowing who he was. I remember how Pasternak himself once stopped, turned around, and, planting himself firmly on both feet, put his tongue out at a girl who had stared at him. "Now look here," I reproached him. "I am so shy, and curiosity embarrasses me," Pasternak replied apologetically.' And the interviewer for *The Paris Review*, in 1960, commented, 'He is very handsome, and conscious of the effect of his extraordinary face. He sometimes turns his head away, half closing his eyes.' Indeed, I think one can see that the events of Dr Zhivago's life would not have happened to the snub-nosed, unimpressive-looking man he is described as being. At least, some of them (his relations with Tonia and Lara) are more likely to have happened to someone who looked like Pasternak.

What gives this, I hope, the status of being more than gossip, is that something similar has been true of nearly all the modern writers we have been discussing, and is discernibly related to the symbolist idea of being a writer. We have pointed out how much of the actor there was in Yeats, Frost, Blok, Rilke, how much determination to embody the poet in manner, gesture, posture, costume—to live out the idea of a poet. Pasternak's case is perhaps deceptive, because there seems so much boyish mischievousness and lightweight self-delight in his posturing. He was a very handsome man, and so it was easy for him to play at as well as to play the rôle of the poet in the flesh. (Though I think that accident of ease, that playing at, was not without significant consequences; I think it made it easier for him to *be* a poet, in every sense.) But if we think of Rilke, whose physical endowment was quite different, we see how important playing that rôle is even to a poet who must do it all by hard work, so to speak. Valéry tells us that Rilke's person, his voice, his glance, his manners, everything about him gave the impression of a magical presence. Any photograph shows us that that effect was a triumph of personality, and any biography betrays the arts by which he achieved it.

This element of theatre in the very heart of the writer's personality, the idea that being a writer involves one in such histrionics, is surely disturbing in itself. It is one of the endearing things about D. H. Lawrence that he took such a bad photograph. Even his beard was more something to hide behind than a manifestation of power, and his other personal devices of that kind—we must expect a hyper-sensitive man to keep trying on armour—seem to have been equally half-hearted and temporary. They weren't the major manifestations of his personality. And our feeling against such histrionics has connections with something quite important. If Lawrence and T. S. Eliot remained private faces in public places, it is surely not fanciful to connect that fact with their being less extravagantly and purely modern poets than the others we have mentioned. They both assigned severe limits to the autonomy of art, they acknowledged other important responsibilities in life, and consequently they never made themselves over into personae and sacred masks in the reckless way of Rilke and Yeats. For it is this idea that anyone with imagination can create meaning and value for himself, can contradict and transcend the common ordinary kinds of truth, which encourages the modern poet to invent a personality for himself. Because he feels that he serves special values, and can ignore ordinary ones, he is in a sense as conscienceless as an advertising man, ready to create an image which expresses in the gaudiest terms the image-maker's desire to dazzle the public. Because he feels that culture as a whole is on the wrong track, and he alone hears the music of the universe, his conscience has no social controls, no social functions. His face, when he is photographed, his opinions, when he is interviewed, his life-story, when he relates it, are so many raw materials for his imagination to work up quite freely, uncontrolled by ordinary respect for the truth or for his audience. In a sense, he gives up being an ordinary man. The theorists of symbolism are always telling us, of course, that the private man must die for the artist to be born, but we need to remind ourselves that part of what they mean is just this— something which when labelled Madison Avenue is the object of general scorn and indignation.

This is obviously just a minor aspect of the transcendent idea of the poet, of poetry, of literature, of art, which I have been arguing against. Perhaps it could be called an aspect of the readiness of the modern writer to become a monster, to exceed the limits laid down for normal decency. (No doubt writers in other ages have been more ready than other groups of people to exceed those limits, but that tendency is exaggerated today by our aesthetic.) And this histrionicism is clearly related to the histrionics of Yeats with his sword and his message to India, and the histrionic nostalgia of Stephen Dedalus. I think that most of the manifestations of the 'modern literary mind' I have been attacking have some interconnections, even though they are also, in other ways, disconnected and disparate. Tolstoy and Lawrence, with their puritan judgments of character, seem very far from Yeats and Rilke with their aesthetic mysticism—from all that is listed in Kermode's definition of symbolism. And indeed there are huge differences between the two pairs. But there are connections.

Let us take Lawrence's definition of 'quickness' from his essay 'The Novel'. Though he is talking about two of Tolstoy's characters here, all he says applies very exactly to Baron von Hügel, and to our whole argument in the second essay. Nothing could put its finger more acutely on that quality in the Baron which disqualifies him for most people today from any real impressiveness.

'Quickness is *necessary* to the novel. ... The man in the novel must be "quick". And this means one thing, among a host of unknown meanings: it means he must have a quick relatedness to all the other things in the novel: snow, bed-bugs, sunshine, the phallus, trains, silk-hats, cats, sorrow, people, food, diphtheria, fuchsias, stars, ideas, God, toothpaste, lightning, and toilet-paper. ... And this is why Pierre, for example, in *War and Peace*, is more dull and less quick than Prince André. Pierre is quite nicely related to ideas, toothpaste, God, people, food, trains, silk-hats, sorrow, diphtheria, stars. But his relation to snow, sunshine, cats, lightning and the phallus, fuchsias and toilet-paper, is sluggish and mussy. He's not quick enough.'

The Baron was no quicker than Pierre—much less—and that more-than-sluggishness, that ruin of the body, is the mark of his total failure at life by Professor Brown's standards, his failure at 'life'.

All this seems remote from the world of 'art'. But we should notice the first two sentences quoted. Lawrence says the man *in the novel* must be quick. This is significant. Not that one can imagine Lawrence saying that outside the novel a man need not be, but that the purest and strongest case (of this saving truth) is the aesthetic one. The difference between art and life for Lawrence was often that in art you could give free play to the really interesting forces in people, and eliminate the dull, distracting, everyday realities. This is, ultimately, a kind of aestheticism —a claim to re-invent life—George Eliot did not eliminate the every-day realities. And it is surprising how many of the items in Kermode's list have some application to Lawrence, surely the least aesthetic of modern writers.

Not that I wish to imply that there is any system of beliefs uniting all these writers: a cloudy conglomeration of beliefs, vaguely analogous and fitfully related to each other, because all animated by the same spirit or family of spirits—nothing more definite than that. But as an atmosphere it is identifiable, it is distinguishable from what it is not, it does amount to an idea. Obviously it excludes from full favour the concept of the Catholic writer and the Communist writer, with their subordinated ideas of the writer's function, their only partial devotion to the values of 'life'. More important, it excludes von Hügel. *All* the people who participate in the modern literary idea agree to find von Hügel's kind of defeats more conclusive than his victories, and to call his kind of philosophic and religious achievements compensations, cowardices, substitute-gratifications or some other dismissive term. Von Hügel stands for all of life that is not 'life'; and when that kind of contrast is drawn, the modern literary mind has no freedom of choice; in all its manifestations, it is previously committed.

Let me protest—for the last time—that I do see how much modern literature, even at its most modern, has to offer to humanist morality and religious spirituality, even in their own terms. I accept, at the same time as I appeal against it, its judgment on von Hügel himself. More, I think Lawrence was right to complain that Christianity has traditionally asked the lion to lie down with the lamb, and that this would be, not a fulfilment for them, but an obscene frustration of their natures. In other words, that one's nature, and its fulfilment, are moral and spiritual values which stand in opposition to traditional Christian teaching. It seems to me that neither Catholicism nor traditional moral wisdom have ever begun to compete with Lawrence or Yeats in the power of their insights into such differences, between the lion and the lamb, the human tiger and the human rabbit. Those differences are of enormous moral and spiritual significance; how one is to feel about them, what one is to do about them, are as fundamental questions as one can ask, in relation to oneself. It is the novelists and poets I have been talking about as 'typical of modern literature' who have most to tell us about those questions—far more than any Catholic moralist or humanist I know of. Von Hügel and Guardini are genuinely wise men about such matters, but their wisdom has a limiting sadness; Lawrence has taught us more. Until the Church can take these matters as seriously as he took them, its intelligent members will read their fiction more attentively, more seriously, than they listen to their sermons. And obviously this is only one aspect of what modern literature has to offer. But just because it has so much to offer that is morally and spiritually powerful, and because so many disparate and disjoined items turn out to be parts of one huge idea, we need to become conscious of it and, if we are humanists, on our guard against it. If we live in England or America now, we need to be more on guard against this than against the Catholic or Communist heresies, and my total argument must begin and end with the same point. This modern aestheticism, this symbolist idea of art and culture, is one I at least cannot accept.

As a humanist, I believe in a rather different idea of what a poem is, what a poet should aim at, what society owes the writer and *vice versa*, what life is all about, and therefore of what reading is. My last essay (more exactly, a lecture) may seem to have little to do with the others, and had better be called an appendix, but it grows out of the same attempt to think about reading in a way that connects that experience with other kinds of experience 'humanistically'. It tries to explain, for instance, just how our response to Rilke's poetry may be inhibited (not simply, and not totally, of course) by our disagreement with his beliefs. It tries to make us see the reading mind as a kind of animal, a creature of instincts and interests, of appetites and feelings, however well trained, and never wholly made over into an instrument of judicious appraisal. It is the whole man who reads, not his aesthetic consciousness alone.

A psychology of critical reading

My thesis is that one can describe what goes on in one's mind as one reads in terms of a certain metaphor; which is adequate and helpful from several points of view, though certainly not the only way to describe that process; and which leads us to better than adequate explanations of three kinds of literary problem. Problems in our response to what we read, problems in the learning and teaching of literature, and problems in our intellectual status as men of letters. It leads us to recognize the voluntary character of all critical response to literature—of all literary judgment. And it is from this marked voluntariness that all those three groups of problems derive. So long as we do not acknowledge that voluntariness, we must always be making unconvincing apologies and over-defensive defences of our profession.

I have some prefatory remarks to make, but perhaps I should give you here some crude version of my model, my metaphor, to return to and refine upon later, but so that it is clear from the beginning what the crux of my argument is. I propose that one can describe what happens as one reads by comparing the mind to the body, and the deeper imagination to the circulatory system. The blood, driven by the heart, carries the oxygen picked up in the lungs all through the vast system of arteries and veins, delivers that oxygen to the cells that use it to make nervous and muscular energy. The oxygen then corresponds to the ideas and feelings picked up in what we read; the blood corresponds to the action of the imagination; and the nervous muscular energy of our first response activates the faculties of choice, of attentiveness, of love, which are crucial to our much deeper final response. Those faculties are crucial to our whole moral life. By the faculty of choice we decide what to respond to, to believe in, to act on; by the faculty of attentiveness, we decide how patiently, how submissively, how passionately we do respond; by the faculty of love, we decide the character of the commitment we make—confident allegiance, rebellious partisanship, sceptical spectatorship. These faculties are crucial to our whole moral life—in politics, in religion in personal relationships—but we shall be concerned here with the way they *re*-act, once aroused, on our reading. It is the reading that first arouses those faculties, that directs their activated attention to certain meanings; but once so aroused, they themselves act on that reading, they *make* those meanings powerful. Just as the blood, set pulsing faster by messages from the eyes and ears carries double energy to those senses, to *make* them doubly acute in registering the outside situation.

One useful thing about this metaphor is that the heart on certain occasions beats more powerfully and thumpingly than usual, drives the blood much faster through the arteries, the pulse runs quicker, the lungs gulp in more air, the blood, if we could see it, is brighter. Conversely, on other occasions, the heart is torpid, languid, slow, the breathing quiet and regular, the temperature low, everything relaxed. There isn't, that is, a fixed amount of energy in the system. The amount of energy depends on the body's judgment of the danger or the delight, the general importance, of the external situation affecting it. That judgment is communicated by the sympathetic and para-sympathetic nervous systems, and it is made by the body, not the mind, as we discover when we try, by conscious will-power, to subdue our excitement on certain occasions. To move back from our metaphor to our subject-matter, the external situation corresponds to what we are reading, and the body's judgment of it—which is of course only partly independent of the mind—corresponds to the involuntary and unconscious part of our reading response.

The other useful thing about this metaphor is the distinction, and the connection, it makes between the circulatory system and the nervous system. The nerves conduct the sensual and muscular messages about the external situation up to the clearing house of the brain, where they are classified, collated, and interpreted, and where decisions are taken. The decisions that emanate from the brain are *mostly* conscious—or we are most conscious of that group. But the decisions that go to the heart and the glands, by means of the sympathetic and para-sympathetic nervous systems, are not conscious or voluntary. They are independent of mind as we usually understand that concept. The nervous system then corresponds to the limitedly apprehending and criticizing activity of the reader's mind. We apprehend the writer's use of metaphor and method of characterization, we evaluate his skill in both. That is what we are most conscious of in serious reading, and what we mostly refer to in discussing it. The point of my metaphor is to direct attention to those things that happen inside a reader's response which are more unconscious and (in terms of my metaphor) organic, but just as fundamental and important, as that *merely* critical activity. My point is also to build a bridge of theory from 'critical judgment' to that affective, emotional experience, which is, after all, in some sense what all reading is *for*. Most theory seems to build no adequate bridge, to take inadequate account of the gap between judging and feeling, between criticizing a writer and responding to him. To say we read *critically* directs our attention to that activity I have compared with the action of the nervous system and the brain in judging an external situation. But if we read responsively, that involves elements which I shall compare with the action of the circulatory system in responding to that situation. Not that the two systems are independent of each other, either in the body, as it acts, or in the mind, as it reads; but you cannot explain what happens, in either case, without describing each separately.

That is my metaphor, my model. It is not, as you will see, relevant to all our concerns. It is not an explanation or justification of literary studies, or the literary profession. Nor is it relevant to the problems of How to Read; it is not the description of critical reading to offer to students asking for help in that way. That is why I call it a psychology rather than a rationale; meaning by psychology what goes on in the mind under the surface, and unrelated to conscious purposes. And it is certainly not *the* psychology. But for certain kinds of critical work, especially with certain authors, it is useful to be able to use this language on occasion.

But I have some prefatory remarks to make on the purely judgmental part of reading, the work of the nerves and the brain. I don't think I have anything new to say about this, but in case my way of thinking about it is odder than I know, in case it contains some crucial hidden differentness, I had better quickly expound it. This will be useful also to show just where such more ordinary critical theory encroaches on the territory I am here concerned with. I quote now from something I wrote for another occasion, and I use the term 'literary sensibility' for the apprehending and criticizing activity of the mind.

'Literary sensibility is a set of aptitudes and habits of response to language; that set which is not specially political, economic, psychological, etc., nor limitedly practical. Limitedly practical meaning that one is reading or listening mostly to acquire information which one will then do something about, in some simple line of endeavour. Specially political—or, for instance, mathematical—meaning that one brings only sharply specified expectations and criteria to what one reads, and most of one's aptitudes of response lie inert, most of one's imagination and experience is locked away inaccessible.

'Literary sensibility takes note of the way things are said. It notes—to be as objective and specific as possible—the number and nature of the adjectives in a description, the mood, tense, voice of the verbs in a narrative, the examples in an argument, the images, the metaphors, the alliterations, the allusions, in a poem. It notes all this while following the argument or seeing the thing described, and this notation is just as important a part of its activity. If the book read is to be judged as literature, the way a thing is said is as important as what is said. Because these details are the literary data it interprets; they become, when interpreted, the literary behaviour it evaluates. And by that behaviour, as much as by his statements, it judges a writer's intelligence and maturity and originality.

'From these details, for instance, it deduces the relationship the writer wants setting up between himself and the things described or discussed; whether he uses the first or third person, whether he claims to know everything about the matter, or nothing, or something. It deduces, and obediently constructs, the relationship the writer wants with his readers; whether he pretends we aren't there, or pretends we're old friends, whether he in effect preaches to us, confesses, chats, or drawls. To take another kind of example, still on the same level of simple interpretation, literary sensibility works out how much irony there is in a writer's tone, how much of what he means he is not saying, and whether a description of a tree in new leaf is romantic, symbolic, or horticultural in its reference.

'Literary sensibility follows the writer's directions in all such things, estimates them and him as it does so, and responds accordingly. The response is the key point.' (And here is where this approach encroaches on the territory I want to explore more in depth here.) 'The reader does not only say, I understand; I see

Q

that this writer uses the third person, and affects omniscience, and makes the reader feel naïve. Nor does he only estimate the writer's behaviour, saying, I admire; this effect is skilfully contrived, and I haven't seen this subject treated for a long time, and this ending is very cleverly managed. Beyond that, the reader responds; saying—only response is not sayable, not verbalizable, that is just the point about it—*feel*ing something like, "This man has the right to ask me to believe what he says and see what he describes and feel what he dramatizes. To see, to feel, to believe, angrily or lovingly or however it is he asks me to respond; the point is, obediently, to some degree unprotectedly. He has the right to make me, for instance, imagine myself present at a child-murder, or to go through the death of Ivan Ilyitch, or—a different sort of case—to ponder the minutiae of some quite trivial social manners."

'Of course, one has to imagine, in some sense, to read at all. When the writer writes "red" we must see "red"; when he says "kick" we must think "kick". We have no choice about that, once granted we are reading. The choice is involved in that profounder imagining we do when it is a Tolstoy or a Dostoevsky who is describing; when we sometimes find ourselves responding to a quite conventionally melodramatic situation without the defensive irony we would use against anyone else's version. Anna Karenina in tears after yielding to Vronsky (Book 2, Chapter 11)—it isn't that Tolstoy makes that more plausible, or more vivid, or more subtle, than the average novelist, is it? Certainly it's not that he deploys wonderful verbal skills in depicting it. If we respond to that scene it is because he has already convinced us that he can handle these themes and the emotions they offer to arouse in us. We have *chosen* to respond.

'Not that all writers ask us to do things we resist or suspect. Though I think most major modern writers do. But all writers ask us to perform some imaginative feat, however easy, natural, unnoticeable it may be; and our only ultimate warrant for obeying them is that we know—we have decided—they have the right to command our feelings. "Ultimate warrant" and "right to command" is melodramatic language; but major writers do more than inhabit our minds for an hour; they make new channels for our feelings to flow along, or they powerfully confirm old habits; if they are handling big themes, what they do to us matters. Many we refuse to respond to at the significant level, in the depths of the imagination; and such refusal is crucial, for what we have called response is in some ways more like co-operation.' (Let me say that this refusal, or acceptance, in the depths of the imagination, is not conscious or voluntary. It corresponds, in our metaphor, to that faster beat of the heart, and rate of the pulse, and brightness of the blood; that *instinctive* alertness and receptivity of the whole body when it responds to its external situation the way the mind responds to its reading. But let me return to word co-operation.)

'The moral excitement we feel when we read *King Lear* is derived in a sense not from Shakespeare at all. It is derived from (a) our own imaginations, and (b) the common vivid facts of growing old, losing power, etc. Shakespeare only connects those facts with our deepest, most naked, most excited feelings. Or rather we connect them, under his direction. He doesn't, that is, tell us anything we didn't know before. The daily paper offers us equal stimulus to pity and terror at the human condition. Shakespeare merely persuades us to feel what we could feel by ourselves if we weren't too lazy, too stupid, or too critically self-protective. But critical self-protection is different from laziness or stupidity. It is an essential part of our moral and intellectual economy, especially in a highly developed civilization, where special interests are ready to exploit our feelings all the time. We must lower that sceptical critical guard over our feelings only when we are persuaded of the truth of the message, the value of the exercise proposed to them. And in literary matters that value can only be guaranteed by the power, the delicacy, the maturity of the intelligence proposing it. Shakespeare's greatness as a writer consists in the completeness with which he does so persuade us.

'How does he do so? By the presentation of that purely literary data we then interpret, and the performance of that literary behaviour we then evaluate. But this does not mean just by being skilful. Mere literary skill, understood in any limited sense, does not constitute a right to command our belief, our co-operation, our imagination. You can be a fine craftsman—very good with the sonnet-form or the triolet—without being a significant artist; and the difference is that the artist *does* persuade us to co-operate, to imagine, to feel along with him. Because he shows—in and through those literary skills—intelligence about life, understanding and experience of, passionate concern for, beliefs and feelings and relationships. Graham Greene's skill, in matters of narrative form, let's say, is often remarkable; George Eliot's is often not. But what George Eliot does, and Graham Greene does not, is to persuade us to respond to her larger meanings, to yield up our self-protective critical scepticism in certain areas. We *respond* to even the details of the Casaubon-Dorothea marriage; because George Eliot's literary skills—with something as technical as sentence form—express also extraordinary understanding of beliefs and feelings and relationships. We are each of us, all the time, judging a writer's intelligence, understanding, imaginative authority, on the evidence of the way he writes, and, if he passes every test, we let ourselves respond to every subtlety as he directs, and even with the big overwhelming feelings.

'That is why in literature the way a thing is said is as important as what is said. Because it is only if we are persuaded to trust the writer that what is said becomes real at all, in the depths of our imagination. Obviously it is Romeo and Juliet dying we are moved by, not skilful verse-writing, but we could not be so moved by that story if it were told by another writer. The skill, by demonstrating intelligence about life, has won from us an attentiveness, a responsiveness, an absorption in the writer's meanings so complete as to constitute belief, in the sense appropriate to literature.' (I need hardly say that I am not here repeating Coleridge's 'willing suspension of disbelief'. What seems to me to happen is almost the opposite; the *un*willing, involuntary, co-operative *activity* of *belief*.) 'Imaginative literature is that kind in which the reality is largely dependent on the writer. In a book of political history, or even a political novel (take Koestler's *Darkness at Noon* as an example) some of the reality is independent of the author. We respond to the story of Russian Communism because of its intrinsic interest. It is important because it happened. Romeo and Juliet never happened. Only Shakespeare (with our consent) makes them happen in our minds, and (with our co-operation) makes us respond to that range and organization of meanings.

'When I talk of our consent, or our co-operation, in responding to something the author presents, I am only describing, from this special point of view, what is more often called his successful evocation of that something. For instance, in the case of the Alpine scenery described at the end of *Women in Love*, a classic case of successful writing, critics usually say that Lawrence makes us see the mountains. My point is that we *try* to see whatever he names once he has convinced us of his authority in this matter; convinced us that he has seen *these* mountains, but also that he knows about natural beauty of all kinds and about the whole morality of the aesthetic life, so that we are ready to follow his every hint implicitly and passionately, to feel in fact more than we would if we actually saw the mountains themselves. So that if Lawrence says, "then in the east the peaks and ridges glowed with living rose", we are ready to imagine that, and respond to it as very beautiful and very significant, while in another novelist exactly the same words would leave us quite unmoved. Those words are not in themselves remarkable; they gain something from their context, of course; but they gain more from the fact that I have granted Lawrence the right to evoke such feelings in my mind—that I am unconsciously working with him to discover and arouse those feelings.

'Most of the time of course Lawrence keeps redeeming that right by finding words and details that are brilliant in themselves; so that one can think of what happens as just skilful describing on his part, with our part reduced to passive, piano-key reacting. In this case, however, I think it becomes clear that we are co-operating actively, and that the brilliant details merely reassure and guide us. We are not passively acknowledging the colour rose, which would be minimal playing fair with the author. We are calling up *all* the associations and powers of the word rose, and east, and living, and peak; *throwing* them into new combinations under his direction, and *presenting* them to our unprotected responsiveness. It is only while we are thus actively engaged in co-operating that we can possibly have the overwhelming emotional experience that reading can be even for—indeed, especially for—the most critical reader.

'There are, then, two parts to the process of critical reading; the recognition of skill and intelligence in the author, literary skills and intelligence about life; and submissive co-operative responsiveness to his meanings in the degree they deserve. Meanings of course not being just what can be translated into abstract formulas; a meaning can be a contrast between two opposed characters, a description of landscape charged with emotion, or a violent action summing up a drama.'

That is the end of what I wrote before. In everything about the second part of the process of reading, I passed on from the 'judgment' of the nervous system to the 'response' of the circulatory system. The heart beats faster when the brain tells it something important impends. The brain has judged the issue on the evidence of the messages sent along the nervous system; but it has not acted only intellectually. It has commanded the body to respond in a variety of ways, which yet add up—in a normal person—to a unity. When the heart is beating faster, and the blood is rushing more oxygen to the cells, the nerves and the muscles are much more selective and intensive in their activity. If the general feeling is danger, they see everything in terms of danger, and take no account of the picturesque or puzzling aspects of the scene. If the general feeling is delight—a beautiful evening, for instance—they see everything in terms of delight, the colours, the sounds, the air, the peacefulness. That is, the nerves, muscles, senses, all co-operate. The circulatory system, the unconscious parts of the body, have somehow directed them to do that. Which is only to translate into the terms of my metaphor the way the reader responds to that phrase in *Women in Love*.

But we must not strain the potentialities of that metaphor. The contrast between the circulatory and nervous systems is useful to indicate a shallowness in our usual understanding of reading, an over-intellectuality, but if we push on to examine further how reading actually works, we have to modify it. In its simple form it is perhaps useful more to the philosophical moralist than to the literary man.

This is so most importantly because any 'operational' analysis of reading reveals much *more* interchange, and more *various*, between 'judgment' and 'response' than we can picture between the circulatory and the nervous systems. In reading there is no single simple message—delight or disapproval—which determines all our responses to a book. There is a complex personal relationship between the reader and the book, between the two systems of value and principles of intelligence, which combines very different degrees of trust of a given author as he deals with different subjects, and even on one sharply specified subject can combine fascination with disapproval. To go back to *Women in Love*, there are other subjects, for instance politics, on which one follows Lawrence's hints far less implicitly than on natural description. And to go back to *Middlemarch*, there are other personal relationships George Eliot describes to which one responds far less than to the Casaubon marriage. Judgment and response interact continuously; there is an enormous range in the degrees to which we 'accept' books; there is an almost infinite variety in the ways in which we take them.

However, this is only to modify the metaphor, and only by extending it. For however sophisticated we may become literarily, we still need the crude but fundamental distinction between good and bad books, between those that satisfy us critically and those that do not. And that distinction needs to be explained by this metaphor. For we find that the bad books, even while we are superficially picturing their most vivid and lurid scenes, do not stir our deeper imaginations. Unconsciously we have refused to co-operate with the writer. Unconscious controls have protected us. It is as if there were filters and locks placed at important junctions in a system of canals, and only what can pass them—pass our critical tests—can reach the powerful and delicate central pump which irrigates the whole imagination.

Now there are two obvious exceptions to this theory, which I should try to take care of. First of all, some bad books do excite us emotionally, and profoundly, because they deal with a subject we, as individuals and not critical readers, always find exciting, however treated. Pornography is perhaps the most general example of this, but most of us have some other weak spot of this kind, in either subject or treatment—a particular landscape, or a certain kind of tough realism. In such cases, one finds one has completely condemned what one read, critically, but one has been powerfully stirred, or stimulated, in one's deepest imagination.

In the second place, we sometimes voluntarily open those protective locks and filters, as some people do for their bedside reading. They voluntarily put their critical apparatus out of action. They neither respond nor refuse to respond, deep down. All the water is equally muddy and sluggish; the irrigation is imperceptible. This is presumably how the wholly untrained reader reads; with more nearly equal responses to everything, all slack and short-lived.

But all these two exceptions prove is, first, that the decision to respond is taken by the whole mind, including its unconscious elements; which represent our appetites and fears, and which are not always subordinated to the purposes the rational part of the mind proposes. Our response, *being* whole, expresses quite profound intentions, some of which may well be in conflict with our conscious purposes. This is why we find ourselves responding to something we have judged to be bad, morally, literally, or intellectually. (Though incidentally our unconscious sometimes proves to be the better critic.)

And secondly, the second of those exceptions shows that only critical, trained, in some sense passionately committed reading makes the full connection between judgment and response. Whenever we voluntarily put our critical apparatus out of action, or even do not strenuously activate it, we find that our response has less to do with our judgment. This may sometimes be quite *in*voluntary. When I was an undergraduate I was very worried by the fact that I enjoyed reading a silly novelist called O. Douglas more than I enjoyed Shakespeare. Now I could see that Shakespeare was the better writer. I mean, I hadn't just been told that; I saw it for myself. But I responded more to O. Douglas. Because my critical apparatus was not deeply enough connected with the rest of my mind. There was insufficient interaction between my critical criteria and my deeper interests. And to some extent this is true today, of course. There is never sufficient interaction, sufficient integration of the mind. Our response is always somewhat independent of our judgment. And indeed this is not simply imperfection. It is how we grow. But the *idea* of critical reading, towards which we always tend, is that response should be wholly determined by judgment.

And that does more or less happen, more or less often. Often enough for us to call it the rule, which these two exceptions help to prove. The rule that when we have a profound emotional experience reading it is because what we are reading has satisfied our judgment, though our emotion is not the direct and immediate result of our critical approval. It is the result of a part-unconscious process by which the protective locks of our imagination have opened before the urgent stream of the writer's discourse—his passionate appeals to our pity, our enthusiasm, our terror—and have allowed his images to penetrate to the most secret, sacred, helplessly responsive sources of our life. Those protective locks and filters are the work of our conscious critical mind, which is ever at work refining, strengthening, developing, its literary criteria, its literary standards. But an intelligence is a larger and more mysterious thing than its conscious analytical and critical activity, and those locks swing open of their own accord. The mind as a whole has taken the decision to co-operate—to some degree—and the activity that results all retains the character of that decision. It is the whole mind that decides, and the activity is not only both rational and effective, it is also importantly voluntary. Unconsciously we *choose* to co-operate with this author and not with that. That choice is not, for a good reader, at all arbitrary; but neither is it forced on him by logic and evidence. It is determined importantly by his large intentions in life, in areas seemingly remote from reading. From this derive all the puzzling phenomena of personal taste, among other things.

The reader's mind is not like a piano, whose notes must resonate in predetermined ways, when hit, whose performance depends wholly on the skill of the player's fingers. The mind is essentially active. It can better be compared to a proud, independent, and temperamental choir, whose performance varies according to the conductor's skill, but also according to their own state of voice and state of mind, their whole relationship to the conductor and intentions towards him. If it co-operates it will be because it has chosen to.

That is my theory, and now I'd like to offer a few examples of the three kinds of literary problem I think it explains. First of all, our passionate response to quite plain pieces of language by great writers. For instance, the Lawrence phrase: 'In the east the peaks and ridges glowed with living rose.' I can find descriptive phrases in, say, Edgar Allan Poe, which seem to my *judgment* as vivid as that. But I respond to the phrase from Lawrence, and not to the one from Poe, because I am working with Lawrence. I'm not testing. I have accepted him as in these matters a master. I take the phrase as a profound directive, which I don't with Poe.

Or take another example, from Salinger's *Zooey*. Zooey looks out of the window and sees a girl in the street wearing a beret the colour of a blanket in a Van Gogh painting. This seems to me very vivid; it conjures up for me, just as Salinger intended, one particular red which symbolizes all the sharp bright colours of life which, though morally indifferent in themselves, nevertheless form a big part of the complex moral experience we have to handle when we talk about 'life'—which is what Zooey is trying to do. Yet I haven't seen that painting; I can't really have a mental image of that colour; and I distrust, consciously, in theory, the over-specificity and self-conscious cleverness of that reference. But I'm eager, *un*consciously, to see what Salinger means; I've decided, in effect, that it's important, I'm seizing on every clue, every directive, I'm co-operating.

R

Or take Wordsworth's famous lines:

The rainbow comes and goes
And lovely is the rose
The moon doth with delight
Look round her when the heavens are bare
Waters on a starry night
Are beautiful and fair.

I take it that one intention here is to communicate visual excite-ment—charged of course with the larger pathos the poem is concerned with. And I take it the intention succeeds—that most of us do feel that visual excitement, as well as the other pleasures the lines afford. But surely that visual excitement must be the result of my own imagination co-operating very actively, on pretty meagre hints and directives from Wordsworth. The rose is lovely, we are told, the waters are beautiful and fair; this could hardly be vaguer, visually. The phrase about the moon in fact gives me a distinct and beautiful image. But I cannot see, when I examine it, that that image has anything to do with Wordsworth's with 'looking round' or 'looking delighted'. Mine is a beautiful lunar effect I have saved up in my memory, and *awarded* to Words-worth, most voluntarily. 'The rainbow comes and goes' is closest to offering us a picture; the picture of the wavering insub-stantiality of rainbows; but after all we could all of us describe that effect more vividly. Wordsworth has not created beautiful images for us. He has named two or three categories of image, and invited us to do the rest. And we have co-operated.[1]

Or let us take a teaching-and-learning kind of problem. A colleague said the other day that when a student says he doesn't like Pope, we tell him, or should tell him, that he must *learn* to like it. Perhaps we think we mean some pure act of the intelli-gence by 'learn' there. But surely we mean something quite voluntary, in fact. This learning is a matter of *trying* to feel the

---

[1] I have had it pointed out to me, since writing that, that Wordsworth is even in these lines showing himself a master worthy of our trust—that the phrasing is more distinguished, more grammatically and rhythmically subtle than it looks at first glance. I think that is true, and it makes this a case rather different from that of the Lawrence phrase. But it is not totally different. The authority on which we are acting may not be so distinguishably the author's rather than the text's, but the experience we 'undergo' results from Wordsworth's distinction of phrasing only because we have activated our sensory apparatus on his behalf.

responses other people feel, trying to find this or that passage witty, trenchant, eloquent, various. The student knows what feelings he is supposed to have already, and in response to what passages. It is the affective response alone he lacks. Teaching at this point can consist only of pointing out which phrases are supposed to evoke which feelings. Learning can consist only of making his mind ready to feel those feelings, by breaking down irrelevant presuppositions, prejudices, resistances. It is a conscious rehearsal of the unconscious decision to co-operate we spoke of. He voluntarily decides to like Pope as a means to the end of later involuntarily liking and appreciating him. And all of us, however early we liked Pope, must have made that involuntary decision. We know we must because our appreciation is so plainly the fruit of active co-operation on our part. This is the heart of what teaching can do, in a subject like literature; rehearse on the conscious level acts which must more really take place unconsciously. That is why good teaching in literature is so close to acting and can slip so easily into self-dramatization.

We should not let conscious and unconscious decisions to like something blend into each other, for this amounts to insincerity of taste. But sometimes we have to employ both. Perhaps the most vivid cases are those of modern movements, in painting, music, literature. A reserved and rigid analysis of new modes is unlikely to produce good criticism; consciously trying to like them, to sympathize, is a necessary preliminary to any adequate judgment.

Last, a problem in the status and character of literary studies. This cardinal significance of voluntariness in the life of the imagination is the source of our greatest contrast with the sciences, and our greatest problems of self-justification. To most non-literary people it seems that the discussion of literature is regulated purely by the values of rhetoric; the more eloquent and generally interesting you are on the subject of your author, the better your criticism. The object itself does not impose any harsh discipline on what you may or may not assert about it, much less on how you should or should not treat it; you can never be absolutely wrong, and consequently never really right. Now this is not true; the great critics differ from the rest just in the harshness of the discipline they have imposed on themselves, and it is they who make the absolute categorical pronouncements. But if that accusation is not true, it is not wholly untrue. The great critics impose a discipline *on themselves*. The sources of that discipline are not wholly in the object. They are also in the subject; the great critic, that is, relates the book he is discussing to a contemporary sensibility which he is creating—creating partly by intention. His theory of that sensibility consults a great range of criteria, and chooses among those criteria which to consult. Whether, like Dr Leavis, he feels himself in opposition to the taste of his contemporaries, or, like Dr Johnson, feels himself at one with them, the great critic obviously feels he knows what people of his time and place *ought* to like, which manifestations of contemporary taste are 'healthy' and which are not. The contemporary situation has, for the great critic, a personality of its own, with its own demands and point of view, which *he* has discovered. Even the literature of the past must be seen from this point of view; from which it may have a quite different profile from what it had a generation earlier. Only by recalling this can we make sense out of the radical shifts in value, of poets as large as Milton, in the judgments of critics as large as Johnson, Matthew Arnold, Leavis. And the great critics *choose* that contemporary point of view. We need only recall the protests of their contemporaries to realize how arbitrary they seemed, how voluntary they were. Voluntary in that they consulted a great range of criteria for poetry, and chose which to measure Milton by. The contrast with the exact sciences is not black and white, ultimately; but there is a marked difference, on the surface, in the narrower range of choices open to a scientist, and the obligatory procedures he must follow.

Indeed, to be frank, this cardinal rôle of the voluntary, the non-intellectual, in literary studies, is the ultimate source of that large element of fraud in them; that rich tropical vegetation of nonsense, of charlatanry or irrelevancy, that is always becoming rampant over one or other of the palaces of art. It is, isn't it, possible to get away with murder in literary studies; certainly it is possible to be hideously deceived, and for intelligent people, and by the worst fakery. How do we explain that, except by admitting that responding to a book, appreciating an author, is quite inevitably to some extent an act of will, a choice. Of course such choices are made as a result of critical thinking, ratiocination. But unlike the models of pure logic, the act of decision does not come at the end of the intellection, when all the evidence has been assembled and all the hypotheses considered, but halfway through, and is itself the source of a great deal more critical thought. And if the decision was wrongly taken, all the responses afterwards, and all the intellectual activity they generate, however conscientious in themselves, are vitiated. In other words, once you've been persuaded to like a bad writer, you can find wonderfully good reasons for liking him, and wonderfully rich experiences while you read him. I sometimes think there is no piece of language in the world which somebody—and I mean some Ph.D. in English—could not be persuaded to find profound meanings and exquisite beauties in. There are so few controls built into either the method or the object. Appreciation depends on the subject, the reader, so completely, that, unless he is really severe with himself, it can get to be quite independent of the book. And being severe with oneself is not a matter of professional scholarly competence.

But that importance of the non-intellectual is also the source of our glory as well as our shame, in that a training in literature is a training of the will. We decide, in a way, what to like; so we must keep checking our liking, to ask both, just what in us is gratified, that makes us respond, and just how our imaginative activity, in which we take such pleasure, is related to the text. Moreover, once having decided, we make ourselves over into the image of what we have chosen, to some extent. It is therefore of prime importance that we should know how to decide rightly. Especially as this is something all men have to do, to some degree, not merely specialists, as is the case in science.

But my point here is neither the glory nor the shame that may derive from that voluntariness, but just voluntariness itself, which is always there, however badly or well we read. I *don't* mean that what we find in great literature is what we put there. What we find is what the artist put there, if we discipline our reading. But the depth and intensity with which we respond to what we find is a function of the attention we pay. And the attention is a partly voluntary faculty of the mind. Not arbitrary, but voluntary, expressing both the conscious purposes and the unconscious intentions of the whole person, not purely appreciative reactions. The laws that govern our attention do not impose themselves upon it necessarily, like the laws of physical matter; they become effective only in so far as they are adopted by the person reading. We are within limits free to decide how we will respond to literary themes and treatments. This is particularly noticeable in the case of contemporary literature, at the moment when certain themes and treatments are new and challenging, and others old and unprofitable. At such moments we may be *conscious* of choosing whether to co-operate with the writer or not. We could do either, within limits. And those limits seem sharply to define the area of the individual's moral responsibility in literary matters. But the acts of unconscious choice that are going on all the time are equally voluntary and responsible, in the broader sense. It is they that characterize the puzzling processes of literary judgment.

The relation between reader and poem therefore seems to me always part of a relationship between reader and poet. Though in some cases this may be only negatively felt—we may think of the poem as a poem while we are reading it, and an entity independent of its maker, but there are always things we may *not* think about it, because we know it is the work of a poet. And the relationship between reader and poet is a relationship between two minds, two persons. In the case of the novel, it seems even more important to deny the fallacy that in literature nothing exists except in a particular verbal formulation, and that everything so existing has a nature radically different from that which exists in life. Novels obviously have characters and plots, that exist independently of particular verbal formulations. But the essential point is that novels have novelists behind them, just as poems have poets, and reading them is an encounter between two minds, according to terms (freshly modified by the writer or not) which the particular culture prescribes.

From this point of view it is largely nonsense for poets to say that the music of the universe is speaking in them, or that the language is writing their poems, or that the world is ripening to Godhead in their art. For the humanist these can only be half truths in the world of thought, though they can be very meaningful in other modes of discourse—anywhere, so long as the poet implicitly acknowledges the limits of the kind of truth he is telling. The modern Symbolist poet has not acknowledged any such limits, and modern literary men have followed him in his defiance. They have insisted on the absolute truth of his figures—or on their being as true as any other kind of truth. Clearly a reader sensitive to literature, ready to hear something important from his writers, but concerned to preserve some self-respect, some sense of intellectual identity, sooner or later has to say no to some of those claims. Humanism is an attempt to define a position that, amongst other things, justifies that saying no.

I must admit that there is something diminishing in that negation; that if a poet believes me (as of course I must wish he would) he will feel limited in his function and status; there are things other poets have believed they could do which he will know he can't. Indeed, even as limiting systems go, humanism has a rather stolid and unexciting character. I am very conscious that von Hügel and Guardini, and even George Eliot (if I may claim them as my sponsors) are none of them great poets. They are the grandmothers of literature, not its bright Apollos, and there is something grandmotherly about the whole idea of humanism.

But then this is a framework of ideas, a setting, a home, within which the children of promise can grow up safely, the men of intuitive and extraordinary gifts can be saved from the self-destructive temptations that beset those who acknowledge no limits. For such a home, surely stolid and grandmotherly furniture—in a roomy and old-fashioned house—is the best; large shabby sofas, hard-wearing carpets, trustworthy fireguards and plenty of books, rooms with sound-proof doors and some whose entry is forbidden. Humanism is old-fashioned and unexciting; but partly for that reason it is the best background of ideas for a literary mind to grow up in.

So much by way of apology to the poets, and those who associate themselves with the poets. My prime concern is with the reader, and those who, like me, associate themselves with him. (If my prime concern were with the poets, I should feel obliged to offer some model of the contemporary writer's duties and opportunities that would fit inside the roomy mansion of humanism but be much more vivid and contemporary in style; but that would be another book.) The reader, as well as the writer, is a literary man. He is as much a part of the literary world—indeed, from my present point of view, he is more central.

As a teacher of literature, my daily work as well as my imaginative sustenance is derived from poetry and novels and literary criticism about them. I must be able to think that I am dealing in the truth, and not in half-truths, lies and sheer silly muddle. I must be able to think that my students, whether they are to become poets or readers, are learning a set of attitudes and responses which are generally useful and healthful. It is by no means sure that they will do so just by reading modern literature or the criticism that goes with it. Only a strenuous and lucky effort by all of us will save them from something quite the opposite.

As a member of the Catholic church, I am made to realize my differences from many modern writers and modern critics particularly often. I cannot glide unselfconsciously into accepting, say, Rilke's or Yeats's ideas for the time of reading—and I am very glad I cannot. Much less can I be satisfied by their treatments of certain major themes in human experience, in which their ideas are implicit. And as a socialist I have other similar problems. Without my being willing in either case to solve those problems either in the wholesale manner of *What Is Art?* —that is, by imposing a radically limited function on literature—or in the even more corrupting manner of many Catholic and Communist writers, by poisoning a seemingly free literary sensibility at its inner source. It is from all these points of view that—as a literary man—I feel humanism the only satisfactory position, and a revival of humanism urgently necessary.

Helen Muchnic quotes interestingly from an essay by Mandelshtam, called 'About the Interlocutor', which distinguishes between the poet and the literary man in terms of the audience each thinks he is addressing. The literary man always addresses his contemporaries and wishes to educate them; but the poet must not address himself in his poems to anyone in particular. The poet is bound to educate, to please, to satisfy, no one but a quite providential interlocutor.

Mandelshtam means presumably a distinction between types of writer which amounts to, more importantly than anything else, a distinction in quality (rather than a distinction in function). A poet is better than a literary man. A literary man is an inferior version of a poet. That is certainly how Professor Muchnic takes up the idea. Gorky, she says, was always the literary man; he made the mistake of bringing his work for judgment to an audience he meant to have an effect on. Many Russian writers of this century have made the same mistake. 'Only Blok and Pasternak, at tragic cost, were able to stand their ground against those ceaseless assaults on poetry which are made by men whom it makes uncomfortable, who find its unpredictable ways disturbing, threatening, incomprehensible.'

As must be clear by now, I am one of those whom 'poetry', thus hypostatized and hypertrophied, makes uncomfortable. I find its ways not exactly unpredictable, but disturbing, threatening, incomprehensible enough. And that is indeed because I am not a poet but a literary man, in a sense only somewhat different from that given the term by Mandelshtam and Professor Muchnic. Literature is my life as much as it is most writers', though I don't write poems, and though I'm not so ready to sacrifice other values to poetry as I'm told they are. The real difference is that I do not regard the literary man as so inferior. And the likeness is that I do see his interests as opposed to those of the poet sometimes—when the latter advances the claims typical of the Symbolist writer. At those times, I am with von Hügel against Yeats.

Bibliography

(Included with each essay is the connecting material that precedes it, and, in the case of the last essay, also the connecting material that follows. Books with bibliographical identification in the text are not listed here, and each book is mentioned only once, except where a second mention seemed the only way to guide the reader to the right source.)

The liberal humanist as Roman Catholic

MICHAEL DE LA BEDOYÈRE, *The Life of Baron von Hügel*, London, 1951.
RICHARD ELLMAN, *Yeats: The Man and the Masks*, New York, 1948.
The Identity of Yeats, London, 1954.
FRIEDRICH VON HÜGEL, *Essays and Addresses*, London, 1921.
Letters to a Niece, Chicago, 1955.
The Mystical Element in Religion, London, 1908.
Selected Letters 1896–1924, ed. B. Holland, London, 1927.
MAURICE NÉDONCELLE, *Baron Friedrich von Hügel*, London, 1937.
M. D. PETRE, *von Hügel and Tyrrell*, London, 1937.
W. B. YEATS, *The Winding Stair and Other Poems*, 1933.

The Catholic as psychological type

ALEXANDER BLOK, *The Spirit of Music*, London, 1946.
NORMAN BROWN, *Life Against Death*, New York, 1959.
GWENDOLEN GREENE, *Two Witnesses*, London, 1930.
ALFRED LOISY, *Choses Passées*, Paris, 1913.
HERBERT MARCUSE, *Eros and Civilization*, Boston, 1955.
RUFUS W. MATHEWSON, *The positive Hero in Russian Literature*, New York, 1958.
MAISIE WARD, *The Wilfrid Wards and the Transition*, London, 1934.
Insurrection versus Resurrection, London, 1937.
WILFRID WARD, *W. G. Ward and the Catholic Revival*, London, 1893.

Two kinds of Catholic sensibility

LOUIS BOUYER, *Life and Liturgy*, London, 1954.
  The Spirituality of the New Testament and the Fathers, London, 1963.
HENRI BRÉMOND, *A Literary History of Religious Thought in France*, London, 1928.
DONAT O'DONNELL, *Maria Cross*, London, 1953
T. S. ELIOT, 'An Emotional Unity', *The Dial*, February, 1928.
  Generation of the Third Eye, ed. Daniel Callahan, New York, 1965.
RANDALL JARRELL, *Poetry and the Age*, New York, 1955.
HANS KUNG, *The Council, Reform, and Reunion*, New York, 1961.
J-L. PREVOST, *Le Roman Catholique a Cent Ans*, Paris, 1958.
KARL RAHNER, *The Christian Commitment*, New York, 1961.
  Theology for Renewal, New York, 1964.
GEORGE SANTAYANA, *Winds of Doctrine*, New York, 1913.
MARTIN TURNELL, *Modern Literature and Christian Faith*, London, 1961.
EVELYN WAUGH, *A Little Learning*, London, 1964.

J. F. Powers and Catholic writing

ROMANO GUARDINI, *The End of the Modern World*, London, 1950.
  Freedom, Grace, and Destiny, New York, 1961.
  The World and the Person, Chicago, 1965.
HENRI DE LUBAC, *Catholicism*, London, 1961.
J. F. POWERS, *The Prince of Darkness and other stories*, New York, 1947.
  The Presence of Grace, New York, 1956.
  Morte d'Urban, New York, 1963.
BRIAN WICKER, *Culture and Liturgy*, London, 1963.

The morality of Lolita

HERBERT E. BOWMAN, *Vissarion Belinsky 1811–1848*, Harvard, 1954.
FRANK KERMODE, *The Romantic Image*, London, 1957.
D. S. MIRSKY, *Contemporary Russian Literature 1881–1925*, London, 1926.
MARTIN TURNELL, *Modern Literature and Christian Faith*, London, 1961.

Sholokhov and the Russian cultural tradition

V. G. BELINSKY, *Selected Philosophical Works*, Moscow, 1948.
ISAIAH BERLIN, 'The Marvellous Decade,' *Encounter*, June, November, December, 1955.
VICTOR ERLICH, *The Double Image*, Baltimore, 1964.
EVGENY EVTUSHENKO, *A Precocious Autobiography*, London, 1963.

ALEXANDER HERZEN, *Who is to Blame?*, available only in Russian and German, so far as I know.

RUFUS W. MATHEWSON, *The Positive Hero in Russian Literature*, New York, 1958.

HELEN MUCHNIC, *From Gorky to Pasternak*, London, 1963.

KONSTANTIN PAUSTOVSKY, *Slow Approach of Thunder*, London, 1965.

RENATO POGGIOLI, *Poets of Russia 1890–1930*, Harvard, 1960.

Doctor Zhivago *and the critics*

MICHAEL ALEXANDER, 'Doctor Zhivago and the Leopard', *The Listener*, 9 September, 1965.

A. BELY, *Reminiscences of Alexander Blok*, available only in Russian, so far as I know.

E. M. BUTLER, *R. M. Rilke*, Cambridge, 1941.

NICOLA CHIARAMONTE, 'Pasternak's Message', *Partisan Review*, Winter, 1958.

J. M. COHEN, 'Servant to the Ages', *Spectator*, 6 April, 1962.

EDWARD CRANKSHAW, *Kruschev's Russia*, London, 1959.

DONALD DAVIE, *The Poems of Doctor Zhivago*, Manchester, 1965.

ISAAC DEUTSCHER, 'Pasternak and the Calendar of Revolution', *Partisan Review*, Vol. 26, 2.

ROMANO GUARDINI. *Rilke's Duino Elegies*, London, 1961.

IRVING HOWE, 'Freedom and the Ashcan of History', *Partisan Review*, Vol. 26, 2.

GEORGE KATKOV, in Boris Pasternak, *In the Interlude*, ed. and trans. Henry Kamen.

BORIS PASTERNAK, *An Essay in Autobiography*, London, 1959. *Safe Conduct*, New York, 1949.

H. F. PETERS, *Masks and the Man*, Washington, 1960.

F. D. REEVE, 'Doctor Zhivago: From Prose to Verse', *Kenyon Review*, Winter, 1960.

R. M. RILKE, *Selected Works*, Vol. 1, tr. G. Craig Houston, intro. by J. B. Leishman, London, 1954.

EDMUND WILSON, 'Dr Life and his Guardian Angel', *New Yorker*, 15 November, 1958.

'Legend and Symbol in Doctor Zhivago', *Encounter*, June, 1959.

NORA WYDENBRUCK, *Rilke: Man and Poet*, London, 1949.

A psychology of critical reading

D. H. LAWRENCE, 'The Novel', *Reflections on the Death of a Porcupine*, 1925.

BORIS PASTERNAK, 'Interview: The Art of Fiction', *Paris Review*, No. 24.

Index

The Contents page is itself a kind of index, and there are no listings here of references to a book or an author within a chapter which is professedly about him or it. Thus there is no listing of references to von Hügel in the first three chapters, only of references to him in the rest of the book.